William Stanley
as Shakespeare

William Stanley as Shakespeare

Evidence of Authorship by the Sixth Earl of Derby

John M. Rollett

McFarland & Company, Inc., Publishers
Jefferson, North Carolina

LIBRARY OF CONGRESS CATALOGUING-IN-PUBLICATION DATA

Rollett, John M., author.
William Stanley as Shakespeare : evidence of authorship by the sixth Earl of Derby / John M. Rollett.
p. cm.
Includes bibliographical references and index.

ISBN 978-0-7864-9660-0 (softcover : acid free paper) ♾
ISBN 978-1-4766-1900-2 (ebook)

1. Shakespeare, William, 1564–1616—Authorship.
2. Derby, William Stanley, Earl of, –1642. I. Title.

PR2947.S73R65 2015 822.3'3—dc23 2014049573

BRITISH LIBRARY CATALOGUING DATA ARE AVAILABLE

Printed in the United States of America

McFarland & Company, Inc., Publishers
Box 611, Jefferson, North Carolina 28640
www.mcfarlandpub.com

To my family and to the memory of my parents

Shall I compare thee to a summer's day?
Thou art more lively and more temperate.
Rough winds do shake the daring buds of May
And summer's lease hath all too short a date.

Sonnet 18
(amended)

Acknowledgments

My first acknowledgments must be to the three pioneers who first envisaged the possibility that William Stanley (later Earl of Derby) might be the real Shakespeare—James Greenstreet, Abel Lefranc and A. W. Titherley, whose researches form the foundation of much of what follows in this book. More recent investigators include the late John Michell, whose book *Who Wrote Shakespeare?* is the best introduction to the Authorship Question, and the late Carl O. Nordling, whose advocacy of Stanley is available on the internet. Next comes John Raithel, whose internet site "The URL of Derby," regularly updated, is a hugely valuable resource for anyone interested in the evidence for Derby.

I have learned much from friends and colleagues met after I became interested in this topic, notably Christopher Dams, Richard Malim, Elizabeth Imlay, Kevin Gilvary and Emma Jolly of the De Vere Society; Oxfordians Nina Green and Daniel Wright; Mark Rylance, Julia Cleave and Bill Rubinstein of the Shakespearean Authorship Trust, independents Pat Buckridge, Wayne Shore, Diana Price, Jerry Downs and Tony Pointon, and also William Niederkorn, who frequently writes for newspapers in the U.S. commenting on recent developments in the search for the real author. Correspondence by e-mail with many people has enabled me to test, refine and often to drop various lines of investigation; my thanks to them all, too numerous to mention. My greatest debt is to Jones Harris, who inadvertently started me off on the voyage of exploration recorded in this book; his crucial contribution is acknowledged more than once herein. To my family, busied with more important matters, my grateful thanks for their support and encouragement.

Table of Contents

Part III: Discoveries

Prologue

In April 1999 I was in a cab in Portland, Oregon. After a while the driver said, "So, what brings you over here?" I replied I was going to a conference.

"What's the conference about?" he asked.

It's about Shakespeare, I replied. After a pause he said,

"Ah, Shakespeare. Back in school, thirty years ago, they told us no one knew who he was. Will that come up, do you think?"

I said it would. The conference was about who wrote Shakespeare.

"Tell me more," he said.

Two minutes, in a cab the other side of the world, to account for 150 years of doubt and incredulity. The writer Shakespeare, I said, was very well educated, well versed in the law, knew all about falconry, a sport of the upper classes, had read more than 300 books, and had spent time in France and Italy. The actor Shakespeare had only a simple education, was too busy acting and making money to read so many books, let alone get access to them, had never been abroad, and signed his name six times with six different spellings.

Another pause. Then the verdict,

"You Brits really messed up back then, not jotting his name down somewhere."

But what if his name *was* jotted down somewhere? It is my contention that someone did just that, and every copy of "The Complete Works of Shakespeare" records it. Untold millions of people have had in their possession the name of the real author for years, and never noticed it.

Many people writing about the "Authorship Question," as it is often called, start by naming their candidate, and continue by reciting all the evidence they can assemble to support their case. Rarely do they mention anything that might tell against their man. In essence, that is what I am doing here, and the name of my candidate is in the title of this book. But as a scientist I have preferred to try to take a more detached view, to rely on facts and reasonable inferences from them where possible, and to avoid too much speculation; moreover, conclusions should arrive at the end of an investigation rather than being promoted at the beginning. The reader will occasionally be told where the argument is weak or where imagination is being called upon—nevertheless I believe the case for my candidate to be very strong. It is based both on substantial new evidence and on evidence which is well-known but which carries implications unrecognized or misunderstood.

So, who was William Stanley? He was born in 1561, a younger son of an earl, and as such had no expectations and few responsibilities. After leaving St. John's College, Oxford, he studied law in London and then toured the continent for several years, initially with his tutor. Returning to London he continued his study of the law and mixed with poets and playwrights. On 16 April 1594, when he was 33, his carefree life came to an abrupt end on the death of his elder brother, and William unexpectedly became the Sixth Earl of Derby and in line to succeed Queen Elizabeth (he and his brother were great-great-grandsons of Henry VII). He was reported in 1599 as writing plays "for the common players," but his closeness to the throne would have necessitated a pen name for his publications right from the start, as the public theaters were regarded as disreputable or worse; in any case it was "not done" (*infra dig*) for a member of the upper classes to publish anything under his own name. He lived to a great age, dying in 1642 just before the Civil War, during which his mansion at Lathom burned down and any papers stored there were destroyed. After the end of the war all the theaters were closed; when they reopened in 1660 on the restoration of Charles II few people would be aware of the identity of the real Shakespeare, and before long his name was forgotten.

This man has been a candidate for the authorship for more than a hundred years, but through a combination of circumstances he has been pushed into the sidelines—off stage, one might say. It will be my endeavor to bring him back into full view, center stage, where he belongs.

Introduction

William Stanley, by now Sixth Earl of Derby, was reported in two letters of 1599 as being "busied only in penning comedies for the common players."[1] Ever since the letters came to light in 1891 he has been regarded as one of the top candidates for the authorship of the works published under the name "William Shakespeare," if that name was a pen name. In this book I aim to show that this possibility is close to a certainty by an analysis of striking new evidence together with much that has been around for centuries but overlooked or misinterpreted.

It is perhaps difficult for a newcomer to the subject to comprehend the apparently outrageous idea that the wrong man has been invested with the authorship of the incomparable poems and plays we know as Shakespeare's. Why was the deception, if that was what it was, not uncovered many years ago? I am going to start in a roundabout way by quoting a remark posted to an internet forum in February 2011.

> If the author of the collection of plays ascribed to William Shakespeare was someone other than the William Shakespeare of Stratford on Avon who had various commercial and acting interests in London around the start of the seventeenth century then, in my opinion, the true authorship would have been unambiguously claimed in some sort of open-sight cipher at the time.[2]

This is a remarkably perceptive observation. There were open-sight ciphers available at the time (though only a few), and the Elizabethans and Jacobeans loved all kinds of word games. If an author did not want to have his name on the title page of his book there were methods for concealing it somewhere in the text which might evade discovery for many years, but which would afford the author the satisfaction of knowing that it was recorded there for as long as his book survived; dozens of people took this course, perhaps hundreds worldwide. So it was in the case of Shakespeare. I am not going to give the game away at this early stage (anyone can look into the later chapter which deals with it if they so choose), but I have right at the beginning to acknowledge the "onlie begetter" of the open-sight cipher which in effect initiated the writing of this book.

In October 2008, I received a transatlantic telephone call from Jones Harris, who had been discussing with me the authorship of Shakespeare for some years, sometimes ringing once a month, sometimes several times a week. On this occasion he confided his great insight, that if the name of the real author had been concealed in the First Folio (the collection of plays published in 1623), then the only page available for the purpose was the one that listed the actors' names. All the rest of the text of the Folio came from outside sources—the plays themselves, the prefatory material signed by John Heminge and Henry Condell (two of the actors in the plays), and the laudatory poems. The one page entirely at the disposal of the editors was the one with the title "The Workes of William Shakespeare," which contains the names of all the players arranged in two columns. "Study these columns," urged Jones Harris, "and see what you find." The result is this book.

My first doubts about Shakespeare arose when reading one of his many biographies sometime in the 1960s. The story was familiar—the gifted young man entranced by a troupe of players visiting Stratford-upon-Avon, joining them and traveling with them to London, where his facility in writing soon began to bear fruit in the early plays. It all seemed entirely plausible, until turning a page one was confronted by the six "authentic" signatures. I could not believe that these were the signatures of a practiced literary pen, although paradoxically it is now thought that some of them were written by lawyers' clerks ([b] and [c] in Figure 1.1).[3] At the time it was taken for granted that these signatures, all spelled differently and with a notable lack of style, were the only remaining words written by our great poet—none of the manuscripts of the poems and plays having survived.

Intrigued by this disconnect between what one might expect—decent penmanship, and what appears—characterless scrawl, I read several books on the authorship question. But the case for the man from Stratford seemed unassailable, and I remained in the orthodox camp for the next 25 years or so. Then in the late 1980s I read a book[4] which set out firstly

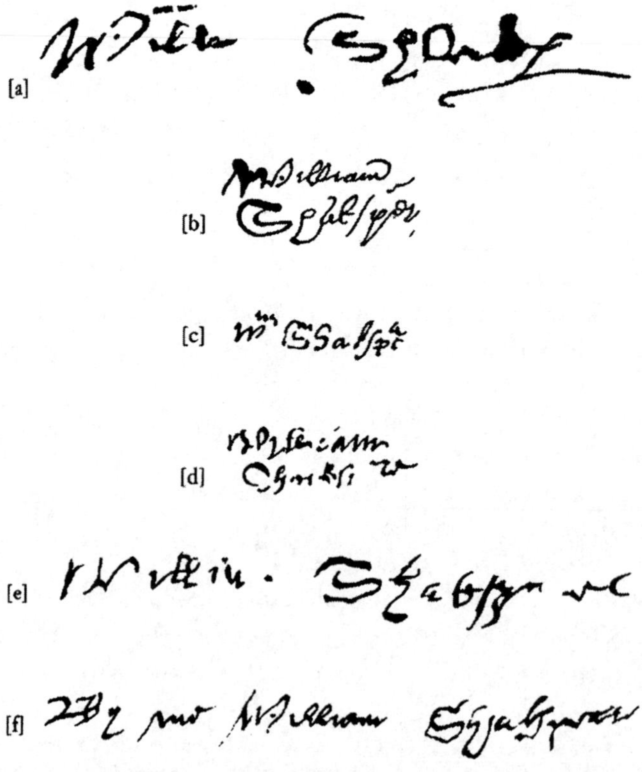

Figure 1.1 Shakespeare's signatures: [a] from the Belott-Mountjoy lawsuit (1612); [b] and [c] from deeds relating to the purchase of the Blackfriars Gatehouse (1612); [d], [e], [f] on his will (1616); the first three words of [f] are in another hand.

to demolish the Stratford man and secondly to put forward the case for Edward de Vere, 17th Earl of Oxford, as the real author. I found the book very interesting, and after a third reading it seemed to me that the case against the Stratford man was strong, while the case for Oxford was rather weak, although not implausible. For a few years I looked for evidence that might support the case for Oxford, but soon found an insuperable barrier. It turned out that Oxford's and Shakespeare's writing habits were incompatible. For example, Shakespeare (as exhibited in the plays) frequently used words for which Oxford (as recorded in his letters) always used alternatives. Thus Shakespeare often used the word "since" to mean "because," for which Oxford invariably used the word "sith," and Shakespeare often used the word "has," for which Oxford invariably used "hath"; there are several other major stylistic incompatibilities as well.[5]

For these and other reasons I discarded Oxford as a possible authorship candidate, and spent quite a lot of time reading about the other top candidates, who included Christopher Marlowe, Francis Bacon, William Stanley and Roger Manners (Earl of Rutland). An excellent introduction to the authorship question is the book by the late John Michell, *Who Wrote Shakespeare?*, already mentioned, and it so happened that he appeared to favor Stanley.[6] When summarizing his findings, however, he finally opted for Bacon, which was a surprise. It has to be emphasized that the case for any of the candidates is purely circumstantial. It is a matter of weighing possibility against possibility and plausibility against plausibility. Perhaps I should add briefly that of those just mentioned, Marlowe died in 1593 before many of the plays had been written and Bacon's equable temperament seemed at odds with Shakespeare's mercurial spirit, while Rutland was born too late to have authored the plays written before 1591.

For the next few years I had no preferred candidate, as there seemed to be nothing which definitely singled out one man ahead of the others. But having now acquired considerable familiarity with all the background issues, I was in a good position to appreciate the force of the clue offered to me in 2008 by Jones Harris. It has been well said that fortune favors the prepared mind.

Although the evidence for any authorship candidate is only circumstantial, in the sense that no contemporary or near-contemporary document has come to light stating that so-and-so was writing under the pseudonym "William Shakespeare," there are a number of remarks made about Shakespeare the playwright and about Shakespeare the man from Stratford-upon-Avon which provide clues. There are also a very few remarks made by the author about himself, and also a few deductions that can be made from his works, all of which obviously demand the very closest scrutiny. It is my opinion, as expressed in this book, that there is in fact enough evidence, both well-known and newly discovered, to resolve the authorship problem once and for all. I should like to invite the reader to embark with me on a journey of discovery, where I shall point out intriguing features, neglected paths, blind alleys and other objects of significance in the literary and documentary landscape. My hope is that we shall together arrive at the goal indicated by this book's title, but if there is a parting of the ways, there will be no recriminations, and the journey may be no less enjoyable if we arrive at different destinations.

Part I: Fundamentals

1. Basic Knowledge

How much do we *really* know about the playwright "William Shakespeare," the spelling adopted by the stationers who published the First Folio,[1] and about the actor from Stratford-upon-Avon, who is almost universally regarded as the same man? As the contention of this book is that they were two different people, it will be convenient to refer to the actor as William Shakspere, to avoid confusion. It is moreover a fact that this spelling (with no "e" after the "k," suggestive of a short "a") was the one used more than 20 times in the church records of the extended Stratford family's births, marriages and deaths (the spelling "Shake-speare" with an "e" after the "k" was never used for the family in these records).[2]

We know quite a lot about William Shakspere. He was born in 1564, married in 1582, fathered three children, and is first recorded in London in March 1595 as one of three payees for theatrical performances given before Queen Elizabeth the previous Christmas.[3] The other payees were William Kemp and Richard Burbage, members of the Lord Chamberlain's Men, one of the leading acting troupes of the time. It is therefore reasonable to assume that by now he had joined them as an actor, and his name occasionally appears on lists of actors for the next thirty years. However, nowhere is there any indication or hint that he might have been writing plays, even where one might most expect it. In particular, when Cuthbert Burbage, founder-investor in the Globe Theatre, wrote a letter in 1635 to the Lord Chamberlain, Philip Herbert, Earl of Montgomery, he referred to "Shakspere" and "Shakspeare" (note the lack of an "e" after the "k," probably indicating a short "a") as one of several "deserving men" and also as one of several "men players."[4] It doesn't sound as though Burbage thought of Shakspere or Shakspeare as the famous playwright "Shakespeare" (whose name was almost invariably spelled with an "e" after the "k," indicating a long "a"). If the actor had been the well-known dramatist, it is virtually certain that Burbage would have referred to the fact in his petition, which sought Montgomery's support in a legal matter concerning the actors, especially as he was one of the two dedicatees of the First Folio. Such a reference would have greatly strengthened the force of his appeal.

We know very little about William Shakespeare, the author. From the plays it is clear that he was an educated man (perhaps self-educated), familiar with Latin, French and Italian,[5] and that he had traveled in France and Italy (or knew people who had done so). From the poet and playwright Henry Chettle, in a poem written just after Queen Elizabeth's death in March 1603, we learn that she had "graced his desert,"[6] which might be interpreted in various ways. And in sonnet 125, published in 1609, he wrote of himself: "Wer't ought to me I bore the canopy?" which appears to indicate that he thought of himself as someone who might have been chosen for that honor. It is not much to go on.

So, from someone who knew the Stratford actor well over a number of years, Cuthbert Burbage, we find no hint that he thought of him as the playwright Shakespeare, the name (with an "e" after the "k") now famous following the publication of the First (1623) and Second (1632) Folio collections of his plays (the actor William Shakspere died in 1616). We also learn that the Queen had "graced" the author's "desert," presumably not long before her death (or the event would not have been fresh in Chettle's mind), and moreover that he thought of himself as someone who might bear the canopy over Her Majesty, or over her successor King James, for by law a canopy could only be carried over royalty.[7]

I have found it difficult to decide how to lay out the evidence which in my view converges on the real author. The following series of chapters may seem somewhat disconnected and haphazard, but they are in effect the building blocks of the edifice which supports my contention. To begin with, then, let us ask the question: "What is the first hard evidence that there was something fishy about Shakespeare and his works?"[8] I pass over indications from the late 1590s that some people were puzzled about the authorship of the long narrative poem *Venus and Adonis* (published in 1593), as little can be deduced from their remarks; I shall refer to these later. The first clear indication that something was amiss with the attribution of the plays to the man from Stratford-upon-Avon comes from the First Folio of 1623, and in particular from the famous portrait of the author on its title page, perhaps the most iconic image of any author of any age. For it turns out to be a caricature—not only that, but a caricature with a devastating hidden agenda.

2. *Shakespeare's Impossible Doublet*

The First Folio collection of 36 plays,[1] published in 1623, is the bedrock on which the conventional view of its author and his identity rests. The name of the author—Mr. William Shakespeare—is at the top of the title page, while the dedication (to the Earls of Pembroke and Montgomery, brothers) and the address ("To the great Variety of Readers") are each signed by John Heminge (elsewhere spelled Hemmings) and Henry Condell, two of Shakespeare's theatrical colleagues. In the laudatory poems that follow, Leonard Digges refers to "Thy Stratford Moniment," while Ben Jonson calls him "Sweet Swan of Avon"; clearly we are being told that the author is Mr. William Shakespeare of Stratford-upon-Avon, although there is nothing else in the introductory pages to confirm the attribution—no dates, no mention of family or friends, or of places of birth or burial, just these two incidental, almost off-hand, phrases. And there on the title page is his portrait, with a poem by Ben Jonson on the facing page saying "It was for gentle Shakespeare cut."

The received opinion concerning the First Folio is that it was a straightforward tribute to our great poet, preserving for posterity his magnificent works for the theater. As will emerge in the following pages, however, it is anything but straightforward, and the key to its darker purpose lies in the enigmatic picture on its title page. It is a masterpiece of duplicity, since it shows a man wearing impossible clothing *when he should have been dressed impeccably.*

Shakespeare's portrait has found few admirers. Various defects have been pointed out from time to time, for example the head is too large, the stiff white collar seems odd, left and right of the jerkin or doublet[2] don't quite match up. But nonetheless the illustration is generally regarded as serving a valuable purpose in giving posterity some idea of what our great playwright looked like. The portrait's deficiencies are frequently ascribed to the youth and incompetence of the engraver, one Martin Droeshout, born in 1601 and aged twenty-one or twenty-two in 1623.[3] It is unlikely that he would have seen Shakspere (who died in 1616), and it is often supposed that the engraving was based on a portrait from the life, now lost.

Many commentators have drawn attention to the image's deficiencies, most finding fault with the details of the face and hair. Several also point out errors in the costume, for example Sidney Lee refers to "patent defects of perspective,"[4] while M. H. Spielmann says that the shoulder-wings are "grotesquely large and vilely drawn."[5] But the nature of the most elusive—and the most extraordinary—peculiarity was first brought to light in 1911 by an anonymous tailor writing in *The Gentleman's Tailor*, under the title "A Problem for the Trade."[6] His expertise allowed him to claim that the doublet "is so strangely illustrated that the right-hand side of the forepart is *obviously* [my italics] the left-hand side of the backpart, and so gives a harlequin appearance to the figure, which it is not unnatural to assume was intentional and done with express object and purpose." The tailor gave no reasons for arriving at his conclusion, and as what was obvious to him may not be at all obvious to the average spectator nowadays (including myself) I shall now present evidence which shows that his assessment was correct, and that there are other peculiarities which cast further doubt on the integrity of the portrait. I should perhaps warn the reader that the rest of this chapter is hard going, but as the portrait turns out to be a time-bomb (with a very slow fuse!) which has the effect of destroying the Shakspere myth, every step of the analysis has to be spelled out in the minutest detail, to construct a cast-iron argument.

When carefully analyzed, the doublet displays four main oddities which fully confirm the tailor's verdict. Firstly, the wearer's right shoulder-wing (onlooker's left, Figure 2.1) is smaller than the left shoulder-wing, when they should be (roughly) the same size, or at least balance pictorially. In addition, the right-hand front panel of the garment is clearly smaller than the left-hand front panel, as is indicated by the different lengths of the embroidery edges labeled "x" and "y" (Figure 2.2). Already we can begin to see why the tailor of 1911 became curious about the wearer's costume.

Figure 2.1 Title page of the First Folio of Shakespeare's plays, 1623.

More significantly, the embroidery on the right sleeve does not correspond to that on the left sleeve (Figure 2.3). On the left sleeve the upper edge of the embroidery (when extended) meets the inside edge of the shoulder-wing (where it is joined to the doublet) a distance of just over two bands of embroidery (labeled "B") down from the top of the shoulder-wing. In contrast, on the right sleeve, the upper edge of the embroidery meets the inside edge of the shoulder-wing a distance of rather over three bands, plus a wide gap (labeled "g," roughly the same width as a band), down from the top of the wing. Instead of corresponding (at least approximately) with that on the left sleeve, the embroidery on the right sleeve is located around twice as far away from the top of the shoulder-wing. This anomaly is immediately evident from the diagram (Figure 2.3), and I apologize for spelling it out in words in such cumbersome detail. (At this point I should like to assure the reader there is only one more difficult paragraph to grapple with, after which it is all plain sailing.)

The most significant oddity of all is that the embroidery on the right shoulder-wing *does not match* that on the left shoulder-wing. From the top of the left wing (Figure 2.4), moving down, there are two bands of embroidery close together, a wide gap, and then another pair of bands, and so on. On the right wing, starting at the corresponding place, there is only *one* band of embroidery, then a wide gap, then a pair of bands, and so on. Symbolically, the pattern of embroidery on the left wing, starting from the top, can be represented by "BBgBBgBB," etc. and that on the right wing by "BgBBgBBg," etc. These two patterns would match on a normal garment, but here they do not: clearly *this is not a normal garment*.

These four points fully confirm the verdict of the tailor of 1911: the garment consists of the left front *joined to the left back* of a real doublet—a sartorial absurdity. The right-hand half of the front of the doublet

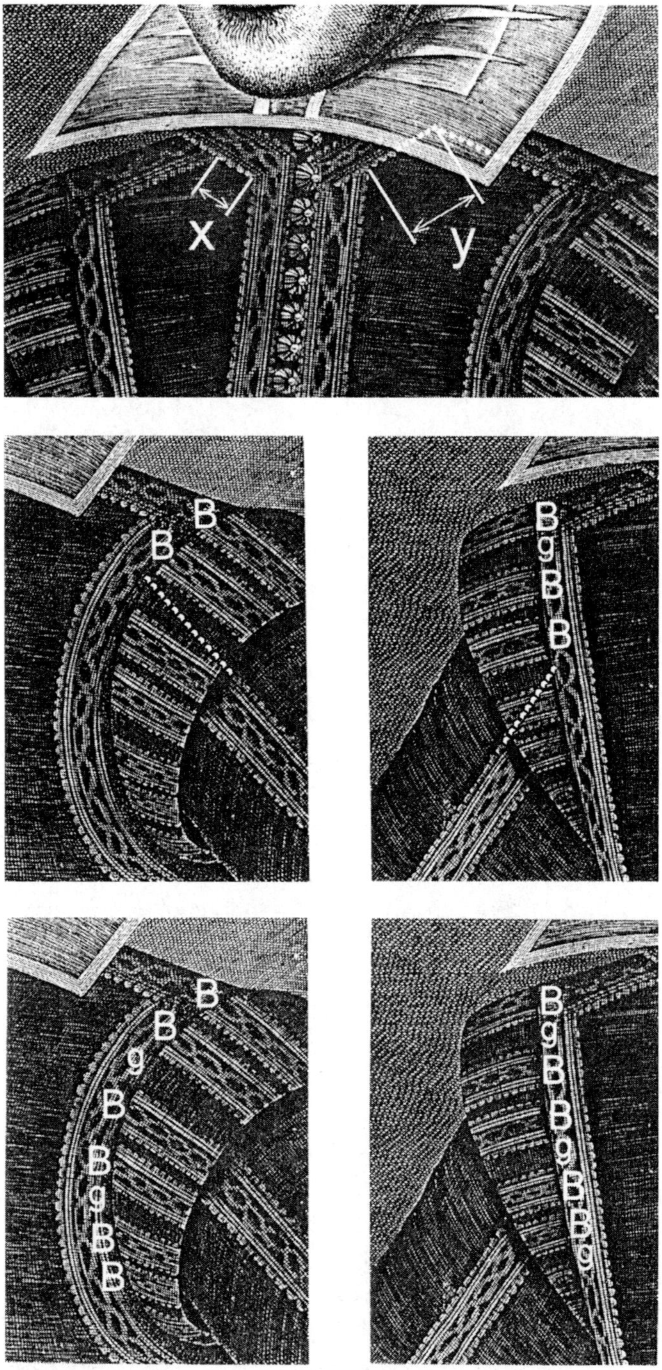

Top: **Figure 2.2 The right-hand front panel is smaller than the left-hand front panel.** ***Middle:*** **Figure 2.3 The embroidery on the right sleeve is placed around twice as far down from the top of the shoulder-wing as that on the left sleeve.** ***Bottom:*** **Figure 2.4 The embroidery on the right shoulder-wing does not match that on the left shoulder-wing.**

(Figures 2.3 or 2.4) is clearly not the mirror image of the left-hand half (even after taking perspective into account), and the embroidery on the right sleeve indicates that this is in fact the *back* of the left sleeve, where it would be suitably positioned. The smaller size of the front right-hand panel (shown by seam "x" being around half the length of seam "y," Figure 2.2) is appropriate for the left-hand panel of the back of the doublet. The (non-matching) embroidery on the (smaller) right shoulder-wing would be what one would expect to see on the *back* of the left shoulder-wing, the "BBg" pattern being repeated regularly around it (Figure 2.5). It is now clear that no tailor-made doublet ever had such a counter-changed or "harlequin appearance," and we are left wondering how this might have come about.

It has been frequently suggested that the engraver was incompetent and that the publishers, principally Isaac Jaggard and Edward Blount, were prepared to accept an imperfect image of the author and his doublet, despite the fact that such a costly undertaking (one of the most expensive to date by an English publisher[7]) would surely demand a flawless frontispiece. Although incompetence in perspective drawing might possibly account for the first three points above, it cannot account for the last, the embroidery mismatch on the shoulder-wings. No tailor, dressmaker, painter or sculptor—or engraver—could ever commit such a gross error, unless it were expressly required by patron or employer. Thus for whatever reason, these so-called deficiencies were evidently intentional, just as the tailor of 1911 supposed, and accepted as such by Jaggard and his colleagues (who would likely have approved initial sketches and might well have kept an eye on work in progress). If they didn't like what the engraver first produced, they had only to withhold payment until he produced something more acceptable. Moreover, a young man undertaking an important commission early in his career is going to make absolutely certain that the finished product is exactly what his employers require. Anxious to gain a reputation and a living, he would strive to avoid errors at all costs, knowing that his work would be subject to severe scrutiny on account of his youth. That the engraver signed with his full name suggests he was fully satisfied with his achievement.

The mismatch between the patterns of embroidery on the shoulder-wings can only

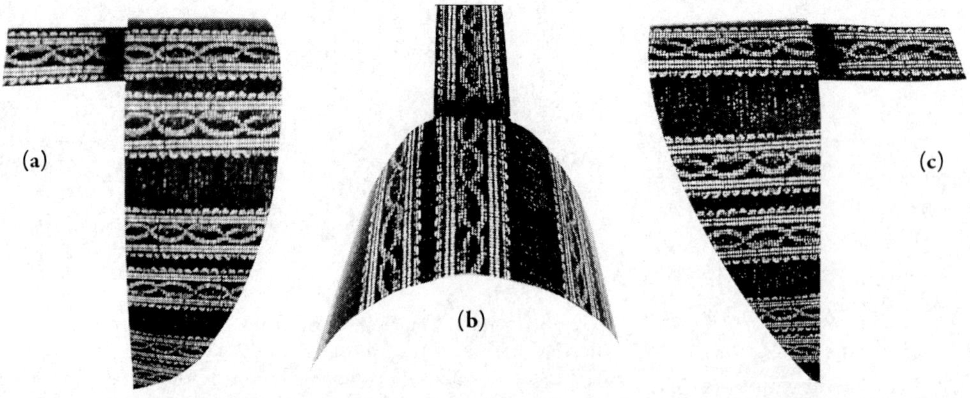

Figure 2.5 A mock-up of the left shoulder-wing; (a) from the front, (b) from the side, (c) from the back. Compare with Figure 2.3 or 2.4.

have been achieved deliberately. To put it another way, even a child of ten would know that the bands of embroidery on the two shoulder-wings should be mirror images of each other. An artist or engraver, having completed one shoulder-wing, would *automatically* make sure the second wing matched the first, unless instructed otherwise. Together with the other peculiarities, this specific feature shows beyond doubt that the engraved doublet was carefully designed to consist of the left half of the front and the left half of the back of a real garment. It would appear that the artist had a real doublet in front of him, and having depicted the front left half with the central fastenings and embroidery, turned it round and drew the back left half. Why the engraver should have distorted reality in such a way as to create sartorial nonsense will be discussed in the next chapter.

3. Shakspere a Stand-In

Before we attempt an assessment of Droeshout's engraving it is interesting to find that it formed the basis of another frontispiece. John Benson's edition (1640) of *Poems* by *Wil. Shake-speare*[1] employs a reversed and simplified version of the engraving, made by William Marshall (Figure 3.1). It hardly comes as a surprise to find that the oddities of the portrait seem to have aroused a certain amount of skepticism. The anomalous right-hand side of the doublet is covered by a cloak, and beneath the portrait are eight lines of verse, the first two of which read:

> This Shadowe is renowned Shakespear's? Soule of th'age
> The applause? delight? the wonder of the Stage.

The use of question marks rather than exclamation marks might appear to suggest that doubts about the engraving had already surfaced (although it is a fact that at the time they were sometimes used where we would nowadays use exclamation marks).

As an example of what could be described as normal practice in this period, consider the portrait of Samuel Daniel which prefaced his *Civil Wars* (1609)[2]; note the modest costume appropriate to a middle-class writer and poet, and the complex ornamental designs surrounding the image.

In contrast, the First Folio title page differs from all other examples by offering *no* surrounding details or embellishments, only the bleak image. Jonson's poem on the left-hand page facing the portrait adds further to the puzzle. It reads, not without a hint of ambiguity:

> This Figure, that thou here seest put,
> It was for gentle Shakespeare cut;
> Wherein the Graver had a strife
> With Nature, to outdoo the life:
> O, could he but have drawne his wit
> As well in brasse, as he hath hit
> His face; the Print would then surpasse
> All, that was ever writ in brasse.
> But, since he cannot, Reader, looke
> Not on his Picture, but his Booke.

Shakespeare, the verses tell us, "is not to be found after all in the compelling image opposite," according to Leah Marcus.[3] It is a "Figure" cut "for" Shakespeare,[4] rather than "of" Shakespeare, and should be ignored in favor of the volume's contents, according to Ben Jonson.

This Shadowe is renowned Shakespear's! Soule of th'age
The applause! delight! the wonder of the Stage.
Nature her selfe, was proud of his designes
And joy'd to weare the dressing of his lines;
The learned will Confess, his works are such,
As neither man, nor Muse, can prayse to much.
For ever live thy fame, the world to tell,
Thy like, no age, shall ever paralell.
W.M. sculpsit.

Left: **Figure 3.1 William Marshall's engraving of Shakespeare for the frontispiece of John Benson's edition of *Poems* by *Wil. Shake-speare*, London, 1640. *Right:* Figure 3.2 Frontispiece of Samuel Daniel's *Civil Wars*, engraved by Thomas Cockson. London: Simon Waterson, 1609.**

Commentary

The findings discussed in the previous chapter reveal a horrendous discrepancy on the title page of the First Folio between what one would expect and what one observes. In place of a lifelike or at least credible portrait of the "Soul of the Age," this "Star of Poets," dressed appropriately, we are offered a picture of a man wearing a ridiculous costume—a mock doublet stitched together from the left front and left back of a disassembled real doublet. What can this mean?

If similar portraits or historical parallels could be found they might supply an explanation, but an exhaustive search has failed to produce a single example,[5] and so we can only offer a few conjectures. The idea that Martin Droeshout might have had a grudge against Shakspere or the publishers of the First Folio, and set out to poke fun at him or them by producing an engraving full of faults (hoping no one would notice), can I think be discarded. Another possibility is that the two left sleeves symbolize the fact that Shakespeare was the servant of two masters, Queen Elizabeth and James I, badges of allegiance being worn on the left sleeve. But the man in the portrait, so far from wearing the clothing of a retainer or actor, is dressed in clothing appropriate to a landed gentleman such as Sir John Petre, later Baron Petre (Figure 3.3). Shakspere might have acquired such clothing as a cast-off to wear on the stage, but could never have worn it in daily life in view of the existing sumptuary laws, which stipulated that a man had to wear clothing appropriate to his station in life.[6] Another suggestion is that since left-handedness is sometimes associated with underhand dealings, the portrait may hint at some subterfuge connected with the publication.

In the absence of a clear interpretation, perhaps something can be learned from other aspects of the engraving. Among the many further peculiarities is that the portrait of Shakespeare is "extremely large."[7] In fact, it is around four times larger in area (six and a half inches by seven and a quarter) than the title page head-and-shoulders portrait of any other author of the period. Why is this? I would suggest that if the image had been of normal size (e.g., that of a playing card or postcard), the details, especially those of the embroidery, would have been so difficult to make out that the implication they were designed to convey might never have been suspected. To ensure that the left-front left-back character would be noticed, the engraving had to be as large as possible, and as a consequence no space was available for the conventional allegorical figures and emblems usually surrounding such an image.

Further evidence of the duplicity of the engraving is provided by the starched white collar or wired band under the head (Figure 2.1). Its support, known as an "underpropper" or "supportasse" (made, e.g., from lightweight material covered in silk), shows clearly through the linen on the left side of the collar (onlooker's right), but is not visible on the right side; both Sandy Nairne and Tarnya Cooper draw attention to this curious omission in the National Portrait Gallery's publication *Searching for Shakespeare* (2006).[8] It is also worth noting that the collar conceals part of the embroidery edge labeled "y" (Figure 2.2), in such a way that the exposed part is the same length as the edge labeled "x." The left and right seams in the neck area therefore appear to match each other, creating a kind of *trompe l'oeil* effect which tends to obscure the differing sizes of the front panels; it may be that the collar was introduced precisely for this purpose. In addition, the triangular sewn darts of the collar are almost comically asymmetrical: left and right bear no kind of mirror relationship with each other, even allowing for perspective; Figure 3.4 draws attention to the chief mismatches.[9] It is no more a real collar

Figure 3.3 Detail of the portrait of Sir John Petre (1603), reproduced by kind permission of Lord Petre, Ingatestone Hall, Ingatestone, Essex.

than the doublet is a real doublet, and it is difficult to resist an impression that the person depicted is being gently and surreptitiously mocked, sent up and ridiculed. Although one or two peculiarities might be ascribed to carelessness, six or seven (some obvious at first glance) seem to point towards a deliberate agenda of some kind.

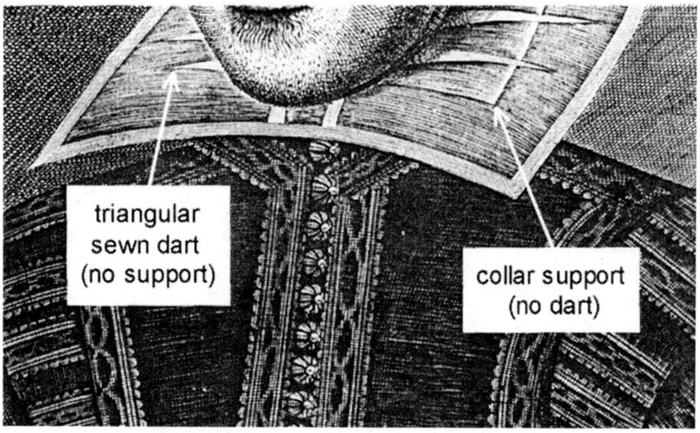

Figure 3.4 Showing the omission of the right-hand side of the collar support, and the lack of symmetry in the depiction of the triangular sewn darts in the wired band.

Here is a summary of the "defects," which we now know to have been the result of a carefully designed and brilliantly executed deception.

(a) The right shoulder-wing is smaller than the left shoulder-wing (Figure 2.1).
(b) The right-hand front panel is smaller than that on the left (Figure 2.2).
(c) The embroidery on the right sleeve is placed twice as far away from the top of the shoulder wing as that on the left (Figure 2.3).
(d) The embroidery on the right shoulder-wing does not match that on the left shoulder-wing (Figure 2.4).
(e) The right shoulder-wing is the back of the left shoulder-wing (Figure 2.5).
(f) The right-hand part of the collar support is missing (Figure 3.4).
(g) The triangular sewn darts in the collar are asymmetrical (Figure 3.4).

Items (a) to (e) are fully explained by the fact (which has now become clear) that the front right-hand half of the doublet has been replaced by the back left-hand half of the doublet. In all garments of a similar design, e.g., a modern gentleman's formal jacket, the panels of the back of the garment are smaller than the front panels since they are of less sartorial interest, and the same is true of the doublet we have just analyzed.

Conclusion

The orthodox community of Shakespeare scholars regards the First Folio as a straightforward tribute to their great colleague masterminded by two members of the acting company he wrote for, the Lord Chamberlain's Men, later the King's Men. These are John Heminge (or Hemmings) and Henry Condell, whose names are subscribed to both the dedicatory letter and to the address to the reader which are printed on the early pages of the volume.[10] The "imperfections" of the portrait are brushed aside as indicating no more than that the artist was incompetent and the stationers indifferent to its shortcomings.

However, as has just been demonstrated, the image turns out to have a hidden purpose, one that is not in the least straightforward. The portrait, which we are told—but only by implication—is that of the author Mr. William Shakespeare of Stratford-upon-Avon ("Thy Stratford Moniment," "Sweet Swan of Avon"[11]), shows someone dressed in a mock doublet, consisting of the left front joined to the left back of a real doublet. In plain material and bold colors, this is the style of dress of jesters, where the front right and left halves are colored (say) red and yellow, and the back halves similarly. By clothing the actor from Stratford-upon-Avon in a ridiculous garment, whoever was in charge was indicating, by a deliberate deception, that the implication that he was the author of the plays was false. The impossible garment clothes an impossible author. The bedrock of the traditional ascription of the plays crumbles to dust, and the man to whom the volume is being attributed is thereby revealed as a dummy, a substitute, a stand-in, a decoy designed to attract attention away from the real author. Those already in the know would spot this, and think to themselves, "What a clever ruse!" Those not in the know would accept the duplicitous portrait at face value and remain unaware of the deception, just as do most people today.

I have perhaps made somewhat heavy weather of this account of the portrait's "deficiencies," and how they deliberately point to calculated deceit and subterfuge on the part of the prime mover or movers of the undertaking. What it amounts to is that whoever was in possession of the great author's works arranged for them to be attributed to someone else, who happened to have a name similar to the pen name. The deception was built into the very foundation of the enterprise. This finding shatters for ever the cozy relationship between the orthodox community of Shakespeare scholars and the man from Stratford-upon-Avon.

It is my hope that readers will find themselves convinced at this early stage of our exposition that there really is something fishy and indeed mysterious about the genesis of the First Folio and about the identity of its author. I am almost tempted to suggest that if you are not happy to accept this, there is little point in reading further. If however you are prepared to keep an open mind, without actually rejecting my conclusion, then I hope you will stay with me on our journey together as we look further into the problem of the authorship of Shakespeare.

4. Shakspere Eliminated

Now that it has been established that the First Folio title page portrait was a clever device (I nearly wrote a *fiendishly* clever device), designed to eliminate (given time) the man from Stratford-upon-Avon from the authorship of the plays printed therein, we need to look in greater detail at what we know of his life and career.

He was born in 1564 and christened on the 26 April as "Guglielmus ... Shakspere" (*ODNB*). He married Anne Hathaway in 1582, Susanna was born in 1583, and twins Hamnet and Judith in 1585. The next relevant occurrence of the name, in the form William Shakespeare, is at the foot of the dedication to the Third Earl of Southampton prefaced to the long narrative erotic poem *Venus and Adonis*, published in 1593.[1] This was parodied shortly after by someone with the initials "T. H.," in a similarly erotic poem entitled *Oenone and Paris*,[2] which included a mocking dedication, modeled on that to *Venus and Adonis*, and referring to its author (T. H.) as "lurking ... obscurely." This may be the first hint (however indirect) that the version of the name with an "e" after the "k" was thought to be a pen name (or it may hint at nothing at all). A second narrative poem, *Lucrece*, followed in 1594,[3] also with a dedication to Southampton signed as before.

The next instance of the name occurs in a document of March 1595 (as already mentioned), recording the payment of £20 to "Willam Kempe, Willam Shakespeare & Richarde Burbage," servants to the Lord Chamberlain, for two comedies played before the Queen at Christmas in 1594.[4] The Lord Chamberlain's Men was an acting troupe which had been formed earlier that year with several players from the break-up of "Strange's Men" following the death of their patron Ferdinando Stanley, Lord Strange (elder brother of our authorship candidate William Stanley), and it is reasonable to suppose that the man from Stratford-upon-Avon (spelled on this occasion with a medial "e") had by now joined this troupe.

Over the next few years we find that the authorship of *Venus and Adonis* is being seriously questioned. John Marston and Joseph Hall appear to think it had been written by someone they term "Labeo." This was the name of a famous Roman lawyer, and it is has been deduced from their comments that they thought Francis Bacon to be its author.[5] Then William Covell, author of *Polimanteia* (1595), writes Shakespeare's name against Samuel Daniel's works, suggesting he thought Shakespeare was Daniel. Thomas Edwards in *Cephalus and Procris. Narcissus* (1595) indicates that someone "masking" and dressed in purple robes was the author, in other words a concealed nobleman. Then Gabriel Harvey, in a note written in the margin of a book sometime between 1598 and 1600, appears to hint at Sir Edward Dyer as the author.[6] What emerges from all these rather vague remarks is that in the period

1594 to 1600 many people were doubtful of the authorship of *Venus and Adonis*, and seem to have thought that the name "William Shakespeare" was a pen name.

I mention these views, conflicting as they are, to show that doubts about whether the name was that of a real person or a pseudonym arose very soon after it first appeared in print. This contradicts the commonly held view that doubts about the authorship only began to arise in the mid-nineteenth century. Although William Shakspere was probably residing in London at this period, no one seems to have thought the actor was the writer, despite the similarity of the names.

Nearer our own time, commentators have found a variety of different reasons for doubting the actor William Shakspere's authorship of *Venus and Adonis* and indeed of anything published under the name William Shakespeare. For example, it has emerged that neither of his daughters was taught to write, although one of them did manage to reproduce two stylized signatures apparently formed with difficulty.[7] One must wonder why a great poet and playwright would fail to have his daughters taught to write. Other reasons for doubting his authorship are now examined.

Shakspere's Penmanship: The Belott-Mountjoy Lawsuit

Evidence about the Stratford man's own facility with the pen is provided by the signature appended to his deposition in the Belott-Mountjoy lawsuit. Shakspere lodged with the Mountjoys in London's Silver Street in the early 1600s, and was required to give evidence in person in May 1612 about a promise of a dowry made by Noel Mountjoy to his son-in-law Stephen Belott in 1604. He is described in his deposition as "William Shakespeare of Stratford upon Avon in the Countye of Warwicke *gentleman* [expanded] of the Age of xlviii yeres or thereaboutes." Charles Nicholl in *The Lodger* (2007)[8] prints all the papers relevant to the Belott-Mountjoy suit. Five of the deponents' signatures are reproduced in his book, all signed in full with good and fluent penmanship. Shakspere's deposition by contrast is signed with an abbreviated and blotchy "Wīlm Sha~k/." It doesn't look as though he was a ready and practiced penman, someone who had recently written *The Winter's Tale* and *The Tempest*. While George Wilkins is thought to be the published author with that name, the other four are ordinary residents of London, not associated with any literary accomplishments, and all have far better handwriting than the Stratford Shakspere.

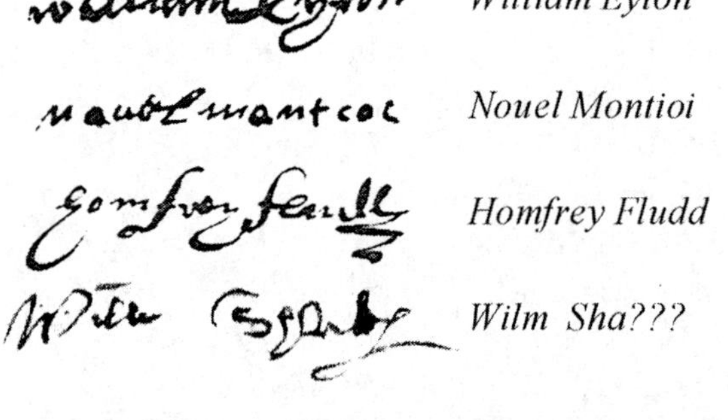

Figure 4.1 Signatures from depositions in the Belott-Mountjoy Suit, Court of Requests, May–June 1612; copyright © The National Archives, TNA REQ 4/1/4/1

Philip Henslowe's Theatrical Records

Philip Henslowe was a businessman and impresario who built the Rose theater in Southwark in 1587, and had interests in other theaters as well. From 1592 until 1609 he kept notes of his theatrical activities in what is known as "Henslowe's Diary,"[9] where he recorded payments for new plays or the rewriting of old plays to twenty-seven Elizabethan playwrights, including Christopher Marlowe, Robert Greene, Henry Chettle, Thomas Middleton and John Marston. Although several plays with titles identical or similar to Shakespearean plays published later are mentioned there as having been staged at one theater or another (*Hamlet, Henry VI, King Lear, The Taming of a Shrew* and *Titus Andronicus*) the name Shakespeare nowhere appears, either as payee for a play or as the recipient of a loan. Just where one might be most confident of finding his presence, among his fellow playwrights, there is a blank, hard to explain if his situation was similar to theirs. (But if the author of these plays was someone of independent means, indifferent to the small sums plays might secure, the absence of his name in the diary is understandable.)

William Shakspere's Litigation

The records show that Shakspere several times went to court to prosecute his neighbors for sums of money. Although the amounts may seem small to us today, they were significant at the time, and it is not recorded how often Shakspere made reasonable requests for the return of what was owed to him. Nevertheless, one particular episode does him no credit. Between December 1608 and June 1609, William "Shackspeare" was proceeding against one John Addenbrocke. The French literary scholar Professor Abel Lefranc gives the following account.[10]

> When John Addenbrocke is prosecuted, in 1609, by Shakespeare his fellow-citizen, for a debt of £6, together with £1 5s. for costs [*in today's money, about £3,600 plus £750 for costs*], he resigns himself to leaving Stratford. But his creditor does not disarm: he avenges himself, as Sir Sidney Lee says, by prosecuting at once Thomas Horneby of Stratford who stood bail for the fugitive. Horneby had succeeded his father as master blacksmith on Henley Street.... The family forge stood close to Shakespeare's birthplace. In this lawsuit plaintiff and defendant had been childhood playmates (per Sidney Lee...), and later in their riper years, not to speak of neighbourly ties, certain common interests brought them still closer together.... [Nevertheless] he had his old comrade and neighbour Thomas Horneby, standing simple bail, thrown into prison.

Richard Grant White, in his *Memoirs of the Life of William Shakespeare* (1866), had earlier commented on this episode as follows.[11]

> The pursuit of an impoverished man for the sake of imprisoning him and depriving him both of the power of paying his debts and supporting himself and his family, is an incident in Shakespeare's life which it requires the utmost allowance and consideration for the practice of the time and country to enable us to contemplate with equanimity—satisfaction is impossible.

Where, one might ask, is "the quality of mercy" displayed in this story? Is this really how our great playwright would have behaved?

William Shakspere's Will

William Shakspere's will, with its three wretched signatures (Figure 1.1), is often claimed not to be what one would expect from the dramatist (but he may have been palsied when he came to sign it).[12] For example, it does not refer to any books or playbooks, or to the eighteen plays which had not yet been printed but which were later to be included in the First Folio together with those that had already been published. Rather it reveals him as an owner of property and a small-time businessman.

While this may be true, I do not think such claims count for much. Little can be deduced from absence of evidence, and it may be that the books (if any) were listed in an inventory now lost, and perhaps special arrangements had been made for the preservation and subsequent publishing of the eighteen unpublished plays. What the will does tell us, however, is that he regarded John Hemmings, Richard Burbage and Henry Condell as his "fellows," and left them "26s. 8d. apiece to buy them rings"; these are three of the King's Men and sharers in the Globe Theatre, where many of the author Shakespeare's plays had been performed. That he was the "man player" later referred to by Cuthbert Burbage (see Chapter 1) is thereby confirmed, if confirmation were needed. Nothing else of note can be deduced from an otherwise mundane but competently drafted testamentary document.

The Monumental Bust in Holy Trinity Church, Stratford-upon-Avon

Inside Holy Trinity Church there is an elaborate monument to "Shakspeare" placed high on the north wall of the chancel. It includes an effigy of the upper half of his body, with his left hand holding down a sheet of paper on a cushion (a poor substitute for a writing desk), and with a pen in his right hand, Figure 4.3. It is clearly designed to commemorate a

Figure 4.2 The image from Dugdale's 1656 *Antiquities*, and the Woolpackers' Arms.

Figure 4.3 The image from Rowe's 1709 publication, and the bust as it is today.

writer. But the earliest printed image of the monument shows something completely different. Figure 4.2 shows a detail from page 520 of Sir William Dugdale's *The Antiquities of Warwickshire* (1656), based on a sketch of his made sometime between 1630 and 1650. Figure 4.3 shows how the bust was represented in Rowe's edition of Shakespeare's works in 1709, markedly different from how it appears today.[13] The image in Figure 4.2 shows someone with both hands resting on a sack. It is quite clear from this image that there are pebbles tied into the corners of the sack, which identifies it as a woolsack; they are there to facilitate lifting. Figure 4.2 shows the Arms of the Association of Woolpackers, which display a sack with pebbles tied into the corners. It is not recorded that William Shakspere was a dealer in wool. Indeed, so inappropriate for a writer was the whole memorial in its earliest state that a distinguished modern orthodox Shakespeare scholar, Professor Brian Vickers,[14] has seriously suggested that it was originally erected to William's father John, who is known to have been a dealer in wool, and later revamped to commemorate William.

The Memorial Inscription in Holy Trinity Church

Immediately below the bust there is an inscription in Latin and English. No first name is given, but the date of death indicates that this is indeed William Shakspere; note the absence of an "e" after the "k," again suggestive of a short "a." The Latin inscription can be translated as follows:

> In judgment a Nestor, in genius a Socrates, in art a Virgil; the earth covers him, the populace mourns him, Olympus cherishes him.

Here Nestor is referred to as "a Pylian," after his birthplace Pylus, and Virgil by his surname, Maro, both identifiers a little obscure. It has often been pointed out that these three are rather inappropriate for a playwright, since Nestor was renowned as a hero (and for his

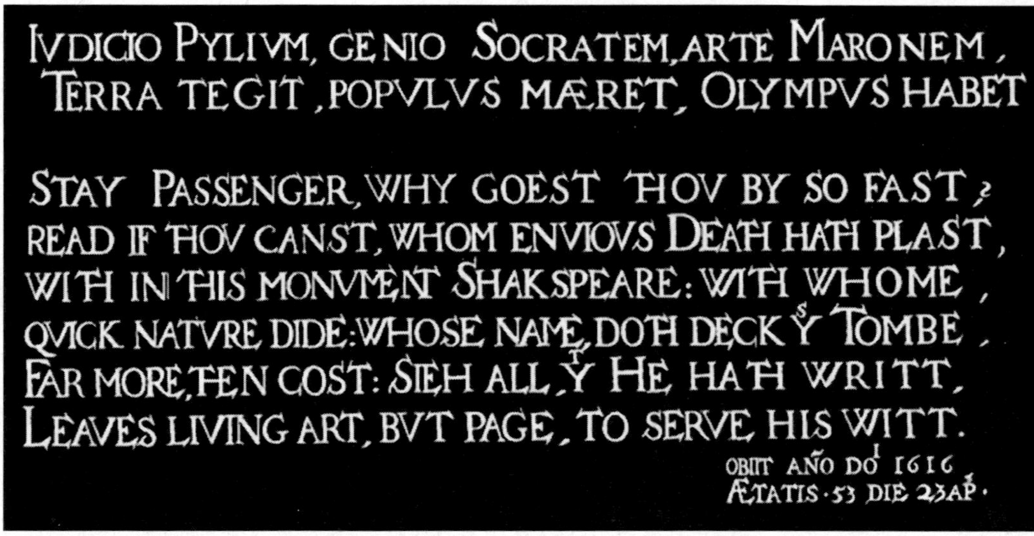
IVDICIO PYLIVM, GENIO SOCRATEM, ARTE MARONEM,
TERRA TEGIT, POPVLVS MÆRET, OLYMPVS HABET
STAY PASSENGER, WHY GOEST THOV BY SO FAST?
READ IF THOV CANST, WHOM ENVIOVS DEATH HATH PLAST,
WITH IN THIS MONVMENT SHAKSPEARE: WITH WHOME,
QVICK NATVRE DIDE: WHOSE NAME DOTH DECK YS TOMBE,
FAR MORE THEN COST: SIEH ALL YT HE HATH WRITT,
LEAVES LIVING ART, BVT PAGE, TO SERVE HIS WITT.
OBIIT AÑO DOI 1616
ÆTATIS·53 DIE 23 AP·

Figure 4.4 The memorial inscription in Holy Trinity Church.

longevity) and wrote nothing, Socrates was renowned for wisdom, and also wrote nothing (his words were reported by Plato), and while Virgil was a poet, his poetry was nothing like Shakespeare's; furthermore none of them was a playwright.[15] If Shakespeare was to be compared to a Roman poet, that poet should have been Ovid, with whom he had far more in common than with Virgil, and there are several classical dramatists with whom he might have been compared, for example Sophocles (whose name fits the scansion of the Latin hexameter, whereas the name "Socrates" does not). Moreover Olympus was the home of the gods, while Mount Parnassus was the home of the muses, a more suitable place for a poet, and so nothing in the inscription quite fits Shakespeare. However, bearing in mind Brian Vickers' suggestion that the original monument may have been intended for John Shakspere, it has to be admitted that the inscription fits him quite well. The three men invoked would then reflect on John's longevity, his wisdom, and since Virgil was a countryman, interested in farming and well-known for his knowledge of bees (expounded at length in the *Georgics*), farming and bee-keeping may have been some of John's other occupations besides glove-making.

All in all, the original monument cannot be said to measure up to what anyone with an open mind would expect to see. The current monument is often supposed to date from around 1760, when it is recorded that the bust was "repaired," or maybe *revised*, to be more in accordance with what an effigy of a writer should be.

Lack of Interest in the Passing of the Great Poet Shakespeare

When William Shakspere died in April 1616, *no one noticed*. Not a single eulogy or even a mention in a letter was forthcoming. When Francis Beaumont died the year before he was buried in Westminster Abbey in "Poet's Corner," as was Michael Drayton in 1631. When Ben Jonson died in 1637 elegies poured forth, and thirty-three were published in a book, *Jonsonus Virbius;* he too was buried in Westminster Abbey. It can hardly be doubted that if the actor and businessman William Shakspere had been the famous writer William Shakespeare someone would have taken notice, but instead he was buried in rural Stratford-upon-Avon "with a gravestone that did not even carry his name."[16] No burial in Westminster Abbey, no eulogies, nothing, for the poet who outshone all his contemporaries. It is inexplicable if the orthodox opinion is correct.

The entry in the Parish Register recording his burial reads "Will Shakspere gent," whereas the name of the dramatist (now at the height of his fame) was almost always spelled "Shakespeare" (occasionally "Shakespere," and often with a hyphen).

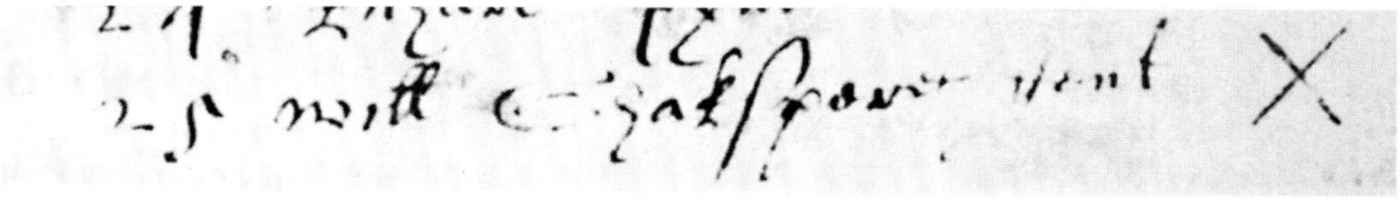

Figure 4.5 Parish Register record of Will Shakspere's burial.

A Seventeenth-Century Authorship Skeptic

The copy of the 1623 First Folio ("Euing")[17] held by the University of Glasgow has annotations on a number of pages, in particular on the page listing the names of the principal actors. It is not known who made the annotations, but against Robert Benfield's name he writes "know," and against others "by report" or "hearsay" or "as I hear." Since Benfield died in 1649, the comments must have been made sometime before that date. And against the name William Shakespeare he writes something quite amazing: "*lease for making.*" "Lease" is a word current in early modern times which is now obsolete, although it was still being used in the nineteenth century (Oxford English Dictionary); it was used by Shakespeare in the form "leasing." It means "false" or "untrue," as first pointed out by Julia Cleave.[18] "Making" means writing poetry, from the Greek *ποιειν*, to make, especially poetry or works of art; "maker" in early modern times meant "poet." So someone who knew one of the actors listed

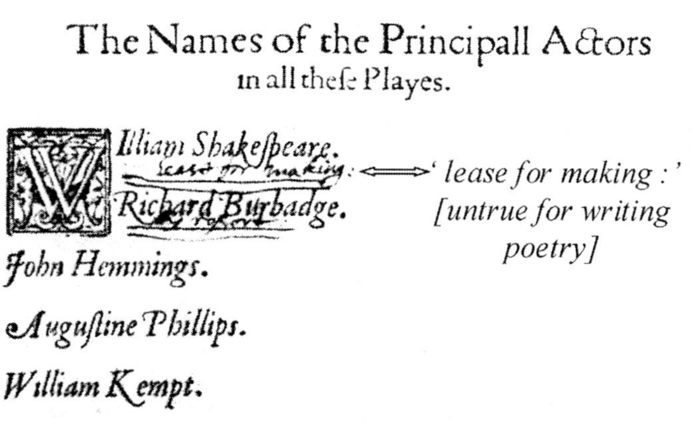

Figure 4.6 Detail from the list of actors' names in the Euing First Folio (by permission of University of Glasgow Library, Special Collections).

in the First Folio made a note recording that the Stratford man was *not* the author. If he got this information from Benfield, it might well be the case that this was the general opinion of the King's Men—that the plays were written by someone else.

Conclusion

Many other reasons have been put forward for doubting the identification of the actor William Shakspere with the playwright William Shakespeare. For example, there is no indication of where Shakspere could have obtained the knowledge normally associated with a university-educated man, or gained access to the 300 or more books the poet is known to have consulted, a number of which had not then been translated into English. Nor is it easy to see how he could have acquired the minutely detailed knowledge of several Italian towns, those which figure in ten of the plays, without traveling abroad, which as far as we know he never did. Orthodox scholars are content to suppose that the Stratford grammar school would have given him a sound basis, after which he would have been self-educated, and clearly that cannot be ruled out. Moreover his knowledge of Italian topography and towns (as convincingly demonstrated by Richard Roe in *The Shakespeare Guide to Italy*[19]) could possibly have been obtained from meeting people who had visited these places. Nevertheless, on balance, it would seem that lack of a university education and lack of foreign travel raise further serious doubts about the Warwickshire man.

I believe the evidence and arguments so far put forward in the last three chapters are enough to eliminate the actor and businessman from Stratford-upon-Avon from the authorship of Shakespeare's works, and for the rest of this book I shall concentrate on exploring those lines of research which in my view bring to light the real poet and dramatist who took such care to ensure that his identity should be hidden from view. Of himself he wrote in sonnet 125: "Wer't ought to me I bore the canopy?" We now ask the question: "Who bore the canopy?" The answer will bring us nearer to the poet of the sonnets, and so on to the poet of the plays.

5. *Who Bore the Canopy?*

Sonnet 125 is one of the most puzzling of all the 154 sonnets, which were first published in 1609.[1]

> Wer't ought to me I bore the canopy,
> With my extern the outward honoring,
> Or layd great bases for eternity,
> Which proves more short than wast or ruining?
> Have I not seene dwellers on forme and favor
> Lose all, and more by paying too much rent
> For compound sweet; Forgoing simple savor,
> Pittifull thrivers in their gazing spent.
> Noe, let me be obsequious in thy heart,
> And take thou my oblacion, poore but free,
> Which is not mixt with seconds, knows no art,
> But mutuall render, onely me for thee.
> Hence, thou suborned *Informer*, a trew soule
> When most impeacht, stands least in thy controule.

The puzzlement starts with line 1. On a first reading, it may seem as though the poet is referring to some event at which he *did* bear the canopy—over either Queen Elizabeth or King James, since by law canopies could only be carried over royalty.[2] After all, he does write "*I bore* the canopy." But in that case he would probably have written "*Was* it ought to me I bore the canopy." What he actually wrote is "*Wer't* ought...," in the subjunctive, so that the sense is more likely to be this: "Would it have meant anything to me if I *had* borne the canopy (which I didn't), or *had* laid great bases for eternity (which I also didn't)." Another reading might be "Would it mean anything to me if I *were to* bear the canopy." Whichever sense the poet had in mind, the underlying thought (expressed later in the sonnet) is, "No—these are matters of general concern that mean little to me—it is my private devotion to you (his young friend[3]) which is all-consuming." Nevertheless, by saying "Wer't ought to me I bore..." the poet seems to be indicating that he might have been one of those selected to do so on some particular occasion, otherwise he could have written "Wer't ought to me *to bear* etc." (with "lay" replacing "layd"), which would have had the effect of distancing himself from any such ceremony.

A number of orthodox commentators allow for the possibility that the poet (for them, the actor William Shakspere) did once bear the canopy, or might have done so.[4] We therefore need to find out more about canopies, who bore them, who might aspire to bear them, and when. Our starting point is Leslie Hotson's finding, already mentioned more than once, that by law they could only be carried over the sovereign (and by extension his consort, or child, or his or their coffins), and over nobody else.

A ceremonial canopy consists of a square or rectangle of richly embroidered fabric carried on four staves (sometimes six or even more) about six or seven feet long, which would often be ornamented with silver finials and bells. Research using the Oxford Dictionary of National Biography and other resources has turned up some thirty state occasions at this period where canopies were employed, always over royalty, and the status or names of the bearers were frequently recorded.[5] Broadly speaking, they were knights or gentlemen, "barons of the Cinque Ports" (commoners) at coronations, and senior academics at Oxford and Cambridge. The three public processions in the early 1600s which involved canopies took place at the funeral of Queen Elizabeth on 28 April 1603, the coronation of James I on 25 July 1603, and the triumphal entry of King James into the City of London on 15 March 1604 (modern dating), which was postponed from the coronation ceremonies of the previous year because of plague.

The Queen's funeral procession involved thousands of people. Her coffin was carried on a hearse drawn by four horses, preceded by office holders of the Court and members of the Household, followed by the Chief Mourner, the Marchioness of Winchester, and other members of the Court; the Household comprised over 1100 officials, retainers and servants, whose names are recorded on a document in the College of Arms. Surmounting the coffin was a lifelike effigy of the Queen, and over this a canopy was carried by six knights, three on either side. The names of the knights and others who were summoned to act as canopy bearers in the Queen's funeral procession are recorded on another document in the College of Arms,[6] and yet another records the names of the "assistant earls"[7] who processed two on either side next to the canopy bearers (according to a marginal sketch). Twelve knights are listed under the heading "Knightes for the Canopie"; they would have formed two teams, turn and turn about, followed by a second list of fifteen knights and gentlemen, who would have stood by in reserve in case any on the first list dropped out. Those marked "x" may have turned out to be unavailable.

Sir ffrancis Knolls,
Lieftenant of the Tower
Sir Jerome Bowes x
Sir Jo: Peeter
Sir Edw. Hobby
Sir Richard Barkley x
Sir Henry Glenmaid
Sir Edw. Wynter
Sir Henry Guilford
Sir Robert Croft
Sir George Moore
Sir Richard Ward
Sir Richard Lea

The names of the "assistant earls" are "E. of Northumberland, E. of Salop [Shropshire], E. of Derby, E. of Cumberland, E. of Hartford, E. of Lincoln"; either all six processed or two attended in reserve.

Three months later a canopy was carried over James on his coronation procession from

Parliament Stairs to Westminster Abbey; the bearers were "barons of the Cinque Ports," as hallowed by tradition. The Cinque Ports (of which there were by now seven) were the ports on the south coast of Kent and Sussex which provided defense against invasion from the continent. In return the inhabitants, including those of adjacent villages, were exempt from all taxes. The Cinque Ports also had the time-honored privilege of choosing and sending members to act as canopy bearers over the new monarch at a coronation. In King James's case, 16 bearers were required, as a canopy was also carried over Queen Anne, and two teams were needed for each canopy, taking it in turns to officiate. The bearers' names are not known, but they were required to wear clothing prescribed in some detail, including scarlet gowns. As "scarlet is valued at £3 10s. the yard at least,"[8] and such a gown would require four or five yards of cloth, it was an expensive honor to be a canopy bearer. (Such a gown would cost between £15 and £18, and the whole outfit would have cost around £20; a university-educated schoolmaster's annual salary was between £10 and £20.)

The following year on the occasion of King James's triumphal entry into London in March 1604 the canopy bearers were Scotsmen from his privy chamber[9]; again their names are not known. Any of these three great occasions of state might have suggested the opening line of sonnet 125, but at none of them would there have been any possibility that the actor William Shakspere might have been one of the bearers; he was neither a knight, a baron of the Cinque Ports, nor a Scotsman.

There are other events of the period, less public, when a canopy was employed, principally at the opening of a parliament, as part of the Garter festivities held in April each year, at the christening of a royal infant, and during the anointing ceremony at a coronation. In addition, a canopy was borne over Queen Elizabeth at a special service of thanksgiving for the victory over the Armada, which was held in St. Paul's Church on 24 November 1588. A canopy is also depicted in the painting known as "Eliza Triumphans."[10]

At the opening of Parliament on 12 January 1563 (modern dating), a canopy was borne over Queen Elizabeth inside Westminster Abbey by an esquire and five knights, whose names were all recorded.[11] The canopy for the procession which was part of the Garter ceremony at Windsor in April 1596 was carried by "four men" otherwise unidentified, on the only occasion of which a record has surfaced.[12] At a royal christening, the bearers were usually related to the monarch, and were often members of the higher nobility, but there were no such christenings during the period we are dealing with.

At a coronation, a canopy is held over the sovereign at the most sacred moment of the ceremony when he or she is anointed with holy oil. These canopy bearers are traditionally Knights of the Garter who are also members of the higher nobility. For example, looking ahead, at the coronation of Charles II two dukes and two earls officiated[13] and at that of James II three dukes and one earl.[14] It so happens that the names of the bearers at James's anointing have not come to light, but it is possible to work out who was available.

On 25 July 1603 there were twelve Knights of the Garter who were also members of the higher nobility, one duke and eleven earls[15]; of these, the Duke of Lennox and the earls of Mar, Pembroke and Southampton had been newly installed earlier that month. The honor of performing the hugely prestigious duty of acting as canopy bearer would have fallen to the Duke of Lennox (James's cousin) and three of the eight more senior earls. Among these the Earl of Nottingham was Lord High Steward, in overall charge of everything relating to the coronation, the Earl of Worcester was Earl Marshal, responsible for ceremonial details, and the Earl of Ormond was too ill to attend. The remaining five were the Earls of Shrewsbury, Cumberland, Northumberland, Sussex and Derby, listed in order of appointment. If the proceedings went according to tradition, the Duke and three of the more senior of these (or four without the Duke) would have borne the canopy, with those remaining perhaps standing by in reserve. I think it likely that James would have wanted his cousin the Duke to be one of the four bearers, but the records are silent.[16]

If this sonnet was prompted (in some sense) by the poet's attendance at some particular ceremony—which is not necessarily the case—then words such as "obsequious" and "oblation" may provide a clue as to what kind of ceremony it was; to these must be added the word "canopy," to which we have already attached so much importance. These words have in the past led commentators to speculate that the poet may indeed have had the coronation of James I in mind. The coronation service (which was essentially an interrupted Holy Communion service[17]) included oblations of a pall of cloth-of-gold and a pound weight of gold, offered by the King (with similar offerings by his Queen), and also oblations of the communion wine and bread, which latter according to the order of the communion service[18] should be *"the purest wheat bread that conveniently may be gotten,"* that is, "not mixt with seconds" (this sonnet, line 11). Furthermore, "layd great bases for eternity" (line 3) resonates with one of the communion service prayers: *"laying up in store for them selves a good foundacion, against the time to come, that they may attayne eternal lyfe."*[19]

We already know that Derby would have attended James's coronation, unless prevented by illness; he was present at the banquet following the installation of the new Knights of the Garter a few days before.[20] Moreover he was the KG earl standing last in reserve. If it was he who wrote sonnet 125 it would seem that he was asking himself if he was disappointed at missing out on bearing the canopy over James as he was anointed, and finding that his devotion to his young friend was far more important to him than a ceremony where outward symbolism meant more than inner feelings. "Let me be obsequious in *thy* [his friend's] heart, and take *thou* [his friend] my oblacion, poore but free" (lines 9–10 of the sonnet).

Do we know whether the actor William Shakspere would have attended? It seems unlikely that he would have done so, as attendance at the ceremony was strictly limited because of plague. Apart from the Lord Mayor and the aldermen, only twelve "distinguished citizens" of London were permitted to be present.[21] Shakspere might have attended in the entourage of some grand personage, but there is no evidence either that he did so or that any others of his fellow actors did so.

Our exploration of the use of canopies in Elizabethan and Jacobean times has revealed the likely presence of Derby standing by at the coronation of James I, waiting to bear the canopy if one of the more senior KGs dropped out. Our account has also highlighted how very unlikely it is that the actor William Shakspere would ever have carried the pole of a canopy. As an aside, it should be added that Derby is the only one of the around 80 authorship candidates who have so far been proposed to come anywhere near to bearing the canopy. He had been appointed KG in April 1601 by the Queen, a gracious act, and this may well be what Henry Chettle was referring to later in 1603 when he said of Shakespeare that the Queen had "graced his desert."[22]

But at this point I must sound a caveat. No account of the coronation of James records the names of the canopy bearers, or indeed whether in fact a canopy really was held over James as he was anointed. All we do know is that this part of the ceremony was traditional and was thought to have occurred at many previous coronations. If James dispensed with it (which seems very unlikely, as he would surely want to abide by the customs of his new kingdom), then we may still imagine William Stanley wondering how much the honor would have meant to him if it had not been canceled and he might have carried one of the canopy poles.

Something else we do not know is whether the canopy of sonnet 125 was a real canopy carried over a real monarch, or whether it was an imaginary canopy, a metaphor involved in some obscure (to us) train of thought running through the poet's mind; other lines in the sonnet are also somewhat difficult to make sense of. But at least we have now found a possible connection between the name of the man in the title of our book and something that Shakespeare wrote. Has the curtain been pulled aside for a glimpse of reality, or does the truth lie elsewhere? In the next two chapters we investigate the way other writers and poets referred to Shakespeare at the time, and make an important discovery.

6. Spenser's Two Gentle Poets

Shakespeare's poetical character was first described by Francis Meres, in his *Palladis Tamia, Wit's Treasury*, published in 1598. There he writes[1]:

> As the soule of *Euphorbus* was thought to live in *Pythagoras:* so the sweete wittie soule of *Ovid* lives in mellifluous & hony-tongued *Shakespeare*, witnes his *Venus* and *Adonis*, his *Lucrece*, his sugred Sonnets among his private friends, &c.

The terms "mellifluous" and "honey-tongued" (or "honey-flowing," etc.) were also applied to Shakespeare by other writers, as follows.

Richard Barnfield (1598)	"hony-flowing Vaine"[2]
John Weever (1599)	"Honie-tong'd"[3]
Henry Chettle (1603)	"Melicert ... his honied muse"[4]
Thomas Heywood (1635)	"Mellifluous Shake-speare"[5]

It is often the case that writers pick up an epithet (or other epithets with a similar meaning) from an earlier writer, and repeat it (or them) as a kind of signal to those "in the know" that they too are "in the know" about some particular topic, in this case Shakespeare. If we ask with Leslie Hotson (in *Shakespeare's Motley*[6]) who it was who linked "honey-flowing" with a writer before Meres and Barnfield, we come up with Edmund Spenser in *The Teares of the Muses* (1591).[7] Here he describes an unnamed poet as a

> gentle Spirit, from whose pen
> Large streams of honey and sweet nectar flow.

Shakespeare's earliest biographer, Nicholas Rowe, was the first to suggest (in 1709)[8] that Spenser's honey-flowing poet was Shakespeare, adding that this had always been the opinion of John Dryden. Perhaps we may learn something from the stanzas which surround this gentle Spirit.

> All these, and all that else the Comic Stage,
> With seasoned wit and goodly pleasance graced,
> By which man's life in his likest image
> Was limned forth, are wholly now defaced;
> And those sweet wits which wont the like to frame
> Are now despised, and made a laughing game.
>
> And he the man whom Nature's self had made
> To mock herself, and Truth to imitate,
> With kindly counter under Mimic shade,
> Our pleasant *Willy*, ah! is dead of late, [inactive

With whom all joy and jolly merriment
Is also deaded and in doleur drent.

In stead thereof scoffing Scurrility,
And scornful Folly with Contempt is crept,
Rolling in rhymes of shameles ribaldry
Without regard, or due Decorum kept,
Each idle wit at will presumes to make,
And doth the Learned's task upon him take.

But that same gentle Spirit, from whose pen
Large streams of honey and sweet Nectar flow,
Scorning the boldness of such base-born men,
Which dare their follies forth so rashly throw,
Doth rather choose to sit in idle Cell,
Than so himself to mockery to sell.

These are stanzas 5 to 8 of Spenser's invocation to Thalia, the Muse of Comedy and pastoral poetry. If the same man is referred to as one of the "sweet wits" of the first stanza, as "Our pleasant Willy" in the next, and the "gentle Spirit" of the last, then we learn that he has written comedies in the past, but as the stage is now being debased by inferior writers ("base-born men") offering scurrility and ribaldry, he chooses to take a break from writing. As "Our pleasant Willy" is called "gentle," and the inferior writers "base-born" and usurping the "Learned's task," we may detect a hint that he is (comparatively) well-born ("gentle"[9]) and not without learning. Can we make a guess at who Spenser is alluding to?

There may be a clue in the dedicatee of these poems, the "*Most braue and noble Ladie*" the Lady Strange. Before her marriage she was Alice Spencer, the youngest daughter of Sir John Spencer of Althorp, with several older sisters and a brother, also Sir John Spencer. Her husband was William's elder brother, Ferdinando Stanley, Lord Strange, eldest son of Henry Stanley, Fourth Earl of Derby. Spenser refers to "private bands of affinity" in his dedication to Lady Strange, and clearly believed himself to be related to her, although in what way has not come to light. It has been suggested therefore that "Our pleasant Willy" was the younger brother of Alice's husband, William Stanley, with the word "Our" indicating a familial relationship.

Further evidence of the closeness between Spenser and Alice and Ferdinando Stanley is provided by a poem written later, *Colin Clouts Come Home Againe*.[10] This was completed after the death of Ferdinando in 1594, and contains a moving tribute to him under the name Amyntas; Amaryllis is Spenser's name for Alice.

AMYNTAS quite is gone and lies full lowe,
Having his AMARYLLIS left to mone.
Helpe, ô ye shepheards, helpe ye all in this, [poets
Helpe AMARYLLIS this her loss to mourne:
Her losse is yours, your losse AMYNTAS is,
AMYNTAS, flowre of shepheards pride forlorne:

After four lines extolling Ferdinando's poetic skills, Spenser then brings in another poet.

And there, though last not least is AETION,
A gentler shepheard may no where be found:
Whose Muse, full of high thoughts invention,
Doth like himselfe heroically sound.

Spenser here refers to "Aetion," than whom "a gentler shepherd may no where be found" (i.e., no other poet is more nobly born), "Whose Muse, full of high thoughts invention, doth like himself heroically sound." By this time William Stanley had inherited the Derby earldom, and the crest of the Derby coat of arms was an eagle carrying a child: "Aetion" is Greek for "man of the eagle."[11] Both Edmond Malone[12] and Sidney Lee[13] were confident that Spenser's "gentle shepherd" was Shakespeare (that is, for them, Shakspere the actor); after all, didn't Ben Jonson call Shakespeare "gentle" in the First Folio (see Chapter 2)? But his appearance in the poem so close to Alice and Ferdinando Stanley, together with the eagle reference, make far better sense if Spenser had William Stanley in mind rather than William Shakspere, who had no documented or familial connection with the Stanleys.

For the second time we are drawn to associate William Stanley with Shakespeare, although the association is weak. We have someone called "Willy" who is well-born and well-known to Spenser and Lady Strange, and who has written plays before 1591, and we have someone nicknamed "Aetion" who is a well-born poet whose muse "full of high thoughts invention" sounds forth "heroically." While we cannot be sure these are the same person, both are very close to Ferdinando and Alice Stanley, as well as to Edmund Spenser.

It so happens that there is another mysterious well-born man named William, otherwise unidentified, who was written about at this period, and in the next chapter we shall find that they are (in all probability) the same man.

7. *Nashe's Gentle Poet*

In 1593 Thomas Nashe, poet, playwright and pamphleteer, published *Strange News*,[1] the latest salvo in his ongoing pamphlet war with Gabriel Harvey. It was written in December 1592 while he was staying as a guest of Sir George Carey at Carisbrooke Castle on the Isle of Wight. Carey was a brother-in-law of Ferdinando Stanley, Lord Strange, who was Nashe's patron at the time[2] (and also Christopher Marlowe's[3]).

The main body of the work is a broadside against Gabriel Harvey, a self-important Cambridge academic, for gloating over the death of Robert Greene,[4] Nashe's friend, in his pamphlet of 1592 *Four Letters*,[5] but it is the epistle (this term is not used) which is of particular interest. It is addressed "To the most copious Carminist [*poet*] of our time, and famous persecutor of Priscian [*a pedant*], his verie friend Master *Apis lapis*," who is called "Gentle M. William" in the next sentence. From Gentle Master William's sobriquet "Master Apis lapis," Nashe is apparently addressing a friend of his who he knows does not wish to be named. The identity of his friend remains a puzzle which has so far defied explanation.

Nashe was not the only person to use the made-up name. In Gabriel Harvey's retort to *Strange News* (*Pierce's Supererogation*, also 1593[6]), he refers to "some of his [Nashe's] favorablest Patrons (who for certain respects I am not to name), M. Apis Lapis, Greene, Marlowe, Chettle, and whom not?"[7] The last three are all poets and playwrights, so it seems quite likely that so is "M. Apis lapis" (whom Harvey also knows as someone who does not wish to be named—"for certain respects"). We may therefore perhaps suppose that Nashe's mysterious friend writes plays as well as poetry.

Leaving the puzzle of his identity aside for the moment, we can learn a lot about Master William from the epistle. Far from being flattering or subservient, it is mocking and insulting, and when reprinted one passage was rewritten and another omitted to remove too scurrilous an implication. Whoever Master Apis lapis was, he cannot have been at all pleased with it.

First of all, Nashe calls him his friend, for all that he treats him so badly. We may therefore assume that they were close friends, of the kind who have a jokey relationship, one that Nashe hoped would not be damaged too much by his remarks; alternatively, this may perhaps be Nashe's way of marking the end of the friendship. He calls him "a copious Carminist," and though this is the only occurrence of the word anywhere in print, it is likely that it means a copious writer of poetry, since *carmen* (genitive *carminis*) means a song or poem in Latin; later passages in the epistle serve to confirm this interpretation. He also calls Master William "a famous persecutor of Priscian." Priscian wrote a systematic exposition of Latin grammar, from which one could deduce that Master William was not someone with scholarly tendencies in Latin (and perhaps someone who is also inclined to play fast and loose with English grammar and language, for example in his poetry).

There then follow a number of more or less explicit indications that his friend is fond of drinking. In fact in the first three paragraphs I can find nine or ten direct or indirect references to drink as a major interest of the man he is mocking so savagely.[8] Then follows one of the more obscure passages which states that his "hospitality" is recorded in the Archdeacon's Court, and that the "fruits" of this hospitality "are of age to speak for themselves." The next sentence refers to Master William keeping "three maids" in his house a long time. When one realizes that the Archdeacon's Court dealt with (among other matters) sexual misdemeanors, and ponders on "fruits" that are now able to speak for themselves, one might suppose that Nashe is teasing his friend for having impregnated one or more of these maids, supposedly three or more years earlier, since the offspring are now of an age to speak for themselves.[9] Nashe is unsparing in dishing the dirt on his friend.

Buried within much inconsequential tomfoolery we also learn that Nashe's friend is a law student, since we are told that he is "among grave Doctors and men of judgment in both Laws every day," and that when because of plague the law term was transferred from Westminster to Hertford (Michaelmas Term, 1592) he was much put out because he would no longer be able to frequent his favorite drinking place, the Steelyard. This was an area in London occupied by a community of traders from the Hanseatic League, seaports along the western coast of the Continent running north from Bruges as far as Novgorod. Exotic wines and foods were available, and we later learn from the main body of the work that Harvey alleged that Robert Greene died of a surfeit of "Rhenish wine and pickled herring," and that Nashe and one of his fellows, Will Monox, were present at this "banquet," which presumably took place in the Steelyard.[10] In all likelihood Will Monox is Master William again, though this identification must remain in doubt.

We also learn that Master William has spent money on "the dirt of Wisdom called Alchemy," which Nashe clearly considers a waste. And still on the theme of money, Nashe alternately praises William for his charity towards scholars and decayed poets, and scolds him for being so mean that Nashe expects to receive nothing for dedicating his pamphlet to him—"Thou ... hadst rather spend jests than money."

So to sum up what we have learned of Gentle Master William Apis lapis, he is wellborn ("gentle"), a law student, has written a lot of poetry and probably one or more plays, is interested in alchemy, and is very fond of drinking. As mentioned earlier, his identity has never been determined. It seems unlikely that he was someone with a name like "Bee-stone," from a literal translation of the Latin words, since that would afford no concealment at all, and it so happens that several possible William Beestons have been tracked down, only to be rejected for various reasons. Yet we have already met a "gentle William" in the last chapter, in the form of Spenser's "pleasant Willy," "a gentle Spirit." Can we establish a connection?

The solution to this puzzle does indeed lie in the Latin, for while "Apis" undoubtedly means a bee, "lapis" has a secondary meaning. Here is the definition for the word given in Thomas Cooper's *Latin Dictionary* of 1565: "a stone: *a negligent person that stirreth not lively in doing*."[11] As if to confirm this meaning, half-way through the epistle Nashe writes: "Sloth is a sin.... What can he [Apis lapis] do better that hath nothing to do, than fall a drinking to keep him from idleness?" So Master Apis lapis is a "lazy bee," which takes us straight back to Spenser's stanza from *The Teares of the Muses* (previous chapter):

But that same gentle Spirit, from whose pen
Large streams of honey and sweet Nectar flow,
Scorning the boldness of such base-born men,
Which dare their follies forth so rashly throw,
Doth rather choose to sit in idle Cell,
Than so himself to mockery to sell.

Here Spenser's "gentle Spirit" produces large streams of honey—a bee, and sits "in idle Cell," much as a bee might.

Thus it seems highly likely that Nashe is calling the poet Gentle Master William a *lazy bee* because he knows that Spenser had earlier called another poet and playwright ("Our pleasant Willy") a *lazy bee*, whom he refers to as "a gentle Spirit," also withholding any further identification. And if we identify Spenser's *Aetion* with William Stanley, we may be pretty confident that Nashe's Master William is the same man. What of the other things that Nashe has told us about his friend?

Firstly, Nashe calls him "gentle" (as does Spenser in the two passages quoted in the last chapter), that is, well-born, which William Stanley certainly was: son of an earl, and descended from Henry VII through his mother. Nashe also tells us that his friend is a law student, and at this period Stanley was a law-student enrolled at Lincoln's Inn (he was admitted having completed his studies in August 1594, after he had inherited the earldom). Nashe further tells us that his friend spends money on alchemy, which the *ODNB* reveals was a special interest of Stanley; he was on familiar terms with Dr. Dee, the magus, savant and alchemist, and they are recorded as meeting on many occasions.

Thus, to sum up, it seems that Spenser's "pleasant Willy," a "gentle Spirit," honey-flowing and sitting in idle cell, is the same as Spenser's *Aetion*, William Stanley, a "gentle shepherd" whose heroic Muse is full of high thoughts' invention, and the same as Nashe's "Gentle Master William," another idle bee, Apis lapis. We can tabulate these findings under the three publications, as follows.

Teares	*Colin Clout*	*Strange News*
gentle Spirit	gentle	Gentle M.
Willy	[*Aetion:* William Stanley]	William
whose pen (poet)	shepherd (poet)	copious carminist (poet)
streams of honey (bee)		Apis (bee)
sit in idle Cell		lapis (negligent person)

The gentle shepherd *Aetion*, man of the eagle, from *Colin Clouts Come Home Againe*, has surely to be identified with William Stanley, grieving like *Amaryllis*, Lady Alice Stanley, for the loss of *Amyntas*, Ferdinando Stanley, his elder brother, the Fifth Earl of Derby (formerly Lord Strange). Recall also that Spenser's "gentle Willy" has written plays, and that Gabriel Harvey includes "M. Apis Lapis" in a list of poets who are also playwrights. I do not think we need hesitate any longer before identifying Nashe's Gentle Master William with William Stanley, whom both Spenser (clearly) and Harvey (indirectly) identify as a playwright. It seems highly likely that they would have met at Lord Strange's house in London when William visited his brother and Nashe waited on his patron. It may also be relevant (if premature) to point out that there is much entanglement between Nashe's writings and the plays of Shakespeare, so much so that there is considerable debate as to who was unconsciously recollecting passages from whom.[12]

It seems that we have identified with some confidence a poet whom both Spenser and Nashe rated very highly. Nashe also insults him disgracefully, never imagining that within a couple of years he would inherit an earldom. It seems unlikely that they were on cordial terms thereafter, and there is no record of any meeting at any time.

As an aside, it seems probable that Harvey also referred to William Stanley in the following passage in *Four Letters*, 1592: "Alas, even his [Greene's] fellow-writer, a proper young man if advised in time, that was a principal guest at that fatal banquet of pickle herring (I spare his name, and in some respects wish him well) came never more at him [Greene]."[13] Once again, his name is withheld (and the word "respects" is repeated). Incidentally, Harvey pretty much confirms that the three members of the "banquet" that supposedly led to Greene's death were Greene, Nashe and Stanley, the "proper young man if advised in time"—advised to drink less, perhaps.

Although (as already mentioned) Nicholas Rowe and John Dryden both thought Spenser's "gentle Spirit" was Shakespeare, and although Edmond Malone and Sidney Lee both thought his "gentle shepherd" was Shakespeare,[14] so far there are no specific grounds for coming to such a conclusion, let alone the further deduction that Shakespeare was William Stanley. But it may perhaps be said that the outlook is not unfavorable for such an outcome.

We now investigate the additions made to several of the plays found in the First Folio which had previously been printed in shorter versions, and when they might have been written. This will throw light on the question of whether the real author was still alive in 1623.

8. Plays: Expanded or Contracted?

A long-standing puzzle associated with the First Folio is that the texts of several of the plays consist of what was printed in the original publication in quarto (a pocket-sized format) together with many extra lines; in three cases over 1,000 new lines appear—*King John, Merry Wives of Windsor* and *Henry V*. The unresolved question is this: were the earlier quarto texts shortened versions of the full texts printed in the Folio, or were the Folio texts expanded versions of the briefer quarto texts (18 plays were published in quarto between 1592 and 1622)? The prevailing orthodox view is the former—that the quarto texts essentially consist of the full Folio text (or something fairly close to it) cut down to a suitable length for playing on the stage.[1] This raises the question of why an experienced playwright would start out writing more, sometimes far more, than could be acted in the time available for an afternoon performance, lasting about two hours, so that what he had written had necessarily to be shortened. Like some other prevailing orthodox views it does seem to go against what (with an open mind) one might expect.

We now attempt to examine this problem, taking *Othello* as a specific example. The 1623 First Folio version of *Othello* was always in the past assumed to have been set up from a copy of the First Quarto, published in 1622.[2] The copy had evidently been carefully edited, since there are many emendations, and moreover an extra 160 lines had been added. The additions are unquestionably by Shakespeare—"among the finest in the play" according to W. W. Greg[3]—and so it appears that there were two different manuscript versions of the play coexisting side by side throughout the early 1600s. The Quarto text was apparently corrected by reference to a superior pre-existing manuscript to provide the Folio text.

However, opinion has changed since then, as research by Ernst Honigmann had led him to put forward a different view, published in 1996.[4] He maintained ("proved" might be too strong a word) that the Folio text had been set into print from a fair copy made by Ralph Crane, a clerk or scribe with handwriting easy to read. It had already been established that Crane had provided fair copies for the First Folio printing of five other plays—*The Tempest, Two Gentlemen, Measure for Measure, Winter's Tale* and *Merry Wives of Windsor*, so this conclusion was not without precedent. Honigmann's theory is that Shakespeare provided the players with an original manuscript which found its way into the Quarto. Then later, for some reason, he produced a second improved and longer version, which remained in obscurity until the First Folio was planned, whereupon it surfaced, and was given to Crane to copy out neatly for the compositors. One might well wonder why it didn't surface a few months earlier in time to provide copy for the Quarto—where was it all this time? Who was hanging on to it?

What really puzzled Honigmann was that Crane's fair copy in a number of cases repeated peculiar spellings and words that made no sense *directly* from the printed Quarto. He therefore had to suppose that while working from Shakespeare's second manuscript version Crane every now and then consulted a copy of the 1622 Quarto, *precisely repeating printing errors*, of a kind he would not have made if he had been simply following the second manuscript, where such errors would obviously not occur. Here are a few examples where the Folio repeats unchanged an error in the Quarto.[5]

Act 1, scene 3, line 43	And prayes you to *beleeve* him (Q) And prayes you to *beleeve* him (F)

This makes no sense in context, and is emended to "relieve" in all modern editions.

Act 2, scene 1, lines 50–51	Therefore my *hope's* not surfeited to death, Stand in bold cure (Q) Therefore my *hope's* (not surfetted to death) Stand in bold Cure (F)

This is clearly wrong, and the apostrophe needs to be removed.

Act 2, scene 3, line 163	Haue you forgot all *place of sense*, and duty (Q) Haue you forgot all *place of sense*, and duty (F)

Clearly the correct reading is "sense of place."

Act 2, scene 3, lines 214–16	If partiality affin'd, or *league* in office, Thou dost deliuer, more or lesse then truth, Thou art no souldier (Q) If partally Affin'd, or *league* in office, Thou dost deliuer more, or lesse then Truth Thou art no Souldier (F)

In this case "league" must be replaced by "leagu'd." It is surely hard to believe that Crane would copy these errors from the Quarto without correcting them.

Further evidence is provided by peculiar spellings.[6] There are several words in common use which appear in unusual identical spellings in Q and F, where alternative more conventional spellings (regularly used by Crane) were available. All these considerations reinforce the idea that the compositor had a copy of the Quarto in front of him (or pages from it) when setting the play into print for the Folio.

Honigmann is honest enough to admit that he can't really explain how these and other instances came about. If Shakespeare's second manuscript was revised and superior to the first version, Crane should have had no need to copy certain passages from the printed Quarto, and if for whatever reason he did so surely he would have corrected obvious errors. Honigmann tries to avoid presenting Crane as a modern editor, collating two conflicting texts, as this would surely be an anachronism. Nevertheless, his theory rests on the coexistence of two manuscripts, with Crane copying the second but *inexplicably reverting to the printed Quarto text* on random occasions and reproducing exactly errors found there.

Let us look at another of Honigmann's examples, which happens to be free of the peculiarities listed above but which is interesting for other reasons. Here in Figure 8.1 are the Quarto and Folio versions of *Othello*, Act 1, scene 3, line 237 onwards.[7] Honigmann's view is that Ralph Crane must have copied this passage into his manuscript from the Quarto text rather than from the second, revised manuscript. Commentators before him thought that the Folio was set into print from a corrected version of the Quarto, which would explain why the two printings below look so very similar. There is nothing new in the Folio version which could not have been derived from annotations on the Quarto page, taking into account the compositor's omissions, misreadings and typos. The question is, who made the Folio corrections (e.g., in the above passage, line four up from the bottom line, "And if," Quarto, changed to "T'assist," Folio), and with what authority—from a revised manuscript, from literary considerations, from common sense, or for a more fundamental reason?

There is an alternative explanation for the anomalies, first put forward by the supporters of Francis Bacon, which is much simpler and altogether more plausible. It is that *the author himself* took a copy of the 1622 Quarto, and went through it making corrections and improvements, adding extra lines and where necessary inserting new sheets of paper containing longer speeches. This resulted in messy copy which might have baffled the compositor, so the bundle of papers was passed over to Ralph Crane to produce the fair copy from which the compositors could reliably set up the Folio text.[8] Where passages in the Quarto were largely unchanged, Crane annotated them rather than transcribing them.

I am not saying that I think this is what happened, only that it is an alternative to Honigmann's explanation, far simpler and (for anyone with an open mind about who the author was) far more plausible. By Occam's razor, the simplest explanation deserves to be given serious consideration before being rejected. A corollary of the alternative view is that *the real author was still alive in 1622.*

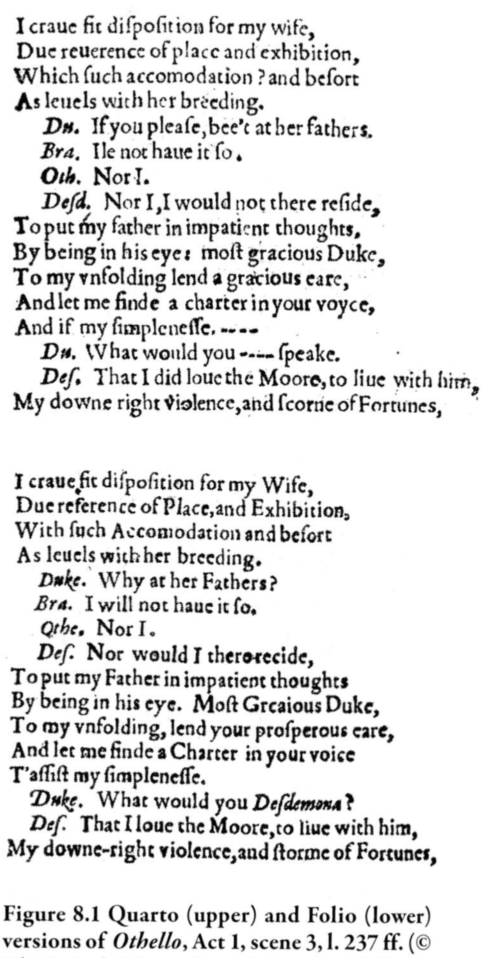
I craue fit diſpoſition for my wife,
Due reuerence of place and exhibition,
Which ſuch accomodation ? and beſort
As leuels with her breeding.
Du. If you pleaſe, bee't at her fathers.
Bra. Ile not haue it ſo.
Oth. Nor I.
Deſd. Nor I, I would not there reſide,
To put my father in impatient thoughts,
By being in his eye: moſt gracious Duke,
To my vnfolding lend a gracious eare,
And let me finde a charter in your voyce,
And if my ſimpleneſſe. ---
Du. What would you --- ſpeake.
Deſ. That I did loue the Moore, to liue with him,
My downe right violence, and ſcorne of Fortunes,

I craue fit diſpoſition for my Wife,
Due reference of Place, and Exhibition,
With ſuch Accomodation and beſort
As leuels with her breeding.
Duke. Why at her Fathers?
Bra. I will not haue it ſo.
Othe. Nor I.
Deſ. Nor would I there recide,
To put my Father in impatient thoughts
By being in his eye. Moſt Greaious Duke,
To my vnfolding, lend your proſperous eare,
And let me finde a Charter in your voice
T'aſſiſt my ſimpleneſſe.
Duke. What would you *Deſdemona*?
Deſ. That I loue the Moore, to liue with him,
My downe-right violence, and ſtorme of Fortunes,

Figure 8.1 Quarto (upper) and Folio (lower) versions of *Othello*, Act 1, scene 3, l. 237 ff. (© The British Library Board: Quarto, C34 k33; Folio, G 11631).

Other Plays

So much for *Othello*. What of other plays?

Richard III. Latest quarto before First Folio (FF): 1622. FF version based directly on last quarto, with 193 new lines added and nearly 2,000 retouched; it also repeated twelve printer's errors from the quarto, showing that the compositor had pages from the quarto in front of him, just as in the case of *Othello*.

King John. Last quarto 1622: new title, 1,000 new lines added including one new scene; much dialogue rewritten.

Henry VI, Part 2. Last quarto 1619: FF version based directly on last quarto, with new title, 1139 new lines added, 2,000 retouched.

Henry VI, Part 3. Last quarto 1619: new title, 906 new lines added and many retouched.

Merry Wives. Last quarto 1619: 1081 new lines added; text rewritten.

Richard II. Last quarto 1615: FF version based directly on quarto, corrections throughout.

Henry V. Last quarto 1608: new title, two new scenes added and text nearly doubled in length.

And so on. These statistics come from Edwin Reed's 1901 book about Francis Bacon.[9] According to Reed, the orthodox explanation is that "the reputed author" (William Shakspere) secretly left revised manuscript versions of some 13 plays at his death, 1616, which remained for a period of seven years entirely unknown to the publishers of the post–1616 quartos. Thus two different versions of 13 plays coexisted throughout the early 1600s up to 1616, and in every single case *the inferior version was printed first*. The orthodox explanation, he says, "would not be tolerated under similar circumstances in other fields of criticism for a single moment," that is to say, in the case of anyone other than Shakespeare.

If so many plays[10] were revised by the author in the years shortly before the publication of the First Folio in 1623, and some six to eight of them copied out legibly by Ralph Crane, presumably at the expense of the author, who might that author be? Of the leading candidates for the authorship only Francis Bacon and William Stanley remain, as the others were all dead by 1622. One of these may be the real author, or perhaps someone else so far overlooked.

We now turn to a striking feature of some of the early history plays, the exaggeration and in some cases fabrication of the parts played by members of the Clifford and Stanley families, ancestors of William Stanley.

9. The Lancashire Connection

From the remarkable way in which Shakespeare enhances the roles of the Clifford and Stanley families in two of the *Henry VI* plays and *Richard III*, we learn that he greatly favored the Lancastrian cause in the Wars of the Roses. According to Ian Wilson (*Shakespeare: The Evidence*), "In the case of the Cliffords, in *Henry VI, parts 2* and *3*, Shakespeare gives unusual prominence to the deaths of Lord Clifford and his son,"[1] developing their characters far beyond anything in Halle's Chronicle,[2] the source he made use of.

Shakespeare also gives even greater emphasis to the parts played by various members of the Stanley family. Thus, although the Stanleys played little part in the reign of Henry VI, Shakespeare brings in Sir John Stanley acting as jailor to the Duchess of Gloucester in *Henry VI, Part 2*, while in *Henry VI, Part 3* he has King Edward IV promising to reward Sir William Stanley; both these events are fictitious.

The most outrageous example of pro–Stanley bias, however, occurs in *Richard III*, where Shakespeare attributes to Thomas Stanley (later created first Earl of Derby) a major contribution to the outcome of the battle of Bosworth Field (22 August 1485), when in fact he prevaricated, and it was his brother William (ignored by Shakespeare) who took the decisive action. I give here Ian Wilson's definitive analysis of these aspects of the play.[3]

> Early in the play Shakespeare represents Thomas as the only Yorkist nobleman not taken in by Richard III, and the only great noble pointedly not cursed by Henry VI's widow, Queen Margaret, among those on-stage in Act I scene 3. Then in a scene for which there is no known historical source he has Thomas conduct a brilliant battle of wits versus Richard, culminating in the increasingly insecure Richard deciding to hold Thomas's son George Stanley as a hostage, prompting Thomas's double-edged response: "So deal with him as I prove true to you."
>
> But it is in the circumstance of the battle of Bosworth Field that Shakespeare makes his most blatant reworking of history. Whereas historically before the battle it was Henry Tudor who sought out Thomas Stanley's allegiance, in *Richard III* Shakespeare has Thomas much more riskily approach Henry. Whereas before the real battle Thomas Stanley hesitated from rendering Henry his full support, saying he "would come to him in time convenient," Shakespeare carefully omits this piece of ambivalence. Whereas during the actual battle it was Thomas's brother William Stanley who at the crucial eleventh hour directed his forces to fight for Henry, Shakespeare ignores this William and gives Thomas all the credit.
>
> Not least, whereas according to the historical chronicles it was a Sir Richard Bray who found Richard's crown in a hawthorn bush, thereupon passing it to Thomas Stanley, Shakespeare attributes to Thomas not only the finding of the crown, but the plucking of it "from the dead temples of this bloody wretch." Finally, as literally the crowning moment of the whole tetralogy, Shakespeare, at last following history, has Thomas set Richard's crown upon Henry Tudor's head, making him King Henry VII, and thus founding the Tudor dynasty of which Elizabeth represented the

third generation. In a moment of the most blatant emphasis of the Tudor debt to the Stanleys, Shakespeare then has the new Henry VII ask, as his first question as crowned king: "But tell me, is young George Stanley living?"

The orthodox view of the prominence Shakespeare gives to the Clifford and Stanley families in these early plays is that he is flattering his patron, Ferdinando Stanley, Lord Strange, patron of the troupe of players of which Shakspere is assumed to have been a member (although there is no evidence for this). For Ferdinando was the son of Margaret Clifford and directly descended from the Thomas Stanley who did indeed crown Henry VII.

As the reader will already know, William Stanley, our potential author, as the younger brother of Ferdinando, had the same descent from the Cliffords and Stanleys, and as an alternative to the orthodox view I would suggest that rather than the actor Shakspere flattering his putative patron, we have the author himself flattering his own ancestors. What more likely, it could be argued, than that a young playwright would choose to write plays about a period of history in which his forbears played important roles, and then proceed to exaggerate those roles to the extreme, with the intention of reminding all who saw the plays that the Tudor dynasty owed its very existence to the Stanleys? Moreover, the *Henry VI* plays are thought to have been first acted by Strange's Men, William's brother's company.

There is of course so far no evidence which would allow one view to prevail over the other. But once again we find that there is no barrier to the view I would favor.

John Weever: Another Lancastrian

John Weever, poet and antiquary, was born in Preston in Lancashire in 1576 (*ODNB*). He was educated at Queens' College, Cambridge, where he was admitted in April 1594. Weever's first tutor at Cambridge was William Covell, himself a native of Lancashire and author of *Polimanteia* (1595), which contains one of the first printed notices of Shakespeare (see note 6 to Chapter 4). After receiving his degree in April 1598, Weever appears to have left Cambridge and traveled to London, where he immersed himself in the literary scene. In late 1599 he published *Epigrammes in the Oldest Cut, and Newest Fashion*,[4] comprising 160 short poems, including a sonnet on Shakespeare, and epigrams on Samuel Daniel, Michael Drayton, John Marston, Ben Jonson, Edmund Spenser, William Warner and Christopher Middleton, all poets or playwrights.

As far as we can tell most of the epigrams concern people he was acquainted with, and a substantial number concern his Lancastrian relatives and local dignitaries, many of them members of the Stanley circle, including one on a cousin of William Stanley's father's second wife, one on the half-brother of his mother (the Earl of Cumberland), one on Edward Stanley (first Baron Monteagle), and two on the death of Ferdinando. Here is his sonnet on Shakespeare (epigram 22), which employs the Shakespearean rhyme-scheme, perhaps suggesting that he had seen some of the sonnets in manuscript.

> Honey-tongued Shakespeare, when I saw thine issue
> I swore Apollo got them, and none other,
> Their rosy-tainted features clothed in tissue,
> Some heaven-born goddess said to be their mother.

Rose-cheekt Adonis with his amber tresses,
Fair fire-hot Venus charming him to love her,
Chaste Lucretia virgine-like her dresses,
Proud lust-stung Tarquine seeking still to prove her:
Romea-Richard; more, whose names I know not,
Their sugred tongues, and power attractive beauty
Say they are Saints, although that Sts they show not
For thousands vows to them subjective dutie:
  They burn in love thy childre[n] Shakespear het the[m] [*heated*
  Go, wo thy Muse more Nymphish brood beget them.

Ernst Honigmann wrote a biography of Weever, and found it particularly surprising that Weever did not address an epigram to William Stanley, especially as they were both involved in writing for the theater.[5] Because of the company Weever kept both in Lancashire and in London, we may be reasonably sure he would have known who Shakespeare really was. So it may be that the omission is only apparent, and Weever's sonnet may have been his tribute to his fellow–Lancastrian poet/playwright.

We now provide a brief biography of the man who has figured several times in our narrative, up to the point at which he unexpectedly inherited the earldom.

10. *William Stanley's Early Years*

William Stanley's name has cropped up many times so far in the course of our journey, though usually as part of the background scenery rather than as a major feature in the landscape. We now present an account of his early life up to the crucial moment, on 16 April 1594, when his elder brother died and he unexpectedly became the Sixth Earl of Derby.

William Stanley was the second son of Henry Stanley, Fourth Earl of Derby, and his wife Margaret, née Clifford, who was the granddaughter of Henry VIII's younger sister Mary, Duchess of Suffolk.[1] Henry VIII's will gave Mary's children precedence over the children of her elder sister, and so Countess Margaret was directly in line to succeed Queen Elizabeth, followed by her children, a fact which had a profound effect on all their lives. Margaret turned out to be a difficult character, and as a result of her lavish spending of her husband's money and other reasons she was banished from his estates in Lancashire and lived in London. Here she incurred the wrath of Queen Elizabeth by repeatedly employing soothsayers and necromancers; it was suspected she did so in order to ascertain whether she would become Queen, and if so when. For some years she was subject to being confined to her house, and died in 1596 without having been restored to royal favor (*ODNB*).

Henry Stanley was directly descended from the Thomas Stanley who placed the crown on Henry Tudor's head after the battle of Bosworth Field. Thomas Stanley's second wife was Margaret Beaufort, who was the mother of Henry Tudor by her second marriage to Edmund Tudor, a Lancastrian; thus Thomas was the stepfather of Henry VII, who created him Earl of Derby after the battle. Henry Stanley held the important posts of Lord Lieutenant of Lancashire and High Chamberlain of Cheshire, and his vast estates made him one of the richest men in the country, so much so that at the Court in London and elsewhere he and his entourage were sometimes described as "the Northern Court."

Henry was patron of a troupe of players, "Derby's Men," and often attended the annual Chester summer festivities with his sons, where plays were performed by professional actors and also by working men—"rude mechanicals"; these shows are thought by many commentators to provide the pattern on which the play within the play in *Midsummer Night's Dream* was based. Visiting players frequently presented plays at his great mansions at Lathom and Knowsley in Lancashire. For example, between May 1587 and August 1590 the Queen's players, the Earl of Leicester's players, the Earl of Essex's players, Sir Thomas Hesketh's players, and three unnamed troupes are all recorded as performing for Henry and his family; each company usually stayed several days.[2] The writer and playwright Thomas Lodge spent some of his childhood years in Henry's household (*ODNB*), and for several years after 1585 John Donne served as one of his waiting gentlemen.[3] John Davies of Hereford, writing-master and poet, was a protégé of his, and Robert Greene sought his patronage. The playwright Thomas Kyd is believed by some to have acted as secretary to his eldest son, Ferdinando, from 1587 to 1593.

As a younger son, William had no prospects and few responsibilities. He was educated with his two brothers at St. John's College, Oxford (1572 to 1575 or 6), at a period when plays were often performed by the students and recent graduates. Details[4] have survived of a kind of festival of plays in early 1582, and some of these later informed several of Shakespeare's plays, including Plautus's "Menaechmi" (*Comedy of Errors*), George Gascoigne's "Supposes" (*Taming of the Shrew*), William Gager's "Meleager" (*Midsummer Night's Dream*), and Richard Eedes's "Caesar Infectus" (*Julius Caesar*, *Antony and Cleopatra*). It might well be the case that some of these plays had been put on earlier while William was still at St. John's (which incidentally was well known for putting on plays at the time, three in the festival of 1582), but no records have come to light.

His friends at this period included Thomas Lodge, John Donne, and Edmund and Robert Carey, whose elder brother George married Elizabeth Spencer, a sister of the wife of William's elder brother Ferdinando. George Carey later became second Baron Hunsdon and in 1597 Lord Chamberlain, patron of the Lord Chamberlain's Men who performed many of Shakespeare's plays.

William is thought to have occupied the years 1576 to 1582 studying law at Gray's Inn, one of the four professional societies for lawyers, to which his father had enrolled him at age two; here he would have met Francis Bacon. He then spent the years 1582–84 touring the Continent with his tutor Richard Lloyd, visiting Paris, where he might have learned of incidents which inform *Measure for Measure*, and also Henri of Navarre's Court at Nérac, the basis of *Love's Labor's Lost* (which features a parody of lines in a poem by Lloyd). He was back in London by January 1585 and then joined his father's grand embassy to Paris to award Henri III the Order of the Garter; other members of the entourage were his tutor, John Donne and Robert Cecil, son of the Lord Treasurer William Cecil, Lord Burghley. Instead of returning home afterwards William continued his travels abroad, perhaps with Donne, and supposedly visited Spain and Italy, though there are no records of his itinerary; as a younger son, albeit of an earl, no one would have taken much notice of him. These travels were greatly embellished after his death and became the stuff of popular and literary legend.

On his return in 1588 he spent time in both Lancashire and London, and was enrolled at Lincoln's Inn. Here he seems to have associated with writers and playwrights, including Thomas Nashe, who has been shown (Chapter 7) to have lampooned him as "Gentle Master William" in his pamphlet published in 1593, *Strange News*. Gabriel Harvey's response later that year (*Pierce's Supererogation*) included "M. Apis Lapis" ("lazy bee," believed to be William Stanley) in a list of Nashe's friends together with Robert Greene, Christopher Marlowe and Henry Chettle, all playwrights as well as poets. Nashe was a protégé of William's elder brother Ferdinando, Lord Strange (hence *Strange* News?), who like his father was also a patron of a troupe of players ("Strange's Men"), and Nashe would have got to know William through the latter's visits to his brother's London residence. Ferdinando's wife Alice, née Spencer, was a relative of Edmund Spenser, who dedicated poetry to her extolling her and two of her sisters (one of whom was George Carey's wife, as mentioned above). As we already know, in one of these poems he refers to "Our pleasant Willy," a kinsman (supposedly) who has written plays but is now resting "in idle Cell"; this is almost certainly William. Strange's Men were the first company recorded as performing Shakespeare's plays. In 1592 William's father, who evidently had a good opinion of his abilities, appointed him governor of the Isle of Man, of which the Stanleys were hereditary kings. The Fourth Earl died in September 1593 and was succeeded by Ferdinando.

On the day his father died, by coincidence, Ferdinando was approached by one Robert Hesketh, a secret Catholic who had come at the instigation of Catholics on the Continent to see whether the father or (failing him) the son would agree to a plan for Catholic armies from abroad to attempt to overthrow Queen Elizabeth and place him on the throne[5] (recall that Ferdinando's mother, Countess Margaret, was in line to succeed Elizabeth, so Ferdinando was next in line after her[6]). Ferdinando waited for a week before apprehending Hesketh and escorting him to London, where he was interrogated by Robert Cecil[7] and others and hanged later in November as a traitor. The delay of a week, together with vague earlier suspicions about his loyalty (almost certainly unfounded) meant that although Ferdinando inherited the earldom, other people were appointed to his father's posts of Lord Lieutenant of Lancashire and High Chamberlain of Cheshire. Ferdinando was greatly distressed at losing these appointments, having felt that he had acted correctly over bringing Hesketh to London and to justice, and his wife complained that he would be "crossed in court and crossed in his country."[8]

Events took a dramatic turn in April 1594 when Ferdinando met a painful death by poison, supposedly administered by Catholic conspirators. He took ten days to die, and the detailed account of his suffering during those days makes harrowing reading. The authorities were unable to decide whether his suffering and death were caused by witchcraft or poison, and amazingly enough commissioned two accounts of the circumstances of his death to be written, one assuming witchcraft and the other poison.[9] Witchcraft was the official explanation, but the real reason for this was not made public; it was that his wife had given birth to a stillborn child a month earlier, when she had apparently been living away from her husband at the time of conception.[10] This last circumstance had to be the result of witchcraft, as the alternative explanation was unthinkable.

Ferdinando while in the agonies of his last days made a will which bequeathed all the Derby estates to his wife and their three daughters, thereby disinheriting William. On his death William thereupon unexpectedly became the Sixth Earl of Derby and also (in effect) heir-apparent to Queen Elizabeth, but found himself dispossessed of the ancestral lands. His legal battle to win back control of the estates (undertaken by Francis Bacon) was not finally settled until fifteen years later, although he had offered a generous settlement right at the outset. He was consequently in financial difficulties for all this time—the few manors he had inherited from his father would have afforded him only a small income. Strange's Men broke up on Ferdinando's death, and most of them joined a new troupe known as "The Lord Chamberlain's Men" under Henry Carey, the Queen's cousin and first Baron Hunsdon, whose son George (as mentioned above) was a brother-in-law of Ferdinando's widow. This troupe, later the King's Men, was the company that frequently performed Shakespeare's plays.

During the early 1590s (as already noted) the household accounts record several visits by troupes of players to Lathom Hall, principal residence of Earl Henry, and William's arrivals and departures were occasionally noted down. Once or twice he is recorded as traveling to London with his brother's wife, and the terms of Ferdinando's will may have been prompted by suspicions about his wife's fidelity—or they may have some other origin; it is impossible to tell. We do know from a letter in the Cecil Papers that Alice had apparently been living separately from Ferdinando in late 1593.[11]

This completes our account of William's life up to the moment he inherited the earldom. There is nothing to suggest he was writing plays apart from what may be deduced from Spenser's and Harvey's remarks as already set out in Chapters 6 and 7. However, if we allow ourselves to suppose he had written plays, whether or not they were later published under the name William Shakespeare, it is apparent that even as a young man, William's closeness to the throne would have necessitated caution on his part and discretion on the part of others. His literary activities (so far hypothetical, since nothing survives under his own name) would have necessitated a pen name from the very beginning, not least to avoid becoming a source of embarrassment to his elder brother were he to succeed Queen Elizabeth.

We now look back on these first ten chapters and review what has come to light.

11. Retrospective 1

It is time to take stock of the ground we have so far traversed on this journey of ours. The portrait of "William Shakespeare" on the title page of the 1623 First Folio has proved to be a deceptive caricature, showing someone clothed in an impossible garment, which can only have been intended to indicate that the person depicted, the actor William Shakspere of Stratford-upon-Avon, was not the real author; evidently *the deception was always designed to be uncovered in due course*. The First Folio was a scam on a grand scale, a bluff that was never called. Notice that if the portrait had shown someone in normal clothing, as in the portrait of Samuel Daniel, Figure 3.2, the deception would never have been spotted, and if those behind the First Folio had wanted the real author to remain concealed for ever, that is what they would have done.

Cuthbert Burbage, who knew the actor for a number of years, refers to him as a "deserving man" and a "man player," and gives no hint that he was the playwright in a letter of 1635 to the Lord Chamberlain, the patron of the King's Men. The superior education apparent from the plays is hard to explain if they were written by someone with no university education, and the minutely detailed knowledge of Italian cities is also hard to explain if the writer never traveled abroad. His daughters were not taught to write (although they may well have been able to read), and the memorial inscription in Holy Trinity Church seems strangely inappropriate as a tribute to a playwright; no other tributes marking his death were forthcoming. Lastly, someone making notes on his copy of the First Folio stated that it was untrue that he was the "maker" or poet who wrote the plays. This will probably be enough to convince many people that the actor William Shakspere was not the playwright William Shakespeare.

If now we look into what little the poet said about himself, we turn first to the line in sonnet 125: "Wer't ought to me I bore the canopy?" This sounds very much as though the poet either had or (more likely) might have borne the canopy over Queen Elizabeth or King James on some specific occasion. The rest of the sonnet contains words and phrases which are reminiscent of the Communion Service, which together with the word "canopy" suggest the coronation of King James. At his anointing with holy oil, the most sacred part of the ceremony, a canopy would have been held over him by four Knights of the Garter who were also members of the higher nobility. Among these we find William Stanley, Earl of Derby, eighth in order of precedence and the fifth available; he had been appointed KG in 1601, and this may be to what Henry Chettle was referring to in 1603 when he wrote that the Queen had "graced his [*Shakespeare's*] desert."[1] It is likely he would have stood by in reserve in case one or two of the more senior KG's fell out, and might well reflect to himself whether such an honor would have meant anything to him compared to his love for his friend. This is the first hint to emerge that associates William Stanley (however tenuously) with something written by William Shakespeare, and also with something written about him.

We have learned that Spenser wrote about two "gentle" poets with great gifts (one of whom had recently taken a break from writing plays), and that Nashe addressed a Gentle Master William Apis lapis who was a "copious Carminist" (prolific poet), and have found reasons to suppose that all three are the same person; furthermore Gabriel Harvey brackets Master Apis Lapis with three well-known poets who were also playwrights. In all likelihood both of Spenser's gentle poets together with Nashe's "Gentle Master William" can be identified with William Stanley, still a commoner at this time. But while eminent Stratfordians (those who support the man from Stratford) in the past thought that Spenser's gentle poets were both references to William Shakespeare, there is no specific evidence which identifies him with William Stanley. The most that can be said at the moment is that there is nothing to rule out such an identification.

Nashe's epistle to *Strange News* tells us quite a lot about William Stanley, the "copious Carminist," some of it not to his credit—drinking heavily, and some very much to his discredit—fathering a child on some maidservant. But if it should turn out that Stanley was Shakespeare, at least it could then be said that we now know a great deal more about our poet than we did before.[2]

From the unresolved problem of the relationship between the Quarto and Folio versions of several of the plays, we have seen that the simplest explanation is that the author himself spent the years leading up to 1623 in revising and enlarging the shorter texts (quartos) that had already been published. This implies that the author was alive in 1622. (But then again, the simplest explanation is not necessarily the correct one.) We have also learned that William Stanley's forbears were closely involved in the setting up of the Tudor dynasty, and their roles were much exaggerated in parts 2 and 3 of *Henry VI* and in *Richard III*, just as one might expect if they had been written by him.

Our account of William's early life up till April 1594 shows a young man eager to journey abroad, even if very little is known about his travels; he is said to have been keen to learn as many languages as possible, though there is no contemporary record to this effect. We have learned that his father was very fond of the theater, and that plays were frequently presented at his mansions in Lancashire. We can imagine (if we so choose) the young William as a boy relishing these occasions, and perhaps attempting to take a part himself with the blessing of the players. Further than this we cannot go. Spenser implies in *The Teares of the Muses* that "Our pleasant Willy," William Stanley, had written plays, but what these were and whether they were later published we do not know.

We now embark on a diversion, to explore and seek to appreciate how much the Elizabethans enjoyed all kinds of word games, and in particular acrostics, one of which will turn out to be crucial to our research into the identity of our great author.

12. *Interlude: Word Games, Acrostics and Ciphers*

The Elizabethans and Jacobeans were fond of all kinds of games with words, such as anagrams, acrostics, and more sophisticated forms which could be used for recording or transmitting secret information. Anagrams may seem to us today rather trivial, though there are some remarkable examples which have a certain charm; for example, (from the book by Elizebeth and William Friedman, *The Shakespearean Ciphers Examined*[1]) the words INTERROGATIVES and TERGIVERSATION are anagrams of each other. But for those in early modern times they had a special attraction, in that they might be supposed to reveal hidden qualities relating anagram to an anagrammatized name.

A prime example of someone fascinated by such relationships is Francis Davison, whose *Anagrammata in Nomina Illustrissimorum Heroum* (1603)[2] gives anagrams, followed by laudatory verses in Latin, on 13 distinguished Elizabethan noblemen and knights, their names being first Latinized. Here are a few examples.

THOMAS EGERTONUS (Lord Great Seal)	*HEROS MAGNE TOTUS* *(Lord wholly great)*
GILBERTUS TAILBOTUS (Earl of Shrewsbury)	*LEGIT TRIBUBUS ALTOS* *(He chooses high men from the tribes)*
EDOUDARDUS VEIERUS (Earl of Oxford)	*AURE SURDUS VIDEO* *(Deaf in my ear, I see)*
HENRICUS URIOTHESLEUS (Earl of Southampton)	*THESEUS NIL REUS HIC RUO* *(Here I fall, Theseus, guilty of nothing)*

It will be noticed that not all of the anagrams are precise, with one or two letters added or omitted in some cases; precision was not regarded as necessary in such matters.

Acrostics were also highly esteemed. Here is one where the first letter in each line spells out the name Sir Francis Walsingham.[3]

S hall Honour, Fame, and Titles of Renowne,
I n Clods of Clay be thus inclosed still?
R ather will I, though wiser Wits may frowne,
F or to enlarge his Fame extend my Skill.
R ight, gentle Reader, be it knowne to thee,
A famous Knight doth here interred lye,
N oble by Birth, renowned for Policie,
C onfounding Foes, which wrought our Jeopardy.

I n Forraine Countries their Intents he knew,
S uch was his zeal to do his Country good,
W hen dangers would by Enemies ensue,
A s well as they themselves, he understood.
L aunch forth ye Muses into Streams of Praise,
S ing, and sound forth Praise-worthy Harmony;
I n *England* Death cut off his dismal Dayes,
N ot wronged by Death, but by false Treachery.
G rudge not at this imperfect Epitaph;
H erein I have exprest my simple Skill,
A s the First-fruits proceeding from a Graff:
M ake then a better whosoever will.

Sir John Davies in 1599 wrote *Hymnes of Astraea*,[4] which consists of a series of acrostic poems in tribute to Queen Elizabeth. Astraea was the Greek goddess of justice and the implication is that Queen Elizabeth is a just queen. The poems are written in adoration of the goddess, but each line of each poem pays tribute to Queen Elizabeth. The first letters of each of the lines of each sixteen-line poem spell out the phrase "ELISABETHA REGINA"—Elizabeth Queen.

Here is poem 7 of the 26, which are all based on the same pattern.

E YE of the Garden, Queene of flowres,
L ove's cup wherein he nectar powres,
I ngendered first of nectar ;
S weet nurse-child of the Spring's young howres,
A nd Beautie's faire character.

B est iewell that the Earth doth weare,
E uen when the braue young sunne draws neare,
T o her hot Loue pretending ; [reaching forward
H imselfe likewise like forme doth beare,
A t rising and descending.

R ose of the Queene of Loue belou'd ;
E ngland's great Kings diuinely mou'd,
G ave Roses in their banner ;
I t shewed that Beautie's Rose indeed,
N ow in this age should them succeed,
A nd raigne in more sweet manner.

Acrostic verses can also be constructed in other ways. The "telestich," for example, takes the final letter of the last word in every line, and the "progressive acrostic" takes the first letter of the first line, the second letter of the second line, the third from the third, and so on. William and Elizebeth Friedman in their book referred to above give rules for their construction.

> In every acrostic, the rules for selecting the letters of the secret text are invariable, and the selection follows a fixed pattern; moreover, the selected letters are chosen in a particular order, and the rules for setting them out in the form of a text are rigid and inviolable.[5]

However, the rules were not always followed too precisely. A devoted practitioner of the art of acrostic verse was Sir John Salusbury, who wrote many such poems; by coincidence his wife Ursula was an illegitimate daughter of Henry, Fourth Earl of Derby, by Jane Halsall, whom he was unable to marry while his banished wife was alive; Ursula was thus William

Stanley's half-sister. Here is an example, illustrating his devotion to the sister of his wife, Dorothy Halsall.[6]

Tormented heart in thra**l**, Yea thrall to loue,
Respecting wil**l**, Heart-breaking gaine doth grow,
Ever DOLABELL**A**, Time so will proue,
Binding distres**s**e, O gem wilt thou allowe,
This fortune my wil**l**, Repose-lesse of ease,
Vnlesse thou LED**A**, Ouer-spread my heart,
Cutting all my rut**h**, Dayne Disdaine to cease,
I yield to fate, and welcome endles Smart.

This conceals the name CVTBERT (Dorothy's husband) reading the initial letters upwards from the seventh line, and the two parts of the name DOROTHY HALSALL as the letters on either side of the breaks in the middle of each line; it will be noticed that there are occasional irregularities. The initials I. S. (for Iohn Salusbury) appear as the first letters of the first and last words in the last line. Aligning the central breaks vertically shows the hidden names more clearly.

Tormented heart in thral**l**, **Y**ea thrall to loue,
Respecting wil**l**, **H**eart-breaking gaine doth grow,
Ever DOLABELL**A**, **T**ime so will proue,
Binding distres**s**e, **O** gem wilt thou allowe,
This fortune my wil**l** **R**epose-lesse of ease,
Vnlesse thou LED**A**, **O**uer-spread my heart,
Cutting all my rut**h**, **D**ayne Disdaine to cease,
I yield to fate, and welcome endles *S*mart.

Salusbury wrote many other acrostic poems, several including his name, which he spelled in six different ways in order to integrate the name with the text of the poem. One poem consisted of a series of acrostics to spell out five names, with Dorothy appearing as DOROTHI HALSALL, Salusbury as IOHN SALESBVRYE, and with other people named FRANSIS WILOWBI, ELIZABETH WOLFRESTONE and ROBERT PARRYE. Exact precision was not needed, since besides being difficult to achieve there could be no doubt about whose name was being concealed.

Another form of word game was used for more serious purposes. It was known to John Dee, the Elizabethan mathematician, alchemist and savant, and first written about by Bishop John Wilkins in 1641. It is a method of concealing a message by writing it in the form of a grid or rectangle of letters, and then transmitting the letters by reading them out from the columns of the grid. Here is an example. Suppose the message is THE SPANISH SHIPS HAVE SAILED. Write this in a rectangular form (in this case a square) going down and up the columns:

```
T H S S A
H S H E I
E I I V L
S N P A E
P A S H D
```

The message would then be sent as THSSAHSHEI.... The message is recovered by counting the number of letters—25—and writing the letters out in a 5 × 5 square. It is amusing to learn that Dee regarded this as "a childish cryptogram such as eny man of knowledge shud be able to resolve."[7]

Here is another example, taken from Bishop Wilkins's book *Mercury, or the Secret and Swift Messenger*.[8]

E	R	F	D	L	E	E	L	L	T
I	E	T	O	O	S	W	I	I	H
L	S	U	U	H	H	S	N	T	E
P	H	O	T	O	A	V	C	S	P
P	A	H	T	T	L	T	R	H	E
U	N	T	H	E	L	S	E	T	S
S	D	I	E	L	N	G	A	O	T
Y	S	W	S	B	O	N	S	D	I
D	P	E	I	A	T	O	E	C	L
E	E	G	E	E	B	M	A	N	E

Here one has to start reading from the top right-hand corner: "The pestilenc[e] doth still increase amongst us wee shall not be able to hold out the siege without fresh and speedy supplie." The 100-letter message would be sent as follows: ERFDLEELLTIET, etc.

Finally, to return to acrostics, here is another method that has been used to conceal a name or a sentence in a book: the letters spelling out the hidden information are taken from the consecutive initial letters of each section of the publication.[9] Perhaps the best-known example occurs in a book with the title *Hypnerotomachia Poliphili*, published anonymously in 1499.[10] The initials of the 38 chapters form an acrostic: POLIAM FRATER FRANCISCUS COLUMNA PERAMAVIT, or "Brother Francesco Columna was very much in love with Polia," and it is thought that Francis Colonna was probably the author of the book. In another example, the sentence "Franciscus Godwinvvus Landavensis Episcopus hos conscripsit," is concealed in the same way: "Francis Godwin, Bishop of Llandaff, wrote these [lines]." This last example comes from the book by the Friedmans mentioned above.[11] About this example and others they write:

> What makes it true that they, and the others, are genuine cases of cryptography is that the validity of the deciphered text and the inflexibility of the systems employed are obvious.... In each case, there is no room to doubt that they were put there by the deliberate intent of the author; the length of the hidden text, and the absolutely rigid order in which the letters appear, combine to make it enormously improbable that they just happened to be there by accident.

They go on to say:

> We should not be surprised if it is claimed that anagrams and acrostics appear in Shakespeare's works, for they abounded in the literature of the time; nor should we be surprised if *these devices*

> *concern the authorship of the works*, for they have often been used to this end. We should even be tolerant of variable and erratic spelling, for this was to some extent a common Elizabethan practice. [*italics mine*]

As will emerge in due course, the names of the two principals in our story were indeed recorded, one in the Sonnets and one in the First Folio, whether for the satisfaction of the author or for the benefit of posterity hardly matters. There they are, preserved for all to see.

After this diversion, with intimations of matters still to be revealed, we turn to the Sonnets, and to speculation about the many mysteries they appear to hold.

Part II: The Sonnets

13. The Sonnets Considered

In 1609 a slim quarto volume was published with the title *Shake-speares Sonnets,*[1] containing 154 fourteen-line sonnets, several of which are regarded as among the finest short poems ever written in the English language. Taken all together, they constitute an impenetrable mystery which has baffled everyone who has attempted to explain how and why they came to be written, and whether they tell a coherent story, or simply hint at haphazard fragments of a disorganized life. At times the reader gains a distinct impression that the emotions expressed and the people referred to are real emotions felt by the poet and real people known to him; at other times the poet seems detached from events and people, and is perhaps writing from the sheer exhilaration of exercising his poetic skills (and some of the poems are rather dull).

The first 126 sonnets are generally regarded as being addressed to a young man—the "Fair Youth"—who is clearly well-born and perhaps a member of the nobility. The next 26 mostly refer to two friends, the young man again (but is it the same young man?) and a "woman colored ill," often called the "Dark Lady"; the identities of these people have been sought for over two centuries, but no consensus has been reached and they remain as elusive as ever. The final two sonnets are variations on the theme of a Greek epigram referring to the "little love-god" Cupid.[2]

In the first 17 sonnets the poet encourages the young man to marry and produce a son: "*... deare my love, you know, / You had a Father: let your Son say so,*" sonnet 13, lines 13–14. Earlier he has said, in sonnet 10, line 13: "*Make thee an other selfe for love of me,*" and from these two extracts alone we can deduce that there is a close relationship between the two men. (It should be borne in mind that at this period "love" expressed between two men meant no more than loyalty and warm friendship.) The urgency with which the poet develops the theme of procreation is at times pushed to extremes, as if some terrible catastrophe will ensue if no son is born. For example, in sonnet 1 the young man is accused of eating his progeny (like Saturn[3]—what a ghastly comparison!) by refusing to produce any:

> ... this glutton be, [lines 13–14
> To eat the world's due, [*his son*

In sonnet 3 he is chided for loving himself more than fatherhood:

> Or who is he so fond will be the tombe, [lines 7–8
> Of his self-love, to stop posterity?

In sonnet 6 he is told:

... thou art much too faire, [lines 13–14
To be death's conquest and make worms thine heir

—rather than a son. He is further accused of "*Making a famine where aboundance lies,*" (#1.7) and "*Within thine own bud [burying] thy content,*" (#1.11) by not wanting to produce a son. He is accused of self-hatred in sonnet 10:

For thou art so possessed with murdrous hate, [lines 5–6
That 'gainst thy selfe thou stick'st not to conspire,

Some of the language verges on the manic, though it requires a sustained reading of all 17 poems to appreciate the full force of the poet's personal involvement in the young man's having a son (and *none* of the other delights of matrimony are mentioned[4]). It could be argued that this is just the normal exaggeration a poet might employ to enrich his verse. But I think it goes deeper than that; something of far greater import than his friend's obligation to continue his distinguished family's line is at stake here.

Whatever the explanation, it is clearly a matter of enormous significance to the poet for the young man to marry and produce an heir, and so, right at the opening of the series of sonnets, we are faced with a problem. For, as C. S. Lewis has said: "What man in the whole world, except a father or a potential father-in-law, cares whether any other man gets married?"[5] Later it will emerge that there is a third possible reason for such an exhortation from one man to another, which will be discussed in due course.

Another theme runs through the sonnets, that of the poet's conviction that his poetry will confer "immortal life" upon the name of the Fair Youth.

But thy eternall Summer shall not fade, [#18.9–14
Nor loose possession of that faire thou ow'st [ownest],
Nor shall death brag thou wandr'st in his shade,
When in eternall lines [*the poet's*] to time thou grow'st,
  So long as men can breathe or eyes can see,
  So long lives this [*the poet's lines*], and this gives life to thee.

Not marble, nor the guilded monuments, [#55.1–4
Of Princes shall out-live this powerfull rime,
But you shall shine more bright in these contents
Than unswept stone, besmeer'd with sluttish time.

From hence your memory death cannot take, [#81.3, 5, 9
... ...
Your name from hence immortall life shall have,
... ...
Your monument shall be my gentle verse,

... ... for't lies in thee [*the poet's Muse*], [#101.10–12
To make him [*the Fair Youth*] much out-live a gilded tombe:
And to be praisd of ages yet to be.

And thou in this shalt find thy monument, [#107.13

Other sonnets elaborate the poet's love for the young man, and brood upon the destructiveness of Time (the great enemy—the word occurs 78 times in the first 126 sonnets), death and the transience of life, his despair at the young man's preferring a "Rival Poet," his ambiguous feelings for his mistress (the "Dark Lady") and her snaring the affections of the young man.

The sonnets' *dramatis personae* thus consist of the poet, the Fair Youth, the Dark Lady, and the Rival Poet. They make appearances more or less at random, and it emerges that some kind of love triangle exists between the poet, his young friend, and the Dark Lady, who is blamed for seducing them both.[6] The sonnets do not seem to be arranged chronologically, and many attempts have been made to reorder them in such a way to allow them to be read as an account of real events.[7] Then again, the prevailing orthodox view is that almost without exception they are simply poetical exercises, with no reference to real people and the emotions they are assumed to experience.[8] This is a view with which a reader with an open mind is unlikely to concur.

I am not going to attempt to provide my own version of "the story that the sonnets tell," not least because so many others have attempted and largely failed to make narrative sense of them. Rather my concern is with what the sonnets tell us about the young man, as a way of finding out more about the poet who immortalized him in his verse: "*Your name from hence immortall life shall have*" (#81.5), a name which paradoxically until very recently had been deemed lost forever, and is still the subject of endless debate. Soon, however, it will emerge that it had indeed been recorded for posterity, so that the poet's promise really was genuine and more than airy rhetoric. First, we will explore one of the main themes of the sonnets, a theme which many commentators prefer to overlook.

14. The Fair Youth Royal?

The sonnets contain many clues about the young man, none more surprising than that he seems to be endued with something akin to royalty, as G. Wilson Knight and Leslie Hotson, both orthodox Shakespearean scholars, declare. For example, in sonnet 57

Nor dare I chide the world without end houre, [lines 5–6
Whilst I (my *soveraine*) watch the clock for you, [*italics added*

he is addressed as "sovereign," while in sonnets 63 and 87

And all those beauties whereof now he's *King* [#63.6

Thus have I had thee as a dreame doth flatter, [#87.13–14
In sleep a *King*, but waking no such matter.

he is addressed as "King." It may be that these are simply extravagant terms of endearment, but it goes deeper than that, for in other sonnets the young man is referred to as "the Sun," "a God," "the Ocean," all terms often applied to royalty, according to Leslie Hotson.[1]

Even so my *Sunne* one early morne did shine, [#33.9
A *God* in love, to whom I am confin'd. [#110.12
But since your worth (wide as the *Ocean* is) [#80.5

Hotson gives numerous examples of Shakespeare and other poets referring to kings as Suns, Gods and Oceans or Seas.

Here are some quotations from Wilson Knight's study of Shakespeare's sonnets.[2]

> The sonnets regularly express love through metaphors from royalty and its derivatives, using such phrases as *my sovereign, thy glory, lord of my love, embassy of love, commanded by the motion of thine eyes*... [p. 6].
>
> At their greatest moments the Sonnets are really less love-poetry than an almost religious adoration... [p. 59].
>
> Royal images recur.... The poet addresses the youth as *lord of my love*, to whom he sends a *written ambassage;* he is *my sovereign* and the poet his *servant or slave*... [p. 60].
>
> The loved one is *royal*... [p. 61].
>
> He is *crowned* with various gifts of nature and fortune, especially *all those beauties whereof now he's King*. Like a *sovereign*, he radiates *worth*, his eyes lending a *double majesty*... [p. 61].
>
> Our final impression is of love itself as king, of some super-personality, the Sun.... The associations are just, since the king, properly understood, holds within society precisely this super-personal and supernal function... [p. 61].

> Kingship is naturally *golden*, and golden impressions recur with similar variations in use.... The Sun is nature's king, and also pre-eminently golden. Throughout Shakespeare *king* and *sun* are compared.... With the Fair Youth, the association of *that Sun, thine eye* comes easily enough... [p. 62].
>
> We have various clusters of *king, gold*, and *sun. King* and *gold* come together in *the gilded monuments of Princes;* and *sun* and *gold*, when the *Sun's gold complexion* is dimmed in the sonnet, "Shall I compare thee to a Summer's day,"[3] or the young man *graces the day* and *gilds the evening* in place of stars. We may have all three. So *great Princes' favorites* are compared to the *marigold* opening to *the Sun's eye...* [p. 63].
>
> These impressions are not just decoration.... That the poet of the Sonnets was deeply concerned with such themes is clear from the many comparisons of his love to kings and state-affairs. His very love is felt as royal and stately. The Sonnets are the heart of Shakespeare's royal poetry [p. 63].

Wilson assumes that the poet is the Stratford man and the fair youth either Henry Wriothesley, the Earl of Southampton, or William Herbert, later Earl of Pembroke. The following are some of Hotson's remarks; for him the poet is again the Stratford man but the fair youth is William Hatcliffe, a member of Gray's Inn who has been elected "Prince of Purpoole," a temporary honor for officiating at Christmas revels.

> Here, then, we have Shakespeare typifying his Friend variously as a *sun*, a *god*, an *ocean* or a *sea:* three familiar metaphors which he and his contemporaries use to represent *a sovereign, prince* or *king...* [p. 28].
>
> Sustained and unmistakable, this language of Shakespeare's lends no support to the common theory that his youthful Friend might be some nobleman or other. For it is obvious that his chosen terms point, *not to nobility, but to royalty* [i.e., for Hotson, his temporary "Prince of Purpoole"] [p. 32].
>
> ... what he sets before us ... is *not* the powers of a peer, but those peculiar to a king: power *to grant charters of privilege and letters patent,* power *to pardon crimes*—in short, the exclusively *royal prerogative* [p. 32].
>
> Clearly these consenting terms, which appear in no fewer than twenty-eight of these Sonnets, cannot be dismissed as scattered surface-ornament. They are intrinsic. What is more, they intensify each other. By direct address, by varied metaphor, and by multifarious allusion, the description of the Friend communicated is always one: *monarch, sovereign, prince, king* [p. 35].

The remarkable comments made by both these orthodox Shakespeare scholars show that the terms which Shakespeare applies to the Fair Youth might well seem to be something more than metaphors, or attributes appropriate to temporary mock-royalty. For there is another word in the sonnets appropriate to royalty: in sonnet 2 the poet tells the young man that his use of his "beautie" will receive praise if he has a "faire child," thereby

> Prooving his beautie by *succession* thine, [line 12

The succession to the throne had preoccupied everyone in the country since early on in the Queen's reign, and in the 1590s, when many of the sonnets are thought to have been written, it had become the burning issue of the day. It is interesting to learn then that this sonnet was the one most frequently copied out into common-place books in the 30 years following publication in 1609, perhaps because of this particular word.

It is a little hard to account for Shakespeare's obsession with royalty, kingship and succession, which runs all through the first series of sonnets. His devotion to the young man is often expressed in extravagant terms, but the recurring theme is royalty, and while at first we might assume it was a metaphor encompassing the young man's remarkable beauty, personal gifts and high birth, after a time we might begin to wonder whether the poet is hinting at some actual attribute of his young friend. Is it possible that he partakes of royalty in some literal sense? The idea is absurd, of course. However, in the next chapter we look into just such a possibility, first put forward sometime during the 1920s or 1930s.

15. The Fair Youth's Lineage

In the late 1920s or early 1930s, an astonishing theory was put forward about Shakespeare's sonnets. The theory proposed that the "Fair Youth" was the Third Earl of Southampton, that he was the son of Queen Elizabeth and Edward de Vere, 17th Earl of Oxford (supposedly the real Shakespeare), and that this was the key to understanding many of the poems.

I was appalled when I first learned about this theory, and I have to add immediately that, for me, these remain open questions. My purpose here is to investigate the theory objectively, as a scientist or advocate at law, seeking and following the evidence wherever it appears to lead, keeping an open mind and forming no conclusions until all the available evidence, such as it is, has been examined. I urge the reader likewise to keep an open mind, and suspend disbelief (the natural reaction) until all the evidence has been laid out, bearing in mind that as described in the previous chapter two eminent orthodox Shakespearean scholars have already deduced that the Fair Youth was regarded by the poet as *royal*, in some so far undetermined sense.

In this chapter, I shall outline how this theory can be derived from the first 17 sonnets (and a few others), and in a later chapter I shall consider what used to be a taboo subject, the question of whether the Queen could have had, or did have, any children. In a subsequent chapter I have assembled evidence which seems to show that from 1592 to 1603 Southampton was indeed thought by many people to have a status not dissimilar to what one might associate with a natural son of the Queen. Amazingly enough, what for some 80 years from the 1920s onwards was regarded as "almost unbelievable" turns out (apparently) to have been "widely believed" in the 1590s.

In a nutshell, there is a case for supposing that the author of the sonnets (whoever he was) believed the Fair Youth (whether Southampton or someone else) to be the son of Queen Elizabeth and Edward de Vere. Unless or until genetic testing throws light on the facts of the matter we shall never know if he was right or wrong in this belief. What we can do is to see if this theory illuminates or makes nonsense of these poems, which have eluded explanation for so long.

The origin of the idea that Southampton was the son of Queen Elizabeth (sometimes known as the "Prince Tudor" theory) is obscure, and I don't know of any systematic account dating from the 1930s or 1940s; it appears to have emerged as a series of guesses. I shall therefore put forward my own arguments, for what they are worth, as originally prompted by a few sentences in Charlton Ogburn's book *The Mysterious William Shakespeare*, which puts forward the case for Edward de Vere as Shakespeare. He opens his chapter on the sonnets by saying:

> We now come to the most tantalizing and provocative, most hauntingly beautiful, most eloquent, most disquieting confession in English poetry.[1]

He calls it "unnervingly outspoken" and "consistently enigmatic," and also "the greatest puzzle in the history of English literature" (quoting A. L. Rowse[2]), and few would disagree. Ogburn had little new to say about the sonnets in this chapter that I hadn't read elsewhere, until near the end, when he said something that really startled me.

> That Southampton was by birth both de Vere's son and, in his eyes, his prince, by virtue of his descent from his mother, Queen Elizabeth, is a proposition on which ... I take no stand.[3]

He then calls it "the one theory so far propounded that would account for the tone and burden of the 126 'fair youth' Sonnets." I was amazed and appalled. To include such an outlandish idea in an otherwise fascinating and well-argued book was a serious blot, I felt, and reduced its standing considerably in my estimation.

At the first opportunity, I got out a facsimile edition of the sonnets, and started reading sonnet 1, keeping in mind the theory indicated by Ogburn that "beauty" shadowed the Queen and "truth" de Vere:

> From fairest creatures we desire increase, [lines 1–2
> That thereby beauties *Rose* might never die, [*italics in original*

If "beauty" is Queen Elizabeth, then "beauties *Rose*" might well be the Tudor line, and it might seem that the theme of the sonnets, or those addressed to the young man, is being announced in the first couplet of the first sonnet, just as in the plays vital information is given to the audience in the opening lines of the first scene. And the theme apparently being announced is this: *the continuation of the Tudor royal dynasty.*

Suspending disbelief, I then went on to sonnet 10, lines 13–14:

> Make thee an other selfe for love of me,
> That beauty still may live in thine or thee.

I already knew of the writer C. S. Lewis's comment on the first of these lines, already quoted:

> What man in the whole world, except a father or a potential father-in-law, cares whether any other man gets married?[4]

And here was a theory with Oxford as both the poet and the father of the young man, urging him to have a son so that "beauty," the Queen and the Tudor dynasty, may live on in her son and grandson. Next, sonnet 14, lines 11–14:

> ... truth and beautie shal together thrive
> If from thy selfe, to store thou wouldst convert, [*have a child*
> Or else of thee this I prognosticate,
> Thy end is Truthes and Beauties doome and date.

It seems that here the poet (whether Oxford or—in my view—someone else) is urging the young man to produce a son so that Truth and Beauty, Oxford and the Queen, shall flourish in their grandson, while if he has no son, Truth and Beauty will be finished, that is, *the Tudor royal line will be extinct.* This new explanation of the sonnets was a revelation, since it was so much more meaningful than any other I had read. The few sonnets I had already looked at certainly seemed consistent with the idea that "Beauty" stands for the Queen and "Truth" for de Vere (whose motto was *vero nihil verius*, "nothing truer than truth," or "nothing truer than de Vere"). Would other sonnets allow the same identification?

Looking ahead, we find Shakespeare in sonnet 101 chiding his Muse for neglecting to praise the Fair Youth, repeating the words "truth" and "beauty" several times (emphasized in italics).

> O truant Muse what shalbe thy amends,
> For thy neglect of *truth* in *beauty* di'd? [dyed
> Both *truth* and *beauty* on my love depends,
> So dost thou [*Muse*] too, and therein dignifi'd:
> Make answere, Muse: wilt thou not haply saie,
> *Truth* needs no collour, with his collour fixed,
> *Beautie* no pensell, *beauties truth* to lay:
> But best is best, if never intermixt.
> Because he [*the Fair Youth*] needs no praise, wilt thou [*Muse*] be dumb?
> Excuse not silence so, for't lies in thee,
> To make him much out-live a gilded tombe,
> And to be prais'd of ages yet to be.
> Then do thy office Muse, I teach thee how,
> To make him seeme long hence, as he showes now.

Here the Fair Youth is being referred to as "*truth* in *beauty* dyed." Are these poetic abstractions, invoked to flatter the Fair Youth, or are they perhaps covert references to his natural parents, Oxford and the Queen?

I must remind the reader at this stage that I am acting as an independent investigator trying to reinvent a theory about which I hold an open mind. As the investigation proceeds there may come a time when the theory collapses, or it may be that no obstacle to its potential validity comes to light. The important thing at this stage is not to let one's immediate reaction (probably negative) color the collecting of evidence.

Sonnet 54 starts:

> Oh how much more doth beautie [*the Queen*] beautious seeme,
> By *that sweet ornament* which truth [*de Vere*] doth give, [*emphasis added*

And if we ask, what is signified by "that sweet ornament," we find the answer in sonnet 1, where the poet addresses the young man as follows, lines 9–10:

> Thou [*the Fair Youth*] that art now *the worlds fresh ornament*,
> And only herauld to the gaudy spring, [*emphasis added*

Here it appears that we are being told that the young man is the "ornament" given to "beautie" by "truth," Oxford fathering him upon the Queen, thereby making her seem so much the more "beautious," perhaps by her achievement in consolidating the Tudor dynasty through having a son. (It may be that sonnet 54 was originally placed second, but was moved elsewhere as too revealing. To retain the number of sonnets in this group at 17, sonnet 8 was perhaps then moved in, but it has little in common with them—no mention of truth or beauty.)

It seems (or seemed) to me that the result of logically combining these two extracts provides quite powerful evidence for the "Prince Tudor" theory (that the Fair Youth was the son of the Queen and Oxford). If "beauty" is the Queen, and if the young man—the "world's fresh ornament"—is her son by "truth," Edward de Vere, then everything fits together and makes perfect sense, whether or not de Vere was the poet. What previously were vague metaphysical musings about "abstract categories of discourse"—truth and beauty—suddenly become passionate outpourings dealing with real people and the poet's hopes for them.

(Here I must interrupt the narrative to remind the reader again that I am exploring these matters as an uncommitted investigator. I am following up the consequences of a hypothesis adopted for the purposes of argument and to see where it and they might lead, introducing such evidence as an independent advocate might rely on. I have no preconceived view on the truth or otherwise of the hypothesis, or of the various stages through which the investigation passes. If some overall deduction emerges from the analysis presented here, it will be found at the end of the investigation.)

Still on this theme of the continuation of the Tudor line, the poet tells the young man in sonnet 2 that his use of his "beautie" will receive praise if he has a "faire child,"[5] thereby (line 12)

Prooving his beautie by succession thine,

introducing what seems to be the main theme of these "dynastic" sonnets, that of "*succession*." It is interesting to learn that this sonnet was the one most frequently copied out into common-place books in the 30 years following publication; 11 manuscript versions have been found,[6] suggesting that it had a particular appeal or significance for readers at the time. During this period James I and Charles I had proved themselves lamentably inferior to the Tudors as rulers, and maybe people were speculating on how things might have turned out differently.[7]

Further reflection suggests that the underlying message of these sonnets, left for the few to appreciate, might seem to be not only the consolidation of the Tudor dynasty by Elizabeth's son marrying and producing an heir, but to point up the need for her to legitimize him, otherwise he will not be able to inherit the throne. There were two ways the Queen might achieve this, either by royal decree, or by marrying Oxford, whose wife Anne had died in June 1588. This last would have been the simplest method through which Southampton (if indeed he was the Fair Youth) could have been legitimized (retrospectively, be it admitted), and his children enabled to take their place in the line of succession. Such a marriage might have taken place before 1591 or 1592, the period within which Oxford married Elizabeth Trentham as his second wife (exact date unknown), but this scenario requires the dynastic sonnets to have been written before that event; most commentators assign them to a later date, making this course of action unlikely to have been in the poet's mind.

So, while the message addressed to Southampton is *"Get married and produce a son!"* the subtext, intended for the Queen's consideration (if she ever saw these sonnets, which I regard as unlikely), is *"Legitimize Southampton!"*—otherwise there is no dynastic point in his getting married and having a son. Thus the line in sonnet 13,

You had a Father, let your Son say so. [line 14

while ostensibly addressed to the young man, could also be regarded, via a "second intention," as an appeal to the Queen to recognize the young man as her son. Hence a line like "Prooving his beautie by succession thine" has a double meaning, since the Fair Youth's son will only inherit the Queen's Tudor "beauty of descent" if the Queen makes the Fair Youth her heir.

It would obviously have been useless (and also unlawful) for the poet (whoever he was) to urge the Queen to nominate her son as her successor, so he adopted (supposedly) the stratagem of urging her son to marry and produce an heir, confident that she would understand the message (again, always assuming she got to see these sonnets). And here at last (it would seem) is a motivation sufficiently strong to explain why these sonnets came to be written. A young man of 17 or 18 will get married anyway, so they are wasted on him, but an aging monarch requires to be coaxed, and to be reminded that the fate of the Tudor dynasty lies in her hands. To urge a young man to marry and have a son *for no other reason* than to perpetuate his "beauty" is verging on the fatuous. To encourage the Queen, whose beauty has been flattered all her life—and who was addressed as "Beauties Rose" by Sir John Davies (see Chapter 12)—to preserve the glory of the Tudor line by acknowledging and legitimizing her son, and thereby securing a peaceful succession, is a theme indeed worthy of the poet, it might seem.

Sonnet 6 urges the young man to make some girl pregnant—any girl, the poet doesn't care who—

> ...   ... treasure thou some place [lines 3–4
> With beauties treasure ere it be selfe kil'd:

Here "beauties treasure" is (supposedly) the Queen's treasure, the Tudor royal blood, which must be passed on before the Tudor line becomes "self-killed"—extinct, killed off by the Queen's failing to legitimize Southampton. The royal bloodline is worthless unless it is legitimate, which requires the Queen either to marry or to proclaim a royal fiat. Incidentally, these two lines might be interpreted as a real give-away, since it is "*beauties* treasure," his *inheritance* of royal blood, which the young man will pass on to his children, not his *own* treasure, which a first reading might suggest.

As we saw in Chapter 14, many of the sonnets appear to attach aspects of royalty to the young man, whether Southampton or someone else. While on the conventional view this obsession with royalty reflects the beauty and other gifts possessed by the Fair Youth, in a kind of exaggerated metaphor, it now seems possible to interpret these attributes as pertaining to someone with genuine royal blood in their veins. Again, please bear in mind that I am exploring a theory, not advocating it. Any conclusions, however tentative, will be offered later on in this increasingly fraught expedition of ours.

So far all this is speculation, based on hypothesis and poetry: what of life in the real world? Could the Queen have had any children,[8] and if so, could Southampton have been one of them? We now turn our attention to these matters, reflecting that we have gotten ourselves into very deep waters indeed.

16. The Queen's Children?

It is well known that there were many rumors about the Queen's alleged children. For example, early in her reign she withdrew from public view for two months, and virtually no one from the Court or Council saw her. It was widely believed that she was in the last weeks of pregnancy, and that she was pregnant by Sir Robert Dudley (later Earl of Leicester). This belief was in no way diminished by the fact that she spent these two months in retreat in Dudley's mansion at Kew, Kew House, which she had given him not long before, in December 1558, six weeks after her accession.[1]

A few years later, in 1571, Parliament was about to pass a law[2] which stated that only the "lawful issue" of the Queen should succeed to the throne, when she insisted that this be changed to "natural issue," throwing a tantrum until it was agreed to. The historian Camden recalled decades later, in 1615:

> I remember, being then a young man, hearing it said openly by people that the word "natural" was inserted into the Act on purpose by Leicester, that he might one day obtrude upon the English some base-born son of his own for the Queen's offspring.[3]

A year later, when the Earl of Oxford[4] began to displace Christopher Hatton in the affections of the Queen, Edward Dyer wrote a letter to Hatton.

> First of all, you must consider with whom you have to deale, & what wee be towards her; who though she does descend very much in her Sex as a woman, yet wee may not forgett her Place, & the nature of it as our Sovraigne.[5]

Further on he writes:

> For though in the beginning when her Majesty sought you (after her good manner), she did beare with rugged dealing of yours, until she hadd what she fancyed; yet now, after satiety & fullness, it will rather hurt than helpe you.

Very few modern writers quote the second of these extracts. One who does makes the comment, "Even the fiction of the Virgin Queen seems to vanish."[6]

On May 11, 1573, Gilbert Talbot wrote to his father:

> My Lord of Oxford is lately grown into great credit, for the Queen's Majesty delighteth more in his personage and his dancing and valiantness than any other.... At all these love matters my Lord Treasurer winketh, and will not meddle in any way.[7]

Here "My Lord Treasurer" is William Cecil, Lord Burghley, father of Oxford's wife Anne. These are just a few of the misgivings that many people at the time felt about the Queen's private behavior.

Historians, starting in the middle of the 17th century, were convinced for some three hundred years that Elizabeth had not led an entirely celibate life, and most of them hinted in various discreet ways that her relations with several of her courtiers were not beyond reproach. For example, the Italian historian Gregorio Leti (notoriously unreliable) wrote in 1693:

> I do not know if she was so chaste as is reported; for after all, she was a queen, she was beautiful, young, full of wit, delighted in magnificent dress, loved entertainments, balls, pleasures, and to have the best-shaped men in her kingdom for her favourites. This is all I can say of her to the reader.[8]

But elsewhere he wrote that she had a child in late 1572.[9] Here is John Nichols in 1788:

> A husband, although a young one, would have been perhaps inconsistent with her private attachments; and the formalities of marriage might have laid a restraint on more agreeable gallantries with the Earl [of Leicester] and others.[10]

And here is Sir Harris Nicholas in 1847:

> ... the notoriety of the Queen's incontinence [lack of chastity] was alleged by the Duke of Anjou as his reason for refusing to marry her.[11]

Frederick Chamberlin, the great 20th-century champion of the Queen's spotless life, names fifty-three 19th-century historians whom he castigates for doubting the Queen's virtue.[12] Fifty-three!

I mention these stories not to approve them, but to show the general climate of opinion in previous centuries. It is of course generally acknowledged that history consists of the stories we agree among ourselves to tell about the past, and what is acceptable often prevails over what is true or what is unpalatable. Somewhere around the turn of the twentieth century the picture of a spotless Queen became more acceptable than the one which had held for the previous three centuries, and the "Virgin Queen," which doubtless meant no more than that she was unmarried and not subject to the control of a husband, became the "Virginal Queen," to general approval. By the date of Chamberlin's book, 1921, the revisionist process was well under way.

Whatever the truth behind all the rumors, I do not think they get us very far, and so I will concentrate on the one child of hers about whom we know the most, for the simple reason that at age 26 or so he wrote out his life story, which in 1895 was included by the Historical Manuscripts Commission in the volumes of the State Papers Spanish.[13]

17. The Queen's Child?

Arthur Dudley was on a pilgrimage to the south of France in mid–1587 when his boat was blown off course and he landed in Spain. He was apprehended and sent to Madrid, where he was interrogated by Sir Francis Englefield, a Catholic exile, previously one of Queen Mary's Privy Council, who had fled to Spain on the accession of Elizabeth and entered the service of Philip II. Arthur claimed to be the son of Leicester and Queen Elizabeth, and Sir Francis's first reaction was that he was an impostor and up to no good, so he gave the young man pen and paper and told him to write an account of his life. This has survived, and in 1895 it was printed by the Historical Manuscripts Commission in the State Papers Spanish.[1] It has been accessible to all subsequent historians of the period, and not one in twenty refers to it.

In his story, Arthur relates how he was brought up by his father, Robert Southern, in Evesham, and when he was about eight, he was taken to London and given the best education available, including Latin, Italian and French, music, arms, and dancing, and if plague threatened he was sent back into the country. When he was about 15, he quarreled with his father and ran away to a port in Wales, but before he could embark for France a horse-messenger arrived where he was staying, with a letter signed by seven members of the Privy Council ordering him back. He was then conveyed to Pickering Place in Kent, where he met Edward Wotton, Thomas Heneage and John Ashley, and was told that John Ashley had paid for his education, and not Robert Southern. Later, he succeeded in his wish to travel abroad, money being provided, and while in France in 1583 he was recalled by his father, who was very ill.

Robert Southern then told Arthur he was not his father, and went on to relate that he had been summoned to Hampton Court by Kat Ashley (the Queen's former governess and her closest confidante, wife of John Ashley), and had been asked by Isabella Harington, one of the Queen's gentlewomen, to get ready to receive a child to bring up as his own, since (I quote) "one of the Queen's ladies had been so careless of her honor that, if it became known, it would bring great shame upon her, and would highly displease the Queen if she knew of it." The next morning Robert duly collected Arthur from Mrs. Harington, and brought him up with his own children in place of one which had died, money being supplied, and his education later provided for. (As a comment on all this, one can see how easy it was for a child to be smuggled out, and how a dutiful retainer would readily agree to bring up someone else's child, a hitherto unsuspected feature of the feudal system.)

Robert Southern at first refused to tell Arthur who his parents were, but later, to salve his conscience on his deathbed, he told Arthur that he was the son of the Earl of Leicester and the Queen. Arthur then traveled to London. Finding there Sir John Ashley and Sir Dru

Drury, he related what Robert had told him. They exhibited great alarm at learning that the secret had been revealed, and told him not to repeat it, and assured him of their best services while they lived. The great fear displayed by these two and others he met alarmed Arthur so much that he fled to France, money being again provided. Later he came back to England and had a tearful encounter with Leicester, who showed him great affection, calling him his son, and told him that they had great plans for him, including marriage to Arbella Stuart (Henry VII's great-great-granddaughter), but that meanwhile he was rather conspicuous, and had better go abroad again, where he eventually ended up in Spain as already described. What happened to him after 1587 is unknown, and no grave has been found.[2]

It is an amazing story, which rings true in every detail. The parts of the story relating to Evesham were investigated by a local historian in 1926, and where verifiable were found to be correct in every particular.[3]

My reason for outlining this story is to show, first of all, how an embarrassing birth could be dealt with—a whole network of feudal retainers was in place to rally round. Secondly, the truth of Arthur's story is reinforced by the fact that all the people that he and his father spoke to at Court were the Queen's very closest and most loyal and long-serving servants and courtiers (see below).

Furthermore, although at first Sir Francis Englefield had doubts about Arthur Dudley, after he had read his story and talked with him at length on several occasions he voices no more suspicions in his subsequent letters to Philip II. He quite clearly accepts Arthur's story as true, and so does the King, who gave him rooms in the palace and a very generous daily allowance. Remember that Sir Francis had been a Privy Councilor in Queen Mary's time, and would have been instantly alert to any flaws in Arthur's story. An impostor would not have remained undetected for long.

It is obvious from all this that neither Sir Francis nor Philip II thought it impossible or even unlikely that the Queen could have given birth to a son. And if they thought it possible, then perhaps we too should consider it possible, since they were closer to these events than we are by some four hundred and fifty years. Those who say that the Queen was always on view, and could never have concealed a pregnancy,[4] are flying in the face of common sense. Here is a woman able to choose exactly what style of clothing to wear, with complete control over whom she saw and when, whether they were three yards away or six, who could cancel any appointment at a moment's notice, and who was surrounded by devoted serving women whose very lives depended on serving their mistress faithfully.

The story of Arthur Dudley lends credence to the view (prevalent in her lifetime and for three centuries subsequently) that the Queen had borne one or more children, so the possibility that the Fair Youth, whether Southampton or someone else, was one of these should not perhaps be ruled out. One can imagine the child being smuggled out in the same kind of way that Arthur was, and later being brought up in the household of the Second Earl of Southampton, perhaps being substituted for a legitimate child who had died in infancy.

We now turn to evidence that shows that the Fair Youth was indeed Henry Wriothesley, Third Earl of Southampton.

People Mentioned in Arthur Dudley's Relation

Katherine (Kat) Ashley: appointed governess to Elizabeth when she was aged 4, in 1537.

Sir John Ashley: relative of the Boleyns; member of Elizabeth's household from circa 1545.

Isabella Harington: one of Elizabeth's gentlewomen from ca. 1550; her son was Elizabeth's godson.

Sir John Harington: confidential servant to Henry VIII; gentleman of Elizabeth's household from ca. 1554.

Sir Edward Wotton: linguist, diplomat and MP, Comptroller of the Household, Privy Councilor.

Sir Thomas Heneage: gentleman of the Privy Chamber, 1558; later Vice-Chamberlain of the Queen's Household; married the Countess of Southampton as her second husband.

Sir Dru Drury: gentleman usher of the Privy Chamber to Henry VIII and then Elizabeth.

Lord Robert Dudley, Earl of Leicester, the Queen's favorite; called Arthur his son.

18. Southampton the Fair Youth

One of the most enduring of literary mysteries is the identity of "Mr. W. H.," the man to whom *Shake-speares Sonnets* were dedicated in 1609.[1] Yet it turns out that his name was recorded, by simple means, in the enigmatic Dedication printed on the second leaf of the quarto. Commentators for more than two hundred years have admitted to being puzzled by its unusual appearance, peculiar syntax, and obscure meaning.[2] If they had only realized it, the key to an explanation of these matters is described in several classical texts and in books on the shelves of every public library.

The Dedication to the Sonnets is unlike any other literary dedication of the period,[3] quite apart from the mystery of "Mr. W. H.," and some scholars have speculated that it may be a cipher. As Professor Richard Dutton says, "The grammar of the piece is almost sufficient to quell interpretation in itself. How many sentences are hidden within the unusual punctuation (which ... [may be] essential to some cryptogram...)?"[4] Who is "the onlie begetter?" Is he the "Fair Youth," the young man to whom many of the sonnets were addressed (and who is identified with "Mr. W. H." by most commentators), or is he the agent who procured the manuscript? Is "T. T." referring to himself as the "well-wishing adventurer," or is he merely signing off as the publisher, Thomas Thorpe? And, asks Kenneth Muir, "Is there any significance in the way the Dedication is set out?"[5]

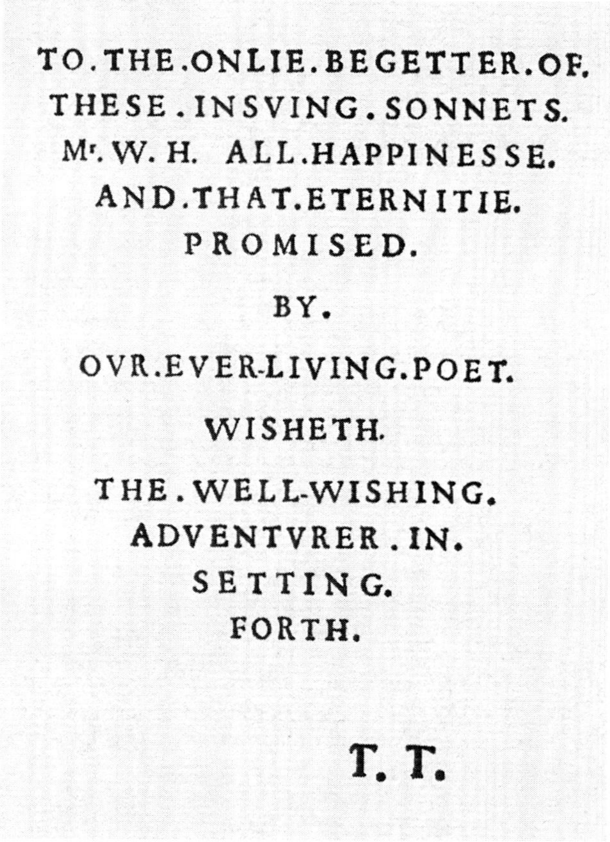

TO.THE.ONLIE.BEGETTER.OF.
THESE.INSVING.SONNETS.
Mr. W. H. ALL.HAPPINESSE.
AND.THAT.ETERNITIE.
PROMISED.
BY.
OVR.EVER-LIVING.POET.
WISHETH.
THE.WELL-WISHING.
ADVENTVRER.IN.
SETTING.
FORTH.

T. T.

Figure 18.1 The Dedication to *Shake-speare's Sonnets*.

Undoubtedly, as Stanley

Wells says, "'Mr. W. H.' provides the biggest puzzle of all,"[6] and Samuel Schoenbaum calls it "a riddle that to this day remains unsolved."[7] The mystery is compounded by the difficulty of understanding what the writer of the Dedication was trying to convey by the rest of the text, which Northrop Frye characterizes as "one floundering and illiterate sentence."[8] This is the more surprising, in view of the fluency and wit displayed in Thorpe's other dedications (see the annex to the next chapter). A student of cryptography might well ask him- or herself whether there was more in this piece than meets the eye, since as Helen Fouché Gaines has said, "awkwardness of wording" may be a pointer to a "concealment cipher," that is, a cipher designed so that superficially it appears innocent of hidden information.[9]

The first person to attempt to decipher the Dedication was the eminent Shakespeare scholar Leslie Hotson, who described it in the following way[10]:

> Thorpe's inscription has been termed *enigmatic, puzzling, cryptic,* recalling the Elizabethans' characteristic fondness for anagram, rebus, acrostic, concealment, cryptogram, "wherein my name ciphered were." In these ensuing sonnets Shakespeare declared, *Your monument shall be my gentle verse,* and Thorpe has set out a monumental inscription TO ... Mr. W. H. Is there possibly something more than initials, hid and barr'd from common sense[11] here in his text, which we are meant to look for? [Hotson's italics].

Hotson's researches had convinced him that the mysterious "Mr. W. H." was a certain William Hatcliffe, who had been admitted as a law student to Gray's Inn in 1586, and a year later chosen as "Prince of Purpoole," an exalted "Lord of Misrule" appointed to preside over Christmas festivities. After detailing several peculiarities of the Dedication, suggestive of a cryptogram, Hotson claimed to find the name of his candidate concealed within it. His method (somewhat simplified) was to start with "Mr. W. H." in line three (Figure 18.1), move down diagonally one line to another "H" in the word "THAT," pick up "HAT" from this word, and then drop vertically down to line seven and pick up "LIV" from "EVER-LIVING." In this way he arrives at "HATLIV," a reasonable approximation to "Hatcliffe."

It must be said at once that no cryptologist would place any credence in this procedure, since it involves so many arbitrary steps. Cryptography (speaking generally) is systematic, and often uses simple mathematics, leaving little room for guesswork. And although Hotson's theory attracted a lot of interest when it was first published, William Hatcliffe has now been ruled out by most scholars as a possible "Mr. W. H."

Hotson was apparently unaware that his hypothesis that the Dedication might contain some kind of secret information seems to receive support from an unexpected quarter—Ben Jonson. In 1616 he published his *Epigrammes*, part of his *Workes*, with a dedication to William Herbert, Third Earl of Pembroke,[12] which begins:

> MY LORD. *While you cannot change your merit, I dare not change your title: It was that* [your merit] *made it* [your title], *and not I. Under which name, I here offer to your Lo: the ripest of my studies, my Epigrammes; which, though they carry danger in the sound, doe not therefore seeke your shelter: For, when I made them, I had nothing in my conscience, to expressing of which I did need a cypher* [clarifications inserted].

According to Edward Dowden, writing in 1881,[13] some critics have supposed that Ben Jonson is here alluding to Shakespeare's sonnets, because of the words "I dare not change your title." It has always been a puzzle that the dedicatee should be addressed as "Mr." if, as is generally supposed, he was a nobleman (invoked in the sonnets as *Lord, prince, king, sovereign*, as we have seen in Chapter 14), especially by or on behalf of one so much lower in the social scale as the son of a Warwickshire glover and dealer in wool.[14] But the most intriguing aspect of Jonson's remarks is the reference to a "cypher." By saying in his dedication that he had *"nothing in my conscience, to expressing of which I did need a cypher,"* he seems perhaps to imply that some other dedication did make use of a cipher, and the reference to a change of title may well point to the Dedication to the Sonnets.

Peculiarities of the Dedication

The peculiarities of the Dedication may be summarized as follows.

(a) The natural order for a dedication of this kind would be, as Hotson stresses: "To the dedicatee: (1) the dedicator (2) wisheth (3) blessings." But in this dedication the natural order is inverted, and it has the form "To the dedicatee: (3) blessings (2) wisheth (1) the dedicator." Hotson comments that it is the *only* dedication he has seen "which puts the sentence backwards." To "expose its conspicuous peculiarity," he reproduces nine other dedications as examples of normal word order, and goes on to suggest that if Sherlock Holmes's remark that "singularity is almost always a clue" holds, then here is a prime example.

(b) It is all in capital letters (apart from the "r" of "M^{r}."). As far as has been ascertained, there are only two other lengthy dedications of the period all in capital letters (those to Spenser's *The Faerie Queene* and Jonson's *Volpone*).

(c) The spelling of the word "onlie" is very unusual; the most common spelling of the word at this time was "onely." In the Shakespeare First Folio of 1623, the word appears as "onely" 67 times, "only" 5 times, "onelie" twice, and "onlie" once. (In the sonnets, "onely" occurs 4 times, "only" twice, and "onlie" not at all.)

(d) There are full stops after every word, a most remarkable feature, which is believed to be unique to this dedication; to date, no other example in English has been reported. However, Roman stonemasons carving an inscription in Latin onto a block of stone or marble frequently separated the words by stops rather than spaces, although the stops were usually placed centrally, rather than as full stops on the writing line. Thus the Dedication appears to have something of the character of a monumental inscription carved in stone, designed (as it were) to last for all eternity.

These peculiarities may be the consequence of a badly worded text and a quirky compositor. An alternative possibility will now be investigated.

The Dedication as a "Transposition Cipher"

The fact that the Dedication is all in capital letters (apart from the "r" of "Mr.") suggests the possibility of a "transposition cipher," a technique familiar in Elizabethan times to scholars such as John Dee[15] and John Wilkins,[16] as already described in Chapter 12 (without mention of the modern technical term). The total number of letters in the text of the Dedication (disregarding Thomas Thorpe's initials, "T. T.," at the end, offset to one side) is 144, which has many factors. In this kind of cipher it is characteristic (though perhaps not mandatory) that information is concealed in arrays of letters which form perfect rectangles, and we therefore need to examine each of these arrays in turn. When I first had this idea, I put it off for weeks, thinking that it would take hours to write out all possible rectangles, not just those indicated by the factors of 144. In the event, when I did get down to it, it only took about twenty minutes.[17]

T	O	T	H	E	O	N	L	I	E	B	E	G	E	T	T
E	R	O	F	T	**H**	E	S	E	I	N	S	V	I	N	G
S	O	N	N	**E**	T	S	M	r	W	H	A	L	L	H	A
P	P	I	**N**	E	S	S	E	A	N	D	T	H	A	T	E
T	E	**R**	N	I	T	I	E	P	R	O	M	I	S	E	D
B	**Y**	O	V	R	E	V	E	R-	L	I	V	I	N	G	P
O	E	T	W	I	S	H	E	T	H	T	H	E	W	E	L
L-	W	I	S	H	I	N	G	A	D	V	E	N	T	V	R
E	R	I	N	S	E	T	T	I	N	G	F	O	R	T	H

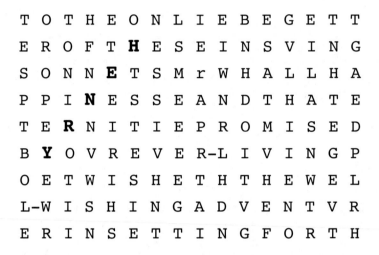

Figure 18.2 The Dedication as an array with 9 rows of 16 letters.

I first looked into the perfect square array of 12 rows of 12 letters, but could find no hidden word, which was disappointing. I then looked into the perfect rectangular array with 9 rows of 16 letters, and soon spotted the name HENRY, running diagonally down and left from the "H" of "THESE" to the "Y" of "BY," as shown in Figure 18.2. In an array with 15 letters in each row (the last being incomplete), the name can be read out vertically in the seventh column, as shown in Figure 18.3.

The reader will appreciate that the letters in this name are *equally spaced;* every fifteenth letter after the "H" of Henry provides the next letter in the name. Once the "H" and "E" have been fixed upon, the remaining three letters are located automatically. Similarly, if someone at the time suspected the name "Henry" to be concealed in the Dedication, they could start with one of the early "H"s and count downwards to an "E," and so on, or better still start with the only "Y" in the text and look for an "R" occurring earlier, and work upwards. The "R" of "promised" fails to reveal a name, but the "R" of "eternitie" yields "Henry" as before. (Many ciphers are solved with the help of preexisting knowledge, or sometimes with just a hunch.)

This finding was intriguing but inconclusive; who was this "Henry"? I wondered whether the rest of the letters in the column, "OLVR," would lead to his identification, but nothing emerged. I next looked at the perfect rectangular array with 8 rows of 18 letters shown in Figure 18.4. I have to admit that at first I could not find any word of interest in

T	O	T	H	E	O	N	L	I	E	B	E	G	E	T
T	E	R	O	F	T	**H**	E	S	E	I	N	S	V	I
N	G	S	O	N	N	**E**	T	S	M	r	W	H	A	L
L	H	A	P	P	I	**N**	E	S	S	E	A	N	D	T
H	A	T	E	T	E	**R**	N	I	T	I	E	P	R	O
M	I	S	E	D	B	**Y**	O	V	R	E	V	E	R-	L
I	V	I	N	G	P	O	E	T	W	I	S	H	E	T
H	T	H	E	W	E	L	L-	W	I	S	H	I	N	G
A	D	V	E	N	T	V	R	E	R	I	N	S	E	T
T	I	N	G	F	O	R	T	H						

Figure 18.3 The Dedication arranged in rows of 15 letters.

this array, and was really disappointed. However, after putting it aside and coming back to it afresh some time later, I suddenly noticed "ESLEY" in the tenth column, and immediately adjacent to it "IOTH," and elsewhere "WR"! This was a real discovery, perhaps even a momentous one, since it surely ends forever speculation about the identity of the Fair Youth.

T	O	T	H	E	O	N	L	I	**E**	B	E	G	E	T	T	E	R
O	F	T	H	E	S	E	I	N	**S**	V	I	N	G	S	O	N	N
E	T	S	M	r	W	H	A	L	**L**	**H**	A	P	P	I	N	E	S
S	E	A	N	D	T	H	A	T	**E**	**T**	E	R	N	I	T	I	E
P	R	O	M	I	S	E	D	B	**Y**	**O**	V	R	E	V	E	R-	L
I	V	I	N	G	P	O	E	T	W	**I**	S	H	E	T	H	T	H
E	**W**	E	L	L-	W	I	S	H	I	N	G	A	D	V	E	N	T
V	**R**	E	R	I	N	S	E	T	T	I	N	G	F	O	R	T	H

Figure 18.4 The Dedication as an array having 8 rows of 18 letters.

Inspection reveals the name "WR—IOTH—ESLEY" located in columns 2, 11, and 10, reading out down, up, down (reminiscent of the examples given in Chapter 12). This is *precisely* how the family name of the Earls of Southampton was always spelled officially. It is remarkable then that the candidate favored by many scholars as the "Fair Youth" and "Mr. W. H." is Henry Wriothesley, Third Earl of Southampton, his initials being reversed in a simple device, occasionally used elsewhere at the time.[18] It was to this man that Shakespeare dedicated the two long poems *Venus and Adonis* and *Lucrece*, printed in 1593 and 1594. (It will be noticed that "Henry" and "Wriothesley" share the one "Y" in the text.) It is a reasonable deduction (though perhaps not an inescapable one) that the full name "Henry Wriothesley" was deliberately concealed in the Dedication in order to record for posterity his identity as "Mr. W. H." and the young man to whom many of the sonnets were addressed, and to whom the poet wrote, "Your monument shall be my gentle verse" (sonnet 81). The odds that this proposed cipher solution might be an accident of chance, and not a deliberate construct, are discussed in the next chapter.

It may be relevant to observe that in February 1601, following the rebellion by the Earl of Essex, in which he played a leading part, he was convicted of treason, attainted, deprived of his lands, stripped of his earldom, and confined to the Tower, where he signed himself "of late Southampton, but now ... H. Wriothesley."[19] Thus during the period up to his release in April 1603 on the accession of James I he was a commoner, plain "Mr. H. W." The Dedication may have been composed during this period, when there was no expectation of his being pardoned.

In the next chapter we examine whether the Dedication is a genuine cryptogram, designed specifically to contain concealed information, or whether the supposed cipher solutions are accidents of chance.

19. The Cipher Solutions Assessed

In search of guidance on how to judge whether a possible concealment cipher is authentic, we turn again to the book by William and Elizebeth Friedman with the title *The Shakespearean Ciphers Examined.* It is of interest to learn that

> ... the science of cryptology ... is a branch of knowledge which goes back far into the past—certainly beyond Elizabethan times. In the sixteenth century it was abundantly used.... The question of course ... is not whether ciphers could have been used, but whether they were used.[1]

In their book (written with a courteous but devastating wit) the Friedmans investigated many such attempts to uncover concealed names or messages, almost all relating to Francis Bacon, and concluded that all were erroneous. They made no mention of the Dedication to the Sonnets, as no decipherment had been proposed before their work was completed.

In the early pages of the book they put forward criteria for assessing whether a solution of a supposed cipher is genuine or not. One of these is that the key to the cipher should be given unambiguously, either in the text or in some other way, and not contrived to fit in with preconceived ideas; another is that the decoded message should make good sense, and have been sufficiently important to have been worth concealing; and a third, that the message should have been hidden where it had a high probability of being found. The last criterion is clearly fulfilled. With regard to the cipher keys, these are the factors of 144, the number of letters in the text, and as to the importance of the information concealed, the "Fair Youth" was promised immortality through the sonnets, although through an irony of fate his name has up till now remained a complete mystery.

Lastly and crucially, it is necessary to assess, on a scientific basis, the likelihood that the supposedly hidden information might have resulted by chance. As a guide to the significance of a probability calculation, the Friedmans state of a cipher solution, in effect, that if "the chances of its appearing by accident are one in one thousand million, [the cryptanalyst's] confidence in the solution will be more than justified."[2]

The assessment of the odds that the name "Henry Wriothesley" might have occurred fortuitously is carried out in Appendix C, and it is found that (very roughly indeed) they are around 1 in 1.6 billion. These odds would more than satisfy the criterion suggested by the Friedmans as sufficient to justify the cryptanalyst's confidence in his solution. Paradoxically, such confidence does *not* amount to certifying that the transposition ciphers are genuine, especially if we bear in mind the fact that very occasionally in daily life we experience what appear to be amazing coincidences: in the final analysis chance cannot be ruled out.

We now discuss various considerations which have a bearing on the authenticity of the proposed solutions we are putting forward. First of all, with regard to the method of writing out a text in the form of a square or rectangle, we have the examples from the 1600s already given in Chapter 12, one from John Dee and the other from Bishop Wilkins.

These examples show that this technique was known about and employed in the first part of the 17th century, though in a somewhat different form. No attempt is made to conceal the fact that in both of these examples the coded text as sent ("THSSA..."; "ERFDL...") contains a hidden message, and it is obvious that it does so (or is nonsense designed to confuse). Thus it is certainly possible that "write across—read down or up" was what the architect of the Dedication had in mind when he crafted it, bearing in mind that he was not just concealing hidden information but concealing the *fact* that information was being hidden. Few people would suspect that "TO.THE.ONLIE.BEGETTER..." contained hidden information, were it not for the mangled syntax and the obscurity of the text.

The next consideration concerns the fact that the name "WR-IOTH-ESLEY" appears split up into three separate segments. The reader may perhaps be thinking to him- or herself that an 11-letter name could readily be built up from (for example) four segments, three with three letters and one with two, and in this way several names might be found in the Dedication. But no experienced cryptographer would ever contemplate hiding a name in such a manner. The objective of the cryptographer[3] is, in this context, not only to conceal a name or message from casual inspection, but also *to ensure that it is recognized as genuine* when the right method of solution (or algorithm) is adopted, otherwise the whole point of the exercise, not to mention the labor involved, is rendered null and void.

We may credit the cryptographer in our case with knowing that when a text like this is written out in rectangular arrays, the columns abound with three-letter words, four-letter words are common, and only with five-letter words can he signal to the decipherer that he may perhaps be uncovering a genuine message, and not simply observing random strings of letters. In the Dedication, examining all arrays with rows containing 30 letters through to 6 reveals, reading down, 180 three-letter words, 42 four-letter words, and 3 five-letter words (HENRY, WASTE, TRESS) plus the segment ESLEY; there are no words of six or more letters. The rarity of five-letter words, and the fact that two of the four (if the five-letter segment is included) are to be found in the full name "Henry Wriothesley," strongly suggest that the name could have been deliberately concealed in the Dedication. In addition it seems to me that by arranging for the segments ESLEY and IOTH to be found adjacent to each other the cryptographer is sending a very strong message to the decoder that he has correctly deduced what was being concealed. It is one thing for chance to produce these segments remote from each other, but to find them so close together is surely to confirm beyond all reasonable doubt that the Dedication was contrived specifically to conceal this name. It is also worth observing that the unusual spelling of the word "ONLIE" was necessitated by the requirement that a letter "E" head the tenth column to form the first letter of the segment ESLEY.

It is often assumed by commentators that the Dedication was written by Thomas Thorpe. But judging by the style of dedications known to have been written by him, reproduced in the annex to this chapter, it seems far more likely that it was composed by someone else, and the initials T. T. added at the end for the sake of form.

The analysis given in this chapter provides strong support for the proposition that the

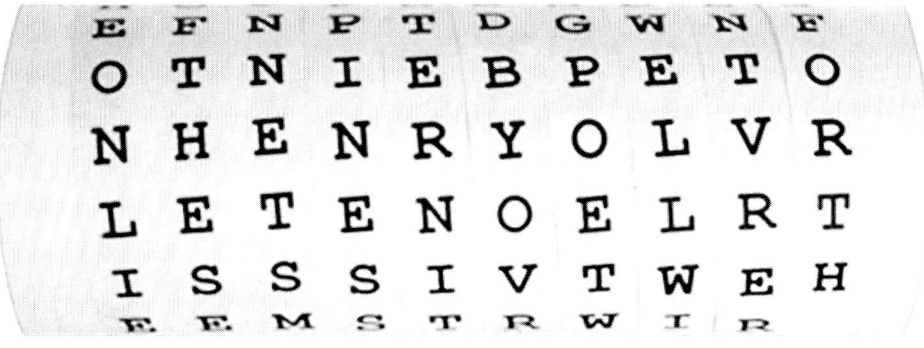

Figure 19.1 Illustrating the *skytale* technique.

Dedication is indeed a well-contrived transposition cipher, of a simple type which calls to mind the σκυταλη (skytale) of the Spartans.[4] This technique was described by several classical authors, and hence would have been familiar to many Elizabethan scholars. To make use of it, a Spartan general would roll a long narrow strip of paper spirally around a baton or staff (the σκυταλη), and write a dispatch across the strip of paper (along the staff). The intervening blank spaces would then be filled up with strings of random letters, and the strip sent out to a distant commander. The strip of paper would be unintelligible to an enemy if it was intercepted, but when wound round a staff of the same diameter by the intended recipient would reveal the concealed message. In a similar way, one can imagine the text of the Dedication written out in a single line on a long narrow strip of paper, which when wrapped around a rod of appropriate diameter yields "Henry," and round a rod of a somewhat larger diameter brings to light "Wr-ioth-esley."

I think it is important to stress that the analysis of these cipher solutions does not amount to *proof* that they are genuine solutions to a genuine cryptogram, for the reason already stated, that in the last resort chance cannot be eliminated. (On the other hand, how else can the fractured syntax and opaque meaning of the Dedication be accounted for?) It is a matter for educated judgment and robust common sense, not always reliable guides. But I think it could be claimed that we now have good reason to suppose that we know who the Fair Youth was with a high degree of confidence.[5] We next investigate whether his biography offers any support for the puzzling idea that there was something about him which led others (including the poet of the sonnets) to think he partook of royalty in some mysterious way, as described in Chapter 14.

Annex: Thorpe's Dedications

We give here the opening sentences of four of Thomas Thorpe's dedications. These demonstrate fluency, wit, and a love of wordplay, qualities all conspicuously lacking in the Dedication to the Sonnets. They are typical of dedications of the time in the use of somewhat extravagant language, the obsequious tone adopted when addressing the nobility, and the frequent alternation of italic and Roman fonts. Thorpe's special flavor lies in subtle and erudite wordplay, involving puns and contrasting pairs of words such as (see below) (1) *Blount*

/ blunt; (2) *late imaginary / now actual, most-conceited / almost-concealed, devised Country / desired Citie, testament / testimonie;* (3) *distressed / fortunate;* (4) *worthily / unworthy, matter / model.* It seems unlikely that a man with such an exuberant and sophisticated style would have freely composed the barely grammatical and nearly incomprehensible sentence which forms this Dedication. Either Thorpe wrote out of character, or someone else with their own agenda wrote the piece and attached Thorpe's initials to it.

1. **From the dedication to *Lucan's First Booke*, translated by Christopher Marlowe[6]:**

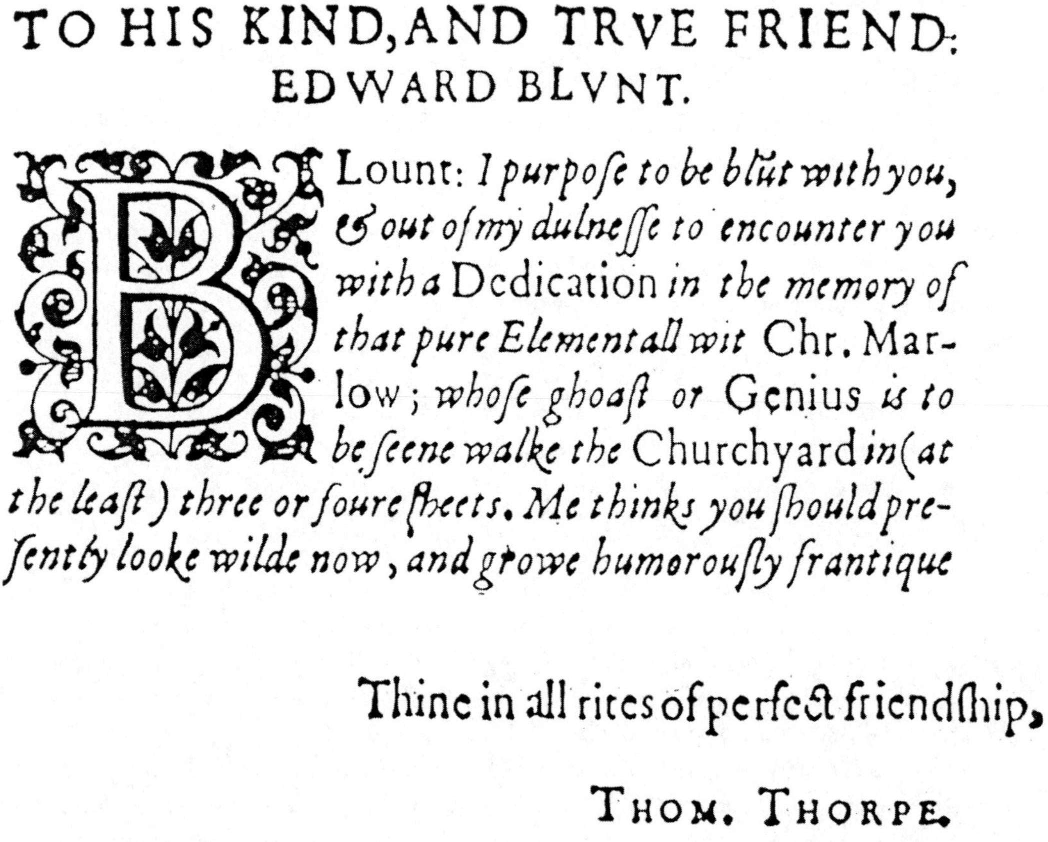
TO HIS KIND, AND TRVE FRIEND:
EDWARD BLVNT.

BLount: *I purpose to be blũt with you, & out of my dulnesse to encounter you with a* Dedication *in the memory of that pure Elementall wit* Chr. Marlow; *whose ghoast or* Genius *is to be seene walke the* Churchyard *in (at the least) three or foure sheets. Me thinks you should presently looke wilde now, and growe humorously frantique*

Thine in all rites of perfect friendship,

THOM. THORPE.

Figure 19.2 Montage of start of dedication to Edward Blunt and the subscription, Thom. Thorpe, of *Lucan's First Booke*, translated by Christopher Marlowe.

To his kind, and true friend: Edward Blunt.

Blount: *I purpose to be blunt with you, & out of my dulnesse to encounter you with a* Dedication *in the memory of that pure Elementall wit* Chr. Marlowe*; whose ghoast or* Genius *is to be seene walke the* Churchyard *in (at the least) three or foure sheets....*

2. **From the dedication to *Augustine, or the City of God*, translated by J. H.[7]:**

To ... William, Earle of Pembroke, *etc.*

Right gracious and gracefull Lord, your late imaginary, but now actuall Travailer, then to most-conceited *Viraginia*, now to almost-concealed *Virginia;* then a light, but not lewde, now a sage and allowed translator; then of a scarce knowne novice, now a famous *Father;* then of a devised Country scarce on earth, now of a desired *Citie* sure in heaven; then of *Utopia*, now of *Eutopia;* not as by testament, but as by testimonie of gratitude, observance, and hearts-honour to your Honor, ...

3. **From the dedication to *Epictetus*, etc., translated by Io. Healey[8]:**

To a true favorer of forward spirits, Maister *John Florio.*

SIR, as distressed *Sostratus* spake to more fortunate Areius, to make him Mediator to *Augustus. The learned love the learned, if they are rightly learned:* So this your poore friend though he have found much of you, yet doth still follow you for as much more: that as his *Mecænas* you would write to *Augustus, Bee as minde-full of* Horace, *as you would bee of my selfe: ...*

4. **From the dedication to *Epictetus*, etc., translated by Io. Healey, another edition of the work above[9]:**

To the Right Honorable, William, Earle of Pembroke *etc.*

Right Honorable, *It may worthily seeme strange unto your Lordship, out of what frenzy one of my meanenesse hath presumed to commit this Sacriledge, in the straight-nesse of your Lordships leisure, to present a peece, for matter and model so unworthy, and in this scribling age, wherein great persons are so pestered dayly with Dedica-tions....*

These dedications are signed (respectively): THOM. THORPE, *Th. Th.*, TH. TH., *T. Th.*; none is signed T. T.

20. *Henry Wriothesley, Third Earl of Southampton*

Henry Wriothesley was born on 6 October 1573. His father, the Second Earl, died on 4 October 1581, whereupon Henry inherited the earldom, became a ward of the Queen, and aged eight was taken into the household of William Cecil, Lord Burghley, the Lord Treasurer (*ODNB*). Here he was brought up in Burghley's "educational establishment for young noblemen," which has been called "the best school for statesmen in Elizabethan England."[1]

In 1592 at the age of 19 he was presented at Court, and before long the first of three events occurred which begin to show that he was held in very high esteem by his contemporaries, an esteem for which only one explanation seems appropriate, as will be seen.

Nomination as Knight of the Garter

In May 1593, Philip Gawdy wrote a letter to his elder brother, Bassingbourne Gawdy, High Sheriff of Norfolk. The passage of interest concerns rumors that are going around about the elections for Knights of the Garter:

> I forgott to wryte to yow ther be no Knights of the garter newe chosen as yet, but ther wer fower nominated whiche wer these—my L. of Southhampton, my L. Keeper, my L. Thomas, and my L. Willoubye of ersby, but it took no effecte.[2]

Commenting on this, the renowned Shakespeare authority Sidney Lee, in the *Dictionary of National Biography* of 1900, wrote:

> In 1593 Southampton was mentioned for nomination as a Knight of the Garter, and although he was not chosen the compliment of nomination was, at his age [19], unprecedented outside the circle of the sovereign's kinsmen.

One may wonder how Sidney Lee explained to himself how this remarkable "nomination" came about; certainly he didn't explain it to his readers. Charlotte Carmichael Stopes, in her biography of Southampton, echoes Lee's view and attempts to provide reasons for the nomination. One is the praise he received when he visited the University of Oxford the previous September, on a visit with the Queen and other dignitaries; another is the brilliance of *Venus and Adonis*, recently dedicated to him; and the third (I quote) "a turn of Elizabeth's favor." She goes on to say:

> .... the fact of his having been proposed was in itself an honour so great at his early age that it had never before been paid to anyone not of Royal Blood.[3]

Just to confuse matters, it turns out that someone else *had* previously been nominated at age 19, unbeknown to Sidney Lee and Charlotte Stopes—Edward de Vere, the 17th Earl of Oxford. But first, to find out what Philip Gawdy meant when he wrote of Knights of the Garter being "nominated," we need to look into the system laid down by Edward III in 1348.

When a KG vacancy occurs, a "Chapter Meeting" is called, and those already members of the Order cast votes for those they want to recommend for the monarch's consideration. (Edward III stipulated that it was the ten most recently appointed members who should take part in these elections, but this rule does not seem to have been strictly observed.) The Queen was not obliged to take any notice of those proposed in the Chapter Meetings, and indeed she mostly ignored the recommendations. The Order of the Garter was an order of chivalry, limited to 22 members (the monarch and heir were *ex officio* members, making the full membership 24 in normal circumstances), and nominees had to have honors or achievements which would in turn bring credit to the order—those that "had done the State some service," or were the offspring or close friends of the monarch. But while some, perhaps many, of those KGs voting in these elections would have voted for those who had done something to merit the honor, others were probably trying to read the Queen's mind, anticipate who she might appoint, and thereby ingratiate themselves.

In 1569, when Oxford was 19, he was high in the Queen's favor. Gilbert Talbot wrote of him (previously quoted in Chapter 16):

> My Lord of Oxford is lately grown into great credit, for the Queen's Majesty delighteth more in his personage and his dancing and valiantness than any other.... At all these love matters my Lord Treasurer winketh, and will not meddle in any way.[4]

This almost certainly accounts for the fact that at Chapter Meetings in that year and the year following he received one vote, and in 1571 all ten votes; the voting for many years was recorded in a book known as the *Liber Caeruleus* (Blue Book).[5] But in the event the Queen never bestowed the honor on him, and it has to be said that he never did do the state any service that might have merited it. What the case of Oxford shows is that KGs casting votes were on occasion inclined to vote for those who were perceived to be the Queen's current favorite, even if they had done the state nothing other than catching her eye.

Returning now to Southampton, it appears that according to Sidney Lee and Mrs. Stopes the general opinion was that the Queen would make him a Knight of the Garter in 1593. The interesting point to consider is how such an opinion could ever have gained currency. What had Southampton done, age 19, to be regarded by the circle of courtiers and hangers-on at Court as likely to be accorded this tremendous honor by the Queen, for which some of her close intimates had had to wait many years before being appointed? For example, Sir Christopher Hatton, one of the Queen's greatest favorites, had received maximum votes in ten elections before he was finally granted the honor in 1588, age 48, whereas Southampton was certainly never one of the Queen's favorites, either then or later; she mostly ignored him, and when in November 1595 he attempted to help her mount her horse she brushed him aside.[6]

The answer, of course, is that Southampton had achieved absolutely nothing, not even the affection of the Queen, and we are driven to the conclusion that the only possible honor he could have brought to the order was the honor accruing to him from his birth and lineage, whatever that might have been; he had nothing else going for him. The comments of Sidney Lee and Mrs. Stopes, to the effect that *"only those of Royal Blood had ever before been considered at such an early age,"* are so extraordinary as to take one's breath away (even if not strictly accurate). Surely these eminent authorities in literature and history must have asked themselves what was so special about Southampton that he should have deserved this distinction in the eyes of his contemporaries. Yet Sidney Lee made no attempt to explain Southampton's teenage candidacy, and Mrs. Stopes' attempts are laughable—praise from an academic, the dedication of a poem, a smile from the Queen: these really will not do.

What is also extraordinary is that Philip Gawdy does not have to supply any reason to his brother in Norfolk to explain why Londoners in the know thought Southampton would be nominated. The reason behind the rumor, whatever it was, must have been common knowledge among a certain class of people for some long time.

In point of fact, Southampton received no votes at the Chapter Meeting in April 1593, and none the next year. In subsequent years the voting went as follows: 1595, 4 votes out of 12; 1596, 10 out of 12; 1597, 2 out of 10; 1598 no voting; 1599, 4 out of 9; 1600, 6 out of 13; 1601, disgraced and in the Tower; 1602, no voting, 1603, 3 out of 6.[7]

In some ways the voting record is even more surprising than the rumor going around in 1593, as it shows that just three years later, aged only 22, Southampton received a massive 10 votes out of 12. Evidently those voting thought there was a strong chance that the Queen would make him KG, although he had still not contributed any service to the realm or achieved any glory in fighting for his country, accomplishments of the kind that candidates normally had to their credit. Post 1596, after only 2 votes in 1597 (perhaps a reaction against high expectations the previous year), he twice gained around half the votes cast, not bad for a raw and untried youth, especially as according to G. P. V. Akrigg he was never in the Queen's good books after 1595.

In contrast, consider the case of Anthony Browne, first Viscount Montagu, who was appointed KG in 1555, aged 27 (*ODNB*). He first served as an MP ten years earlier; he was knighted in 1547, appointed Sheriff of Sussex and Surrey in 1553, and elected MP for Petersfield that year. The next year he was elected Knight of the Shire for Surrey and appointed Master of Horse to Philip of Spain and given an annuity of £200. In 1555 he was created Viscount Montagu, the same year that he was appointed KG, after several years of service to the country. Consider also the case of Edmund, Baron Sheffield, elected in 1593 (the year in which Southampton was expected to have been nominated), aged 29 (*ODNB*). He had served with distinction under Leicester in the Netherlands in 1585, and served as captain of three ships in the Armada campaign of 1588 (the *Victory*, *Dreadnaught*, and *White Bear*, in which he sailed), for which he was knighted and praised in reports to the Council by the Lord Admiral.

Southampton had done nothing comparable with either of these two men, who were among the youngest of those appointed KG without having royal blood; he had neither served as an MP nor fought for his country. While it is true that he had expected to accompany Essex on the expedition that captured Cadiz in 1596, this expedition was launched *after* the Garter election at which he received 10 out of 12 votes, so that his possible involvement could hardly have influenced the voting. In the event the Queen forbade both him and his friend Derby from taking part in the campaign.

Perhaps the most extraordinary event in the whole of Southampton's life was James writing to the Council within a few days of being pronounced King to order his release from the Tower (where he had been imprisoned after Essex's abortive uprising in 1601), and then appointing him KG at the first opportunity.[8] Not only that, but when on his progress south the King arrived at Hinchingbrook, Southampton was chosen to bear the Sword of State in front of the King as he entered the house of Sir Oliver Cromwell—a traitor convicted of treason against the previous sovereign! We are driven to the conclusion that there was something uniquely special about the esteem in which Southampton was held both by the King and by his contemporaries at this time, an esteem which remains inexplicable unless accruing to him from his birth.

"Shine Immortally!"

The second strand of evidence testifying to Southampton's exalted status as perceived by his contemporaries is provided by George Peele, who published in this same year of 1593 a long poem with the title *The Honour of the Garter*.[9] The work was written to celebrate the Installation Ceremony of June that year, and is dedicated to the Earl of Northumberland, one of the five people who were duly appointed Knights of the Garter on this occasion. The poem is a long eulogy, firstly of the Order of the Garter, and secondly of those appointed this year. What is astonishing from our point of view is a remarkable passage extolling Southampton, who was *not* one of the new knights, and had received not even a single vote in the Garter election that year, despite the prevailing opinion that he would be appointed (or at least nominated). What on earth was Peele driving at?

The poem begins with a prologue of 70 lines devoted to the Earl of Northumberland, which leads into the main body of the poem. Here Peele tells us how (in his imagination) he lay down to sleep on a bank of the Thames outside Windsor Castle, and had a dream about the founding of the order by Edward the Third in 1348. In the dream (after about 200 lines) he sees a procession of the first knights to be appointed, Edward Prince of Wales, the Duke of Lancaster and so on, and then "the brave Earles of Stafford and South-Hampton." While the other knights mentioned were all founding members of the order, the "Earle of South-Hampton" mentioned is a fiction, since there was no earl of that title at the time of Edward the Third. But the introduction of this imaginary earl was done for a purpose, as it gives Peele an excuse to bring in the modern earl of that title, and he proceeds to praise him in the following amazing lines.

> Then the brave Earles of *Stafford* and *South-Hampton*,
> To whose successors, for his sake that lives
> And now survives in honour of that name,
> To whom my thoughts are humble and devote,
> Gentle *Wriothesley*, South-Hamptons starre,
> I wish all fortune that in *Cynthias* eye [Queen Elizabeth's
> *Cynthia* the glory of the Western world,
> With all the starres in her faire firmament,
> *Bright may he rise and shine immortally.* [*emphasis added*

Southampton is the only living person, besides Cynthia, the Queen, to appear in the main body of the poem, and Peele says of him: "*Bright may he ... shine immortally with all the stars in* [the Queen's] *fair firmament*." To deserve, at age 19, to share immortality with the Queen is to bear a very special relationship to her indeed. It is hardly necessary to add that neither Sidney Lee, Mrs. Stopes nor Southampton's later biographers (G. P. V. Akrigg and A. L. Rowse) quote even a single line from this poem.

Peele now goes back to the time of Edward the Third, and continues his roll-call of the rest of the original Garter Knights and other past heroes for another 140 lines, until eventually he comes to the five appointed in June this year:

> Northumberland, and Worcester, noble Earles,
> Boroughe, and Sheffeilde, Lords of lively hope,[10]
> And honourable olde Knowles ...

The ages of these five are, in order, 39, 40, 35, 29, 79, the youngest being only 10 years older than Southampton—but Sheffield had served with distinction under Leicester in the Netherlands in 1585, and (as already mentioned) had commanded the *White Bear* and two others of the Queen's ships in the Armada, and fully merited the great honor. Southampton had done nothing even remotely comparable, basically because he had done nothing. The final 60 lines are devoted to eulogizing the new knights, and the poem is rounded off with an epilogue of 15 lines.

Figure 20.1 Royal Coat of Arms prefaced to Peele's *The Honour of the Garter*.

Thus not only is the compliment paid to Southampton extraordinary in itself—wishing him *immortality with the Queen*—it is placed in a unique position, where it is totally irrelevant, in the middle of 364 lines of verse devoted to heroes from antiquity and from three hundred years earlier. In effect, Southampton is being bracketed with the Black Prince, with Caesar, Hector, Jason, as if he were already a living legend. And to justify this insert, Peele invents *a completely fictitious ancestor*, whom he then falsely numbers among the founding members of the order.

Clearly, it was no ordinary teenager who was being extolled in this way, in a poem commemorating one of the most prestigious events of the year, and which would therefore come to the notice of all those in high places. In such a publication, which carried a full-page representation of the Queen's arms and motto on the second page, a poet takes very great care to say the right things and to avoid offending the powerful. No one at the time could have read the poem and missed the significance of the lines on Southampton.

And as if to emphasize their significance, Peele ends the poem with one-and-a-half lines of Latin[11]:

Procul hinc turba invidiosa,
Stirps rudis urtica est; *Stirps generosa rosa.*

These may be translated as:

[Stay] far away from here, detested turmoil, [civil war
[while] the nettle yields [only] coarse weeds,
the Offspring of the rose is noble.

where I have italicized the most significant words in both passages. Since the poem has the Queen's arms on the second page, and contains numerous references to her, and since one of the commonest ways of apostrophizing her was as a "rose" ("par excellence the flower of the Queen," according to Roy Strong[12]), and since Southampton is the only other living person to be mentioned in the poem in connection with the Queen, it is hard to avoid the conclusion that Peele is coming very close to telling us that Southampton is the noble offspring of the Rose, Queen Elizabeth, who has it in her power to dispel the "detested turmoil" of potential civil war over the succession by making him her heir.

"Dynasta"

The third strand of evidence is provided by John Sanford, chaplain of Magdalen College, Oxford, who wrote a set of Latin verses to celebrate the visit of the Queen and her entourage to the university in September 1592. The title of this poem is *The Idylls of Apollo and the Muses*,[13] and the lines devoted to Southampton, identified both in the margin and in the poem, are truly astonishing. Here they are in the original.

Post hunc insequitur *clarâ de stirpe Dynasta,* [*emphasis added*
Iure suo dives quem South-Hamptonia magnum
Vendicat heroem; quo non formosior alter
Affuit, aut docta iuvenis praestantior arte;
Ora licet tenerâ vix dum lanugine vernent.

I could hardly believe my eyes when I read them and tried to make out what they meant. This is how G. P. V. Akrigg translates them in his biography of Southampton.

> After him there follows a lord of lofty line, whom rich Southampton claims in his own right as a great hero. There was present no one more comely, no young man more outstanding in learning, although his mouth scarcely yet blooms with tender down.[14]

The second sentence is fine, but the translation of the first has been badly botched. Mrs. Stopes does somewhat better, since the start of her version reads

> After him there followed a Prince of a distinguished race...,[15]

but she too misses its significance, and also makes a mess of the rest of the sentence.

It is the word "Dynasta" (see sidebar) which is so astonishing, because its meaning is precise: *a lord inheriting great power, a prince, a ruler*. My own translation of the first sentence is (after taking advice):

> After him there follows a hereditary Prince of illustrious lineage, whom as a great hero the rich House of Southampton lawfully lays claim to as one of its own.

It is a rare word in Latin, and is taken over directly from the Greek. Its root is the same as that of "dynamic," and means "possessing power" or "great power." The only rulers or princes "possessing great power" in Tudor England were the Tudors, culminating in Elizabeth. To call Southampton "Dynasta," or in modern English a "Dynast," can properly mean only one thing, that he was held to be in the line of succession of the Tudor dynasty.

It might be thought that the meaning was something like "belonging to the dynasty of the Earls of Southampton." But the word "dynasty" in English did not acquire this broader meaning until the nineteenth century (according to the *Oxford English Dictionary*), over two hundred years later, and it certainly never had such a meaning in Latin. A "dynasty" in English could then only mean "a line of kings or princes," not a line of earls, and "dynasta" in Latin could only mean a "prince possessing great power." (The Greek word *τυραννος*, English "tyrant," was used of a ruler who assumed power by force; Greek *δυναστης*, English "dynast," of one who inherited power.)

Bibliotheca Eliotae, edited by Thomas Cooper (1545)

Dynasta, vel Dynastes, ae, m. g.: a lorde of great power, a prince, a ruler

Webster

dynast: a ruler, esp. a hereditary ruler; one of a line of kings or princes [first usage 1631, *OED*]

dynasty: a succession of rulers of the same line of descent; a line of kings or princes [first usage 1460, *OED*]

The remark about the earldom of Southampton "lawfully" claiming Henry as "one of its own" is also very revealing. If Henry had been the birth son of the Earl and Countess, there would be no need for him to be "lawfully claimed" by the earldom; such a claim would have been automatic, and not worth commenting on. But if effectively adopted by the Earl (whether in full knowledge or not), and accepted by him as his own, he automatically became legitimate in law, from the maxim *pater est quem nuptiae demonstrant;* a son accepted as such by his supposed father is *legally* his son, whatever his true parentage.[16]

Thus the second half of the sentence adds to the meaning of the word "Dynasta" in the first half, by (apparently) indicating how Southampton could be both a prince in line to succeed and also the legitimate Third Earl. The writer of the verses chose a rare word to convey his precise meaning, and would only have felt safe in doing so if it was widely believed among well-placed people that Southampton was indeed the Queen's son. If we also take into account the fact that these Latin verses were an official publication of the university, with the university's coat of arms occupying most of the title page, it is clear that the university authorities approved this graceful reference to Southampton's supposed status, and that it would be expected to bring credit to the university if he ever ascended the throne. The combination of these lines calling Southampton (in effect) *"the heir to the Tudors"* with George Peele's poem wishing him *"to shine immortally with the Queen in her fair firmament"* shows beyond reasonable doubt that Southampton was considered by many of his contemporaries in Oxford and London to have a status commensurate with or appropriate to that of a son of the Queen.

Moreover, Philip Gawdy's letter to his brother shows that people were expecting her to make him a Garter Knight at this time, for which there was a precedent. Sixty years previously Henry VIII had made his illegitimate son Henry Fitzroy, Duke of Richmond, a Garter Knight (aged six!), and subsequently planned to make him his heir at about the age that Southampton now was, a plan frustrated by Fitzroy's early death (*ODNB*). Maybe not a few were hoping that Elizabeth would copy her father's example, and at long last provide the country with an undoubted heir. The threat of the horrors of the Wars of the Roses had hung over the country for the whole of the Queen's reign in the absence of a named successor, and now it was (supposedly) in her power to put an end to uncertainty.

Early in her reign, Alexander Nowell, Dean of St. Paul's, had spelled all this out to Elizabeth in no uncertain terms in a sermon preached on 11 January 1563.[17]

> And whereas the Queen's majesty's most noble ancestors have commonly had some issue to succeed them, but her majesty yet none; which want is for our sins to be a plague unto us.... When your majesty was troubled with sickness [*smallpox*], then I heard continual voices and lamentations, saying, "Alas, what trouble shall we be in! ... For the succession is so uncertain, and such division for religion! Alack! What shall become of us!"

Here perhaps we may glimpse the real motivation for the poet's exhortation to the Fair Youth to produce a son. A possible successor who has already produced a son would be far more desirable to the people than one without. If Southampton had any claim at all to the throne in the eyes of his contemporaries, the possession of a son would have greatly increased it.

Needless to say, the unpredictable Elizabeth had other ideas, and she rarely favored him, even if near the end of her life she did spare him the axe. Any hopes that the Queen might name Southampton her heir came to nothing, and uncertainty over the succession continued to remain the order of the day.

In the next chapter we attempt to fathom the motive and mechanism by which the child Southampton came to be placed where he was, and record the manner in which at the end of his life he was interred.

21. *Henry Wriothesley: Early Years and Last Days*

Henry Wriothesley was born on 9 October 1573, six months after his father, the Second Earl, had been released from imprisonment in the Tower on suspicion of disloyalty to the Crown (*ODNB*); it has to be assumed that his Countess was allowed to visit him there, since if she did not, scandal could hardly have been avoided. There were no royal forbears of either the Earl or his Countess, so if Henry had any aura of royalty hovering over him, his true parentage must differ from his apparent parentage. How could this have come about? (May I again remind the reader that I am investigating this extraordinary scenario as an independent observer with an open mind, in an effort to get close or closer to the truth.)

At birth, Henry would have immediately been placed with a wet-nurse, since mothers in the upper layers of society never breast-fed their babies.[1] In the normal course, he would have been left with the wet-nurse for his first two years or so, and then taken back into the Southampton household. If the man who grew up as the Third Earl was really the son of someone else, then a switch must have occurred, and one might guess that the baby born on 9 October 1573 died some time in the next two years (presumably unknown to the Second Earl), and that some other child assumed his place. It seems unlikely that the true identity of the changeling child would have been made known to the Countess, just that he was an indiscretion of a lady of high birth (as in the case of Arthur Dudley, narrated in Chapter 17); she may have learned the truth later. The Countess would have been keen to take on a substitute child, since it was her duty to provide an heir to inherit the estate and the earldom, which otherwise would be forfeited to the Crown. In their seven years of marriage, for two of which her husband was in the Tower, she had only produced one other child who had survived, a daughter, and further children seemed unlikely to be forthcoming. In any case, her relationship with her husband was fraught with problems, as described below.

Seeking to discover how the switch might have been arranged, I have ascertained that the Second Earl's sister, Lady Katherine Cornwallis (née Wriothesley), was for 30 years one of the Queen's closest and most devoted ladies-in-waiting, and ideally placed for smuggling a child of the Queen (if there was one) out of the Court, subsequently to be handed over to her sister-in-law.[2] The two-year period of wet-nursing would have offered plenty of time for one child to be substituted for another who had died while in the care of the wet-nurse (several instances have been recorded where this really did happen).[3] Lady Katherine was a die-hard Catholic, but was excused all penalties by the Queen (and later by James I) in recognition of her devotion to her mistress.[4] Her husband, Thomas Cornwallis, was "groom-porter" to the Queen, a kind of major-domo of the Queen's outer chambers (he was never knighted, perhaps because of ill health; his nephew often stood in for him). They were thus two of the people closest to the Queen during this period. The Second Earl and Countess were also notorious Catholics (and probably Southampton himself, secretly, until about 1590 or maybe later). The need to foster the Catholic religion would have been a powerful additional incentive for the Countess to take on another's child in place of one of her own who had died.

The relationship between the Countess and the Second Earl was difficult, and in about 1577 or 1578 he accused her of "incontinence" (sexual misdemeanors), and forced her to live apart from him, bringing up Henry (then aged five) himself until he died in 1581. In letters later written to the Earl of Leicester (a relation) at the time of the earl's death, the Countess on several occasions referred to Henry as "the child," "the boy," rather than "my child" or "my boy," and at least once referred to him as "it."[5] This has to be an odd way for a birth mother to refer to her own son, aged eight, but is consistent with the child having been born to someone else.

It is interesting to note that the home of Thomas and Lady Katherine Cornwallis was at East Horsley, on the edge of the estate of Lord Howard of Effingham (and possibly part of it); it was he who was later granted the wardship of Southampton by the Queen through Lord Burghley, and might have been party to such a secret. In his youth he had been regarded as a possible consort for the Queen, and they remained friends throughout her reign (*ODNB*).

After an eventful life, frequently finding himself at odds with King James, Southampton spent his last days, accompanied by his elder son, James, in command of a troop of English volunteers who went to assist the Dutch in their 1622 campaign against Spain. After landing in the Low Countries father and son were both attacked by fever and died shortly after. Their bodies were preserved in honey and transported back to Titchfield for burial.

In 2000, efforts were made by the Titchfield History Society, chaired by a retired Admiral, to secure permission to have DNA samples taken from the remains of Southampton and his parents, all three having been preserved in lead coffins in the vault under St. Peter's Church,[6] but it was not then forthcoming. Permission to make such tests was rarely granted at the time, but is now becoming more acceptable. In recent years the Duke of Edinburgh has been involved in not dissimilar cases involving disinterring distant relatives for DNA testing.[7] So the possibility of checking whether Southampton was Countess Mary's son may not be as remote as it might once have seemed. A substantial donation towards the upkeep of Titchfield Church might help towards a favorable decision.

The vault had been opened in 1947 to see whether recent floods had damaged the lead coffins. A nine-year-old boy from the village observed the proceedings, but when asked 53 years later where the entrance was, refused to say, as he disapproved of disturbing the dead. According to a guidebook of 1946, the vault is somewhere underneath the floor of the South Chapel, between the Southampton memorial and the east wall. It may also be relevant to mention that Queen Anne Boleyn's remains lie under a marked stone in St. Peter's Ad Vincula Chapel in the Tower of London (*ODNB*).

As mentioned earlier, we find ourselves in very deep waters indeed—we began our journey looking for the author of the works published under the name Shakespeare, and are now contemplating the near-impossible possibility that one of Elizabeth's earls might actually have been her son. It may be that the aura of royalty with which the sonnets appear to invest the Fair Youth is a mirage, a result of taking metaphor too literally. But when we find Southampton's name carefully concealed in the Dedication to the Sonnets, and also find that he is treated as someone of exalted status by his contemporaries (*"Bright may he rise and shine immortally in* [the Queen's] *fair firmament"*) one begins to wonder.[8] It may be that the poet of the sonnets was misinformed about Southampton's lineage, and that his contemporaries were under the same delusion. We defer to a later opportunity any further discussion of these matters.

22. *Retrospective 2*

In Chapter 15 we encountered the theory, derived from the sonnets, that the "Fair Youth," Southampton, was the son of the Queen, or thought by the poet of the sonnets to be her son, supposedly fathered by the Earl of Oxford. Suspending disbelief as far as possible, we then looked at some of the rumors that abounded during the Queen's lifetime to the effect that she had given birth to two or more children, the first a son fathered by Robert Dudley, Earl of Leicester, then a daughter[1] (not mentioned so far, supposedly fathered by Sir Christopher Hatton), and then another son by Oxford, supposedly brought up as the Third Earl of Southampton. The story of Arthur Dudley, preserved in the State Papers Spanish, was then outlined in Chapter 17, and it emerged in Chapter 20 that Oxford and Southampton were the two youngest noblemen ever to achieve ten votes in the KG elections during Elizabeth's reign, Oxford aged 21 in 1571 and Southampton aged 23 in 1596.

The chronology of these supposed events is shown below, incorporating the premise that Southampton was thought to be the Queen's son. To sum up, then, from purely literary evidence, the dynastic sonnets, it was hypothesized some 80 or more years ago (correctly or otherwise) that Southampton was the son of Oxford and the Queen. However unlikely that hypothesis may have seemed, it is now apparently confirmed by documentary evidence from 1592 and 1593, outlined in the previous chapter, which shows that several writers really thought that Southampton was, or might be, the son of the Queen, one publication actually styling him *Dynasta*, a prince, one of a line of hereditary princes or rulers. If the procreation sonnets were partly written in an oblique attempt to urge the Queen to legitimize Southampton, then, although the attempt failed, we are as a consequence left with what might be interpreted as evidence that it was someone privy to Court secrets who wrote them, under the pen name "Shakespeare." Alternatively, the rumor that Southampton was the Queen's son may have stoked up the imagination of a number of writers for a short period, including Shakespeare (whoever he was) before being seen as no more than wishful thinking and never referred to again.

In the fractured narrative presented in Chapters 15 to 17 and Chapter 20, we have encountered hypothesis, speculation, and an interpretation of some of Shakespeare's sonnets which appears at best fanciful and at worst delusional. We have visited a young man imprisoned in Madrid who calls himself Arthur Dudley, brought up in humble circumstances in England but given the education of an aristocrat, who claims to be the son of the Queen, and whose claims are apparently accepted by King Philip II and his right-hand man, previously one of Queen Mary's Privy Councilors. On more solid ground, we have listened to the voices of contemporaries extolling the virtues accruing to him on the grounds of his birth

Chronology

1559–61	Birth of Arthur Dudley	[Henry VII's sons were
1573–75	Birth of Henry Wriothesley (HW)	named Arthur and Henry
1587–88	Death of Arthur Dudley; HW now eldest son of QE	
1588 June	Death of Anne de Vere, wife of Oxford	
1591 July to 1592 March	Oxford marries Elizabeth Trentham sometime during this period, the Queen having failed to make him her consort	
1592 September	Southampton styled "Dynasta" by Oxford University panegyrist.	
1593 April 18	Venus and Adonis registered, dedicated to HW.	
April 23	Garter Election in secret: HW receives no votes.	
May	HW expected to be made KG (cf. Henry Fitzroy).	
June	Extolled in exalted terms by Peele; not made KG.	
1594–96	Dynastic sonnets written on the assumption that HW was the Queen's son.	
1595 on	Southampton ignored by the Queen, though receiving many votes in Garter elections.	
1601 February	Joins Essex rebellion; imprisoned and reduced to commoner status—"Mr. H. W."	
1603 July	Restored to Earldom and appointed KG by James I.	

and heritage of another young man, brought up as the Third Earl of Southampton, and who is regarded as having a very special relationship with Queen Elizabeth (extolled as one destined to "*shine immortally in her fair firmament*").

These findings are enough to stretch the imagination almost beyond breaking point. Can these things be true? Until recently, there was no way to investigate further, but with the advent of DNA testing a means exists to settle the matter in the case of Southampton. Whether it is considered important enough to merit disturbing the dead remains to be seen.[2]

Part III: Discoveries

23. The Hidden Name

So far on our travels, apart from evidence that eliminates the man from Stratford-upon-Avon, we have not really achieved very much in the way of new discoveries. Spenser's "pleasant Willy" may well be William Stanley, but is only linked with Shakespeare through the wishful thinking of past Shakespeare experts (Chapter 6). That Nashe's Gentle Master William was gentle Master William Stanley was interesting, but only marginally links him with playwriting (Chapter 7). The identification of the Fair Youth with Southampton is also interesting, but most commentators already believed this to be the case (Chapters 18, 19). And speculation about children of Queen Elizabeth is just that—speculation (Chapters 16, 17, 20, 21).

However, we have now arrived at the threshold of the amazing discovery of the real author's name, a discovery prompted by Jones Harris's remarkable insight as described in the Introduction. To recapitulate, during a phone call from America in October 2008, Jones Harris told me of his brilliant hunch, that if the name of the real author had been concealed in the First Folio, then the only page available for the purpose was the one that listed the actors' names. All the rest of the text of the Folio came from outside sources—the plays themselves, the prefatory material signed by John Hemmings and Henry Condell, and the laudatory poems. The only page entirely at the disposal of the editors was the one with the title "The Workes of William Shakespeare," Figure 23.1, which contains the names of all the players arranged in two columns. "Study these columns," I was told, "and see what you find."[1]

Shown in Figure 23.2 is the left-hand column, indicating that the last letters of the middle seven names reveal the name "STENLEY" or "ST(E)ANLEY," an acrostic pointing to William Stanley, Sixth Earl of Derby, as the real author. As we shall see, the unique spelling "Kempt" proves beyond reasonable doubt that the acrostic was deliberately contrived. The publishers had complete control over the contents of this page, its layout, and—crucially—the order in which to list the actors' names in the two columns. It was therefore the only page available for introducing concealed information, Jones Harris's original and superb deduction.

It so happens that E. K. Chambers, the great 20th-century Shakespeare scholar, commented in 1930 that the order was anomalous, since Robert Armin was one of the original sharers in the Globe Theatre, built in 1599, and should be listed in the first column together with the other founding members, rather than being relegated to the second column along with players who joined the troupe years later.[2] In addition (perhaps a minor matter) one might expect Condell's name to come immediately after Hemmings's name, as the two of

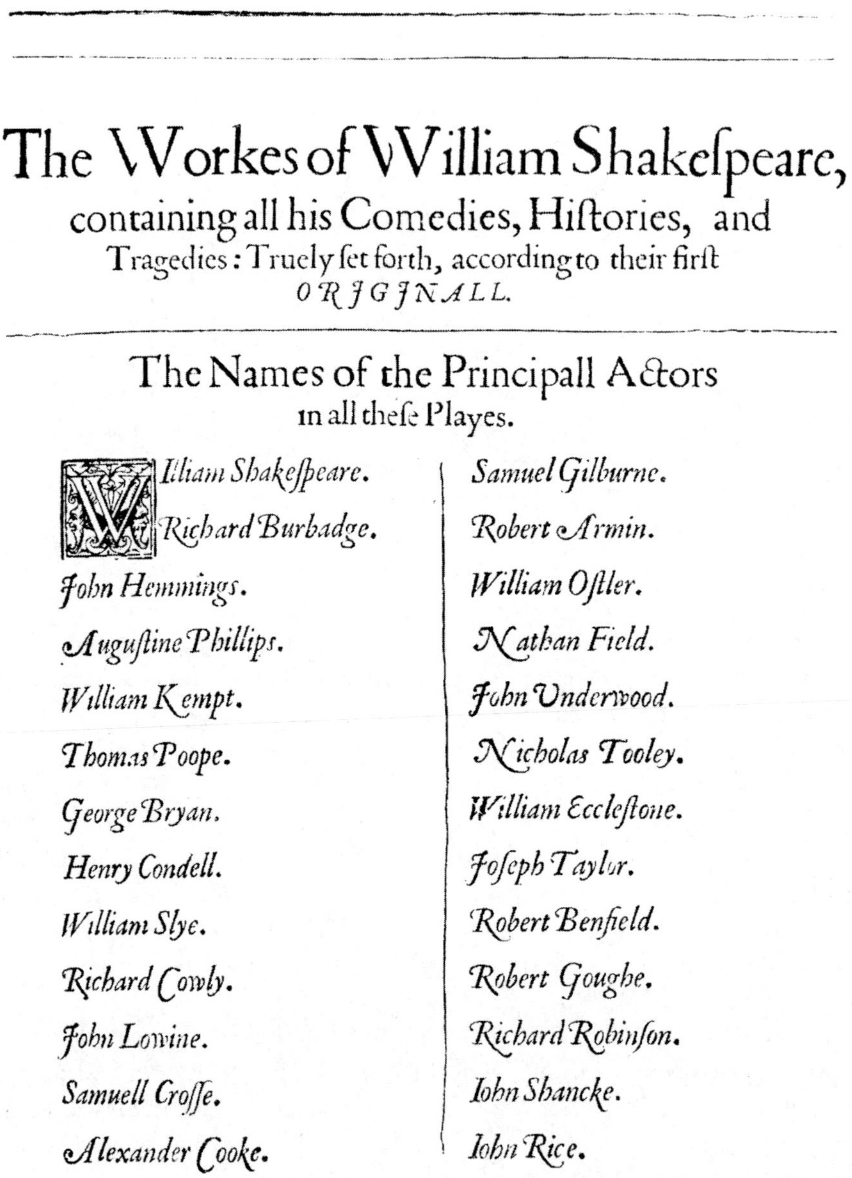

The Workes of William Shakeſpeare,

containing all his Comedies, Hiſtories, and Tragedies: Truely ſet forth, according to their firſt ORJGJNALL.

The Names of the Principall Actors in all theſe Playes.

William Shakeſpeare.
Richard Burbadge.
John Hemmings.
Auguſtine Phillips.
William Kempt.
Thomas Poope.
George Bryan.
Henry Condell.
William Slye.
Richard Cowly.
John Lowine.
Samuell Croſſe.
Alexander Cooke.
Samuel Gilburne.
Robert Armin.
William Oſtler.
Nathan Field.
John Underwood.
Nicholas Tooley.
William Eccleſtone.
Joſeph Taylor.
Robert Benfield.
Robert Goughe.
Richard Robinſon.
Iohn Shancke.
Iohn Rice.

Figure 23.1 List of actors' names, Shakespeare First Folio, 1623.

them jointly signed the Folio's dedication and the address "To the great Variety of Readers"; moreover their names are listed consecutively in six of the other players' lists quoted by Chambers[3] (they were friends and lived close to each other in the parish of St. Mary Aldermanbury, per the *ODNB*). It is interesting to note that the spelling "Kempt" and the order of the actors' names are repeated identically in the later three Folios of 1632, 1663/4 and 1685, despite thousands of changes in each reprint. (They are also repeated identically in many modern editions of the Complete Works, which explains my remark in the Prologue.)

There are very strong reasons for supposing that this acrostic was deliberately contrived.

1. This is the *only* place in print and in surviving documents where the name "Kemp" or "Kempe" is spelled "Kempt."[4] None of the players' names ended in "T," so a "T" was tacked on to the end of Kemp. None of their names ended in "A," so one ending in "E" (Poope, pronounced "Pope") was used as the best available substitute.[5]
2. Rather than use either of the names "Lowin" (minus the "e"), or "Armin" (listed in the right-hand column of actors' names) to provide the letter "N," the name of the player George Bryan was brought in, although he had stopped acting in 1596, and was neither a shareholder in the Globe Theatre, built in 1599, nor a member of the King's Men, formed in 1603; all the others on this list were both (apart from Kemp; he was a share-holder but not one of the King's Men). Bryan's name was (supposedly) included to provide both the "N" and also the "A" before the "N," as if to provide confirmation for the name "Stanley."
3. The odds of the name STENLEY occurring as an acrostic are minute. The odds of a T following an S in the sequence of final letters are (from a cryptographic table of final-letter frequencies) 1 in 30. The odds for either an A or an E following the T are 1 in 13, and the odds for N, L, E and Y are 1 in (respectively) 30, 110, 15 and 110. So the combined odds are 1 in the product of these numbers, i.e., 30 × 13 × 30 × 110 × 15 × 110. This works out to 1 in around 2,100,000,000 (2.1 billion).

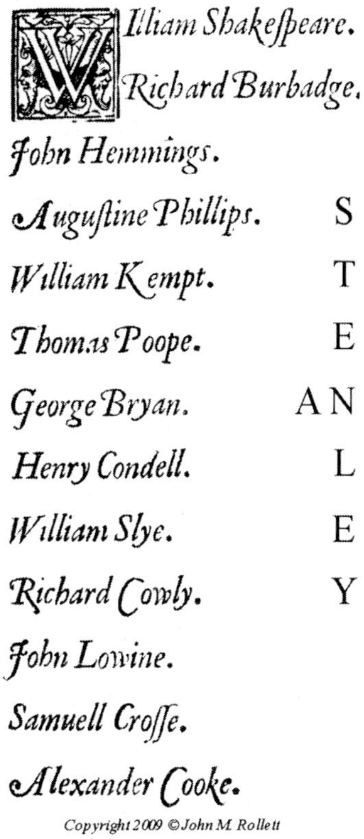
William Shakeſpeare.
Richard Burbadge.
John Hemmings.
Auguſtine Phillips. S
William Kempt. T
Thomas Poope. E
George Bryan. A N
Henry Condell. L
William Slye. E
Richard Cowly. Y
John Lowine.
Samuell Croſſe.
Alexander Cooke.

Copyright 2009 © John M. Rollett

Figure 23.2 Left-hand column of actors' names.

This last consideration does not amount to proving that the acrostic was deliberately contrived, since chance can never be ruled out, but it does make it unlikely that it occurred accidentally. If we then factor in (notionally) the odds against the *unique spelling* of "Kempt," and against the *astonishing coincidence* that someone with the name "Stanley" is one of the top few candidates for the man writing under the name William Shakespeare, then it does seem almost beyond dispute that we now know the name of the real author. It is as if the whole landscape has suddenly been lit up by a dazzlingly bright light, reaching into the furthest corners of confusion and doubt. Behold the man, the real Shakespeare, William Stanley, resurrected after four centuries of obscurity![6]

For confirmation, we repeat what William and Elizebeth Friedman say about acrostics in their book *The Shakespearean Ciphers Examined* (already quoted above, Chapter 12).

> We should not be surprised if it is claimed that ... acrostics appear in Shakespeare's works, for they abounded in the literature of the time; nor should we be surprised if these devices concern the authorship of the works, for *they have often been used to this end*. We should even be tolerant of variable and erratic spelling.[7] [*emphasis added*]

They also say that what matters is that the letters must occur in precisely the right order, and that there should be enough of them for there to be no doubt what word or words were intended. Both of these stipulations are fulfilled: Stanley was the only person heavily involved with players and playwriting whose name needed to be concealed (because of his closeness to the throne, as already discussed).[8]

There is another matter to take into account, which was mentioned when we were considering the hidden name "Wr-ioth-esley," and that is the need (ideally) for the cryptographer to conceal hidden information in such a way as to give the solver some reassurance that he has found something that was *deliberately* hidden, and not just something produced by chance. In the case of Wr-ioth-esley it was the fact that "ioth" was found in a column adjacent to "esley." Chance might have placed the two segments apart, but to find them as close as possible looks like a nod from the cryptographer to indicate that the full name had indeed been deliberately concealed. In the case of the acrostic found in the list of actors' names, is there something else unexpected which is similar to the nod just mentioned confirming the Fair Youth's name? I believe there is, and that is the placement of the name of Robert Armin. As Chambers observed in 1930, it should have been located in the first column of actors' names. Instead it was placed in the second column, in between Gilburne and Ostler. Gilburne became a sharer in the Globe in 1605 (according to Chambers), Armin in 1599, and Ostler in 1609 (*ODNB*). I believe the anomalous positioning of Armin's name may be a hint that the names had been deliberately moved around, thereby helping to reassure the solver that he has found something deliberately hidden. As Helen Fouché Gaines remarked in her book on cryptography, "awkwardness of wording" may be a pointer to a "concealment cipher" (see Chapter 18, note 9), and so might also be an unexpected departure from the largely chronological listing of the actors' names.

We now look into the history of authorial acrostics. The British Library and other resources together list over 80 manuscripts and books written between 900 and 1700 where the author's name is given by an acrostic, and in many cases this is the only indication of the identity of the author. A writer unwilling to allow his name to appear on a title page, but nevertheless wanting to record it somewhere, would immediately think of an acrostic, since it was a commonly used device of great antiquity dating from Roman times (and the only really practical one). When the first letters of consecutive lines were employed, the device would often be obvious to an alert reader. In the present case this was not an option, as the initial letters of the actors' names do not provide enough of those needed to spell out "Stanley." Instead the more unusual technique was employed of utilizing the final letters, which provide all but two of the required letters, "E" being substituted for "A," and the missing "T" being affixed to the name Kemp (thereby pretty much confirming that the acrostic was deliberate and not an accident of chance). Some examples of acrostic authors' names are given next.

Examples of Acrostic Authors' Names

We here give examples of authors' names concealed in acrostics; in each case the name of the writer appears nowhere else. The use of the device as a means of allowing authors to attach their name to an otherwise anonymous manuscript or publication was widespread across both Europe and the Middle East for several centuries and in many languages. Most examples use the first letters of consecutive lines of verse, but there are also some which use final letters (sometimes called "telestichs"). A fine example of this technique occurs in a 36-line Latin poem written by St. Dunstan in around 940: "Indignvm abbatem dvnsantvm christe respectes"—"May you deign to look, O Christ, on your unworthy abbot Dunstan." The use of final letters for hidden names or messages is just as well established as the use of first letters, though employed far less frequently. Notice that in two of the examples below, more than one letter from the same line is employed to make up the full name, not dissimilar to the case of "St(e)anley" outlined above.

(a)	*(b)*	*(c)*	*(d)*	*(e)*	*(f)*
I...	**I...**	**A................i**	**R...**	**J...**	**...v**
A...	**O...**	**D................o**	**O...**	**O...**	**...v**
C...	**S...**	**A................h**	**G...**	**H...**	**...l**
O...	**Q...**	**L................a**	**E...**	**N...**	**...f**
B...	**V...**	**S................n**	**R...**	**H...**	**...s**
V...	**I...**	**T................n**	**M...**	**A...**	**...t**
S...	**N...**	**A................e**	**A...**	**R...**	**...a**
S...	**Des...**	**N................s**	**R...**	**R...**	**...n**
EX...	**P...**		**B...**	**I...**	**...v**
T...	**R...**		**E...**	**S...**	**...s**
V...	**E...**		**C...**		
S...	**Z...**		**K...**		
			E...		

(a) This is how the name of James VI of Scotland (later James I of England) appears in his otherwise anonymous book of poems in the Scottish dialect, *The Essayes of a Prentise in the Divine art of Poesie*, published in Edinburgh, 1584: Iacobus Sextus.

(b) The spelling of the composer's name was in doubt until this acrostic of 1495 was found: Josquin des Prez.

(c) The name of the author of this ms. Latin poem of 930 is identified by this double acrostic, using both the first and last letters of the eight lines: Johannes Adalstan.

(d) The author of this book, *A Defence of tabacco*, etc., published in 1602, is revealed by an acrostic in the dedication: Roger Marbecke.

(e) The name of the author of *The divine Physician: prescribing rules for the prevention and cure of most diseases*, etc., by "J. H. M.A.," 1676, is given by an acrostic: John Harris.

(f) This name is made up of the final letters of the opening lines of a "substantial poem" in a Latin ms. of 1000: Vulfstanus.

I do not think there can be any doubt that the acrostic "Ste/anley" was deliberately encoded into the list of actors' names, and very little doubt that it was intended to record the name "Stanley." If we then ask why, the most probable answer (I would suggest) is to record the name of the real author. The purpose of the deceptive portrait of William Shakspere on the title page of the Folio was to record the fact that he was not the author, thereby creating a vacancy which the name just found (located a few pages later) fills admirably. In the next chapter we continue the biography of William Stanley, who has now unexpectedly inherited the earldom of Derby following the death of his elder brother Ferdinando.

24. William Stanley, Sixth Earl of Derby

We here continue the biography of William Stanley, now—since 16 April 1594—the Sixth Earl of Derby following the poisoning of his brother Ferdinando. Strenuous efforts were made to identify whoever had procured or administered the poison.[1] Suspicion briefly fell on Countess Alice, perhaps because of her miscarrying a baby not fathered by Ferdinando, thereby seeking to forestall his inevitable wrath. It also briefly fell on William, who might have had designs on the earldom.

It was also suspected in some quarters, amazingly enough, that the instigator was Lord Burghley. The following is quoted from Hotson's *I, William Shakespeare*.

> [Henry] Young tells us that '[Edmond] Yorke spake, being at dinner with [Sir William, a cousin of Ferdinando and William] Stanley, [Richard] Williams being present and myself, about the death of the young Earl of Derby [Ferdinando]; they musing how he came by his end, Yorke said, "It is no marvel, when Machiavellian policies govern England. I durst pawn my life," said he, "that the Lord Treasurer [Lord Burghley] caused him to be poisoned, that he [Ferdinando] being dead he might marry the young Lady Vere unto the brother [William Stanley] of the said Earl of Derby. It is time," said he, "to cut them off that go about to be kings."' [*Information in* brackets *was supplied by Hotson and myself.*][2]

Machiavellian indeed! Burghley, having first tried and failed to marry Elizabeth Vere (his granddaughter and for whom he acted as guardian) to Henry Wriothesley, son (just possibly) of Queen Elizabeth (and her potential successor?), then gets rid of Ferdinando in order to marry her to William, now Earl of Derby and the legitimate heir-apparent to the throne. If you believe that of Burghley you will believe anything! I should add that Sir William Stanley, Edmond Yorke and Richard Williams were all Catholics and traitors, having gone over to the Spanish side in 1587 during the war in the Low Countries, and had no reason to speak well of Burghley. Sir William's children were being brought up by Earl Henry while he was abroad, and Ferdinando had continued to do so on becoming Earl. This might have been another reason for Burghley's not fully trusting Ferdinando—bringing up the children of a Catholic and a traitor, even though they were the sons of his cousin.

An inescapable fact concerning Ferdinando's poisoning is that one of his waiting gentlemen, Robert Dowtie, had ridden off immediately after his death and was never seen again in England.[3]

As already described, Ferdinando during his appalling illness had left all the Derby lands to his wife and daughters, so William, while inheriting the earldom (and also the heir-apparency to Queen Elizabeth) found himself in financial straits; the few estates left to him by his father would have afforded him only a small income. After his sister-in-law Countess Alice failed to agree to a more equitable distribution of the ancestral lands, he embarked on a lawsuit to regain control of the estates that was not finally settled until fifteen years later.[4]

We learn from a letter written by Alice on 9 May 1594 to Robert Cecil that William now had plans to marry (leaving aside the suspicions of Edmond Yorke).

> I hear of a motion of marriage between the Earl, my brother, and my lady Very, your niece, but how true the news is I know not, only I wish her a better husband.[5]

It is not recorded where William first met Lady Elizabeth Vere, one of Her Majesty's ladies in waiting, though it has been suggested that it was at the entertainment arranged by the Earl of Hertford for Queen Elizabeth at Elvetham in September 1591, where the festivities lasted four days and her entourage comprised over 500 people.[6] At this time an engagement between the younger son of an earl and Lady Elizabeth would probably have been unacceptable to the lady's grandfather, Lord Burghley, her guardian, but it seems that within three weeks of his inheriting the earldom William had lost no time in approaching him. He was now 32 or 33 years old and his intended bride 19, and evidently the match met with Burghley's approval.[7] There was, however, a snag. It was possible that Countess Alice might be carrying a child, and so the nuptials were delayed until the possibility of William being "unearled" by the birth of a son to her was timed out.[8]

It is evident from Countess Alice's letter to Cecil that she did not think well of William, and pretending to be pregnant when she was not in an effort to delay his marriage is further evidence of disapproval. Her brother-in-law Sir George Carey had previously written on 22 April to his wife, Alice's sister, about his relief on learning that the Derby estates had been saved from "this nidicock"—that is, "nincompoop."[9] It seems that the whole family, Ferdinando, Alice, George Carey and his wife thought little of William and would have liked to deprive him not only of the earldom and his inheritance but also of his marriage. If one were to hazard a guess as to the reason for this dislike, it may be that they disapproved of his playwriting and more particularly his publishing *Venus and Adonis* the previous year. There was a real stigma attached to a nobleman publishing poetry, and for someone so near to the throne to do so was an added affront to propriety and good sense. George Puttenham wrote in 1589 that anyone who shows himself excellent in poetry is called in disdain "phantasticall" and "light headed."[10]

Nonetheless, the marriage was celebrated in grand style on 30 January the following year at Greenwich Palace and in the presence of the Queen.[11] It is often claimed that *A Midsummer Night's Dream* formed part of the festivities, but there is no clear evidence for this. At this time his friends at Court included the Earls of Southampton and Rutland. He was also a close friend of Dr. John Dee, and visited him frequently at his home in Mortlake, where his library was one of the largest in the country (and may have contained many of the over 300 books which the plays tell us that Shakespeare had read).

The marriage started well, with a daughter born sometime towards the end of 1595 or early 1596. She would have been passed immediately to a wet-nurse and was being brought up in her uncle Robert Cecil's house at Pymmes in Edmonton (a gift from his father Lord

Burghley on the occasion of his marriage). Burghley wrote to his son Robert complaining about his granddaughter's lack of concern for her child,[12] but sadly she soon died.

Around this time rumors of Elizabeth's flirtations started tongues wagging at Court. Lady Anne Bacon wrote to the Earl of Essex in December 1596, castigating him for imperiling Elizabeth's reputation, and added, about William, "it is said he lovethe her, and greatly, as with grief, laboureth to win her."[13] As a consequence, either at this time or the next year William was prevailed upon to frame a challenge of "combat of life" to anyone who thought he doubted his wife's honor; it was written down, signed by him and witnessed by Lord Burghley and Robert Cecil and one other, but not issued.[14] In July 1597 William collected Elizabeth from the Court and they returned to Knowsley escorted by a huge following, perhaps to escape the rumors.

But there was no escape. The next month letters[15] arrived at Knowsley reporting her alleged infidelity with the Earl of Essex, causing Derby great torment ("jealous frame," "storm," "madness"[16]) and putting his marriage in jeopardy. He treated his wife so badly that the domestic staff (over 100 strong) threatened to walk out, but within a week matters were patched up through the mediation of friends.[17] However, suspicions broke out again some months later,[18] and for a time the Countess decided to live apart from her husband, causing William to be very downcast. She asked her uncle to find her a suitable place to live, though where it was we do not know. It is recorded that they did meet occasionally, and that William was very distressed when she left to return to her self-imposed exile.[19]

Eventually they were fully reconciled and the marriage prospered, with several children being born over the next few years. At his Lathom estate he bred horses and raced them, and it has recently been established that he founded the "Derby" race, so that the term "derby" originated with him (*ODNB*). Other interests besides the theater included alchemy and bridges ("which he passionately built, maintained, and repaired," *ODNB*).

In January of 1599 Derby was expected to serve with the Earl of Southampton and the Earl of Rutland in Essex's ill-fated expedition to Ireland, but it seems he did not embark. In May of this year Derby and his wife visited Castle Hedingham, ancestral home of Elizabeth's father Lord Oxford, apparently for a short holiday, but stayed no more than a day or two.[20] Later that year he was reported in two letters by a Catholic agent, George Fenner, as being "busied only in penning comedies for the common players," as already mentioned.[21] The letters were intercepted and never reached their intended recipients.

In the same year Derby financed ("to his great paines and charge") the revival of the Children of Paul's acting company, in partnership with John Marston and (later) Thomas Middleton,[22] and according to the *ODNB* "one or two of their probable extant plays could be his as well." In this year he is also believed to have financed the launch of the Boar's Head Inn playhouse in Aldgate, with Robert Browne in charge; Browne was the leading actor of the Earl's own company, Derby's Men.[23] This troupe performed several times at Court at around this time, breaking the duopoly held by the Lord Chamberlain's Men and the Admiral's Men. Derby was more closely associated with players and playwrights than any other nobleman of the period.

It was probably at about this time his wife wrote an undated letter to Robert Cecil.

> Good uncle, being importuned by my Lord to entreat your favour that his man Browne with his company may not be barred their accustomed "plaing" in maintenance whereof they have con-

sumed the better part of their substance, if so vain a matter shall not seem troublesome to you, I could desire that your furtherance might be a means to uphold them for that my Lord taking delight in them it will keep him from more prodigal courses and make your credit prevail with him in a greater matter for my good. So commending my best love to you I take my leave

Your most loving niece
E. Derby[24]

It would be interesting to know what "prodigal courses" might otherwise have been followed by the Earl.[25]

Derby proved an able representative of the Crown in the counties of Lancashire and Cheshire, and Elizabeth appointed him Knight of the Garter in 1601.[26] He was consequently one of the five KG noblemen available to bear the canopy over James I at his coronation anointing in 1603 (see Chapter 5). His wife was a great favorite of her uncle Robert Cecil, who had been secretary to the Privy Council for some time and was by now Viscount Cranborne. She was also a favorite of King James, and frequently took part in Court masques in the early years of his reign.

Derby was represented by Francis Bacon in his protracted legal battle with his sister-in-law Alice, the Dowager Countess of Derby, over the estates in Lancashire and elsewhere. The dispute was finally resolved in 1609,[27] and shortly after Derby was appointed Lord Lieutenant of Lancashire and devolved to his wife the governorship of the Isle of Man, to which he had been reinstated as hereditary king.

In 1614 Derby carried the Sword of State before King James as he rode to Parliament. In subsequent years he and his wife divided their time between the Court and his Lancashire estates. In 1617 the Earl was visited by King James at Lathom House. After his wife's death in 1626 he made over his estates to their eldest son, James; two of the three trustees were his brother-in-law the Earl of Montgomery, and the latter's elder brother the Earl of Pembroke (the dedicatees of the First Folio). About this time he moved to a house on the side of the River Dee, near Chester, where we are told "he retired and passed the evening of his life in quiet, peace, and pleasing enjoyment of ease, rest, and freedom of body as well as mind."[28]

In 1627 William was visited by his son James's wife, Charlotte de la Trémoille (they had married at The Hague), and she reported back to her mother that they had spent the whole day talking in French, and that the Earl had greatly charmed her with flattery and compliments.

> I wrote you word, Madame, that I had seen my father-in-law at Chester, where he always lives, never desiring to go to any of his other houses; he has been there now three or four years. He spoke to me in French, and said very kind things to me, calling me lady and mistress of the house, a position which he said he wished no other woman to hold; that I had the law in my own hands entirely.[29]

Derby's Men were still performing in the area as late as 1637. He died in 1642 and was buried first in Chester and subsequently reburied in the family church at Ormskirk. His castle at Lathom was sacked during the Civil War, and any papers or manuscripts that might have been stored there were destroyed. He published nothing under his own name, and some fifty letters, mostly short, are all that survives of his handwriting. Many of these letters (we are told) were designed to help others, for example to try to save a servant of his wife from hanging,[30] to recommend a troupe of players to the mayor of Chester,[31] or to commend some worthy individual to Robert Cecil[32]; a few letters are reproduced in Chapter 29 and in Appendix D. One of his biographers wrote: "There are many indications of his devotion, help in distress and service to others, but none of hatred or even dislike by him or towards him."[33]

There are many more details of Derby's biography which could be assembled to fill out the story of his life, but nothing more to support directly or indirectly the idea that he was a poet and playwright. We next take another look at the sonnets, to assess the relationship between the poet and the Fair Youth.

25. *The Poet and the Fair Youth*

Now that we know with a high degree of confidence both who the poet was—William Stanley, and who the Fair Youth was—Henry Wriothesley, we can attempt to ascertain what their relationship was as hinted at by the poet in many of the sonnets.

It has emerged from the analyses of two orthodox Shakespeare scholars that the poet invested the Fair Youth with an aura of royalty, metaphorical in the view of G. Wilson Knight, and temporary "pretend" royalty in the view of Leslie Hotson (see Chapter 14). We have also found that his contemporaries behaved towards Henry Wriothesley, Earl of Southampton, as if he merited a uniquely high esteem, of the kind that might well seem appropriate for someone who was thought to be the son of the Queen (Chapter 20). (Let me remind the reader that I am not advocating this view, merely recording and investigating it.)

The reader will also recall that William himself was a fully legitimate great-great-grandson of Henry VII, and had a strong claim to succeed Elizabeth after his brother Ferdinando died in 1594.[1] Strictly, their mother Margaret (née Clifford) was the next heir to the throne, but she would never have been chosen by the Great Council[2] as the next monarch since the country would not have tolerated three queens one after another. William was descended from Henry VIII's younger sister, so it might be supposed that a great-grandson of his elder sister Margaret Tudor would have precedence. There was only one such, James, now James VI of Scotland, but he was barred for two reasons, firstly because he had not been born in England (and was termed "alien"), and secondly because Henry VIII's will, ratified by Parliament, had given precedence to the children of his younger sister Mary.

Now consider William's position after his brother's death. He had unexpectedly inherited both the earldom and also the heir-apparency. Other potential heirs were James VI of Scotland, whose chances of inheriting were hampered for the reasons just given, and Southampton, whose chances (if he was the Queen's son) were hampered by his being illegitimate. Let us now for the sake of argument assume that Southampton really was of royal birth, purely as a hypothesis, and see whether this offers any insight into the Fair Youth sonnets.

The first seventeen sonnets (Chapter 13) urge the Fair Youth in the strongest possible terms to produce a son, in order to preserve his beauty, no other reason being given. It has been suggested that this was a covert reference to his inheritance of royal blood. Why, then, was it so important to the poet, William Stanley, that Southampton should have a son? I would like to suggest that this can be explained by two considerations, firstly that William did not want to ascend to the throne (this is conjectural), and secondly that the Great Council, following the Queen's demise, would be far more likely to choose a successor *who already had a son*, so that the country would have the reassurance not just of a new king but also of a son to succeed him. The threat of civil war had hung over the whole country throughout the whole of Elizabeth's reign, and there were many who had terrible family memories of events during the Wars of the Roses ("father against son, son against father"). The repeat of such a catastrophe had to be avoided at all costs.

By this time, Stanley (if he was Shakespeare) had written several of the history plays, and had thoroughly explored what it meant to be King of England—*"uneasy lies the head that wears a crown."*[3] I think it likely that he had decided that he was temperamentally unsuited to fulfill the office of the King of England, and felt that Southampton was the better man for the job, or at least would remove the burden from his own shoulders.[4]

Let us take a moment to explore this conjecture, that Stanley felt himself unsuited to undertake the role of King. The poet of the sonnets more than once refers to himself in self-effacing terms—he did not want his name to be remembered,[5]

> My name be buried where my body is, [#72.11–2
> And live no more to shame nor me nor you

and most strikingly in this passage, indicating that he did not *expect* it to be remembered.

> From hence your memory death cannot take, [#81.3–8
> Although in me each part will be forgotten.
> Your name from hence immortal life shall have,
> Though I, once gone, to all the world must die:
> The earth can yield me but a common grave,
> When you entombed in men's eyes shall lie.

He also in effect abases himself before the Fair Youth, addressing him as *Lord* and *sovereign*, calling himself the Fair Youth's *vassal* or *servant* or *slave*. Here and elsewhere we get an impression of someone unwilling to shine in the limelight of public approbation, content to be a bystander and commentator on life, not a leader or the kind of person who would seek power over others.

Additionally, we learn from the sonnets that Stanley regarded Southampton with an almost religious devotion, merited (on the basis of our conjecture) by his royal blood inherited from his mother, the Queen. He as it were prostrates himself before him, promises him love and affection both personal and as a kind of patriotic duty towards the next in line. It was also the case that Southampton was extremely handsome, with an almost feminine beauty at this time, which many people had commented upon; the charisma of beauty is a desirable quality in a ruler. For example, there seems little doubt that Richard Barnfield was enamored with Southampton, and wrote his (anonymous) homoerotic sequence of poems *The Affectionate Shepheard* (November 1594)[6] with him in mind, apostrophizing him as "Ganymede," the cup-bearer to the Gods. Two months later, in January 1595, he published his second volume, *Cynthia, with certain Sonnets*,[7] and this time signed the preface, which was dedicated to William Stanley in terms which imply close personal relations. It seems likely moreover that Barnfield was the "Rival Poet" of the sonnets, something that will be explored later, and that they both had special (though different) reasons for their devotion to Southampton.

We have just put forward the idea that the poet of the sonnets, shown with a high degree of probability to be William Stanley, urged the Fair Youth, Southampton, to have a son in order to make it more likely for him to be selected to succeed Queen Elizabeth (on the hypothesis that he really was her son), and to reduce the likelihood of being selected himself. Thus we can now amplify C. S. Lewis's remark: "What man in the whole world, except a father or a potential father-in-law, cares whether any other man gets married?"[8] by adding "someone wanting another man to increase his chances of being chosen to succeed to the throne by producing a son." There is no way of substantiating this idea, but there does not (so far) appear to be anything that would make it untenable, and moreover it provides *the first rational explanation* for one of the most puzzling aspects of the Fair Youth sonnets.

Our travels seem to have brought us into strange territory—either to the wilder shores of fantasy, or to areas of Elizabethan history hidden so deep under the sands of time that they might never have been suspected, let alone uncovered. We shall press on boldly, and look into those plays of Shakespeare with which it can be claimed that Stanley was closely linked. But first, a detour to allow us to investigate the mystery of the Rival Poet.

26. The Rival Poet

In a sequence of sonnets about two-thirds of the way through the series devoted to the Fair Youth, numbers 78–80, 82–86, occur references to a mysterious "Rival Poet"; there are in addition other poets whose poems addressed to the Fair Youth the author finds disturbing.

> As every *Alien* pen hath got my use, [#78.3–4
> And under thee their poesy disperse.

Other poets are attracting the notice of the Fair Youth, and distracting him from giving his full attention to the poet of the sonnets, whom we believe with a high degree of confidence to be William Stanley. But throughout this chapter I prefer to refer to the poet as Shakespeare, for reasons that I find quite hard to explain; it may be simply that the sonnets being the quintessence of Shakespeare's poetry, they are so closely attached to the name that to attach any other name to them (even the name of the man I think he almost certainly was) seems somehow *lèse majesté* (irrational, I know).

These are some of the people who have been suggested as the main Rival Poet: Spenser, Marlowe, Drayton, Nashe, Daniel, Gervase Markham and Barnaby Barnes. Our poet is especially disturbed by one poet in particular, "a better spirit":

> O how I faint when I of you [*his friend*] do write, [#80.1–2
> Knowing a better spirit doth use your name,

The rival poet is seen to be a threat to Shakespeare, who finds himself "tongue-tied" (line 4). The use of the word "spirit," both here and in sonnet 86

> Was it his spirit, by spirits taught to write [#86.5

has led some commentators (together with other considerations) to suppose that the rival poet was Chapman, who claimed to have been directly inspired by Homer's spirit. The sonnet continues with a similar thought:

> He nor that affable familiar ghost [#86.9–10
> Which nightly gulls him with intelligence,

but now an element of mockery can be detected, and we might begin to wonder how serious Shakespeare is being throughout the Rival Poet sonnets.

These sonnets offer almost no clues as to the identity of the rival—hence the large number of poets who have been put forward. But recently a new dimension to the puzzle has been added, with the discovery by Professor Leo Daugherty[1] of echoes between a number of the sonnets and poems by Richard Barnfield. What seems to have happened is that Barnfield saw several of the sonnets in manuscript soon after they were written, and responded in his own poems, to which in turn Shakespeare responded.[2] Daugherty has found that two phrases used by both Shakespeare and Barnfield are unique, in that they were not used by anyone else at the time.[3] These are "**renew thy force**" and "**mend/amend thy style.**"[4] (I use boldface type following Daugherty.)

Thus, in sonnet 56 Shakespeare writes:

Sweet love **renew thy force**, [#56.1

chiding his devotion ("Sweet love") to his friend for neglecting to offer him the highest praise. Then, in Sonnet IV of *Greene's Funeralls*,[5] Barnfield admonishes an unnamed living poet ("my friend so pretty") to join him and others (one mythical, Minerva, and two dead, Ferdinando Stanley and William Elderton) in praising the dead Greene.

Come thou hither, my friend so pretty, [IV.13–18
All riding on a hobby horse[6]:
Either make thyself more witty
Or again **renew thy force**.
Come and deck his brows with bays [Greene's
That deserves immortal praise.

The reader will recall that Stanley is associated with Greene by Gabriel Harvey in *Pierce's Supererogation* (Chapter 7), and there is good reason to suppose that Stanley was present at the "banquet" of pickled herring and Rhenish wine, which Nashe tells us Harvey claimed was the cause of Greene's demise. Barnfield is therefore calling upon a fellow-poet whom he knows knew Greene; in any case it will emerge that Barnfield and Shakespeare were friends, which accounts for each knowing the other's poetry before it was published.

Next, in sonnet 78, Shakespeare addresses the Fair Youth as follows:

Yet be most proud of that which I compile, [#78.9–14
Whose influence is thine, and borne of thee:
In others workes thou doost but **mend the style**, [Barnfield's
And Arts with thy sweete graces graced be;
But thou art all my art, and doost advance
As high as learning, my rude ignorance.

What he is saying is that the *style* of others' poetry is improved (mended) by his friend's approbation, while the *whole* of his own poetry, style *and* content, is dependent upon the approval of his friend (whom we know to be Henry Wriothesley, Chapter 18).

Barnfield responds in his Sonnet V, in which he addresses the dead Greene, saying that *no one* could amend *his* (Greene's) style, in contrast with the case of Shakespeare.

Amend thy style who can: who can **amend thy style?** [V.1–5
For sweet conceit?
Alas the while
That any such as thou should die [Greene
By fortune's guile
amidst thy meat.

This last phrase may perhaps refer to the alleged surfeit of pickled herrings and Rhenish wine, the meal at which both Stanley and Nashe may have been present.

Leo Daugherty makes a very good case for Barnfield as the Rival Poet, who is therefore to be presumed to be enamored of the Fair Youth, whom he addresses by the name "Ganymede" in *The Affectionate Shepheard.* The "affable familiar ghost" of sonnet 86, who "nightly gulls him with intelligence," is therefore Greene's ghost, who was "the most famous literary ghost of the entire Tudor-Stuart period" according to Daugherty, citing several publications[7] where authors summon up his ghost to entertain their readers. Daugherty also identifies the "compiers by night" from the same sonnet with Nashe and Chettle. It will not escape the notice of the reader that these people are all known to have kept company with Stanley.

Figure 26.1 The ghost of Robert Greene in his winding sheet.

Daugherty is especially intrigued by Barnfield's Sonnet V from *Greene's Funeralls.* The first five lines are printed above, and the poem continues

Pardon (Oh pardon) me that cannot shew, [V.6–11
My zealous love.
Yet shalt thou prove
That I will ever write in thy behove [Greene
'Gainst any dare,
With thee compare.

Barnfield is expressing his support for Greene and his reputation, against any detractors, who were not lacking as the next line indicates:

It is not *Hodgepoke* nor his fellow deare, [12–14
That I do feare:
As shall appear,

Daugherty suggests that "Hodgepoke" refers to Gabriel Harvey, who was lowly born and wrote in disgraceful and gloating terms about the squalid circumstances of poor Greene's death. "His fellow dear" Daugherty thinks may be Harvey's publisher John Wolfe (an anagram of "fel(l)ow"), with whom he was lodging at the time. Barnfield continues:

But him alone who is the Muses' owne, [15–20
And eke my friend, [Stanley
Whom to the end,
My muse must ever honor and adore:
Doe what I can
To praise the man.

For Daugherty, this is Stanley in the shape of Barnfield's beloved Ganymede, but I think it far more likely that this is Stanley being saluted as *il miglior fabbro*, the better poet. The rest of the poem seems to confirm this view, although some doubts must remain.

It is impossible for me that am [21–36
So far behind,
Yet is my mind
As forward as the best, if wit so would
With will agree;
But since I see
It will not be,
I am content, my folly to confesse,
And pardon crave.
Which if I have,
My Fortune's greater than my former fall:
I must confesse.

But if he otherwise esteem of me [Stanley
Than as a friend, or one that honors thee [Greene
Then is my labor lost, my care consumed,
Because I hate the hope that so presumed.

Perhaps I should have pointed out earlier that for Leo Daugherty, the poet is the man from Stratford, and William Stanley is both Shakspere's Fair Youth and Barnfield's Ganymede. These assignments encounter a problem right from the outset, since Stanley was three years older than Shakspere, while the Fair Youth is universally regarded as being younger, perhaps as many as ten years younger, than the poet (he is addressed as "sweet boy" in sonnet 108). In my view the Dedication to the Sonnets indicates beyond reasonable doubt that the Fair Youth is Southampton, who therefore also becomes Barnfield's Ganymede.[8] Barnfield remains the Rival Poet under both scenarios.

While *The Affectionate Shepheard* was published anonymously, with a dedication to Lady Penelope Rich (thought by some to be the Dark Lady of the sonnets), Barnfield's next collection of poems, *Cynthia, with Certain Sonnets*,[9] was dedicated to Stanley (now Earl of Derby) with an effusive signed epistle indicating that they knew each other well (it is printed as an annex to this chapter). Included in the collection is a commendatory poem (signed

"T. T.") saying that Barnfield's pen was "eagle-winged" and "new tasked," suggesting (perhaps) that he had been encouraged to write them by Stanley ("Aetion," man of the eagle, the Derby crest).[10]

Francis Meres, in *Palladis Tamia* (1598), gives a list of twelve of Shakespeare's plays, and also refers to "his sugred Sonnets among his private friends." One of these friends has now been identified as Richard Barnfield, whom Meres calls "my friend master *Richard Barnefielde*."[11] It may be that it was through Barnfield that Meres heard about Shakespeare showing his sonnets to his "private friends" (and it may even have been he who gave Meres the list of Shakespeare's plays). At this time (1593–1594), Stanley was a law student at Lincoln's Inn (where his childhood friend Thomas Lodge resided) and it is known that Barnfield had friends at Gray's Inn. Other law students Stanley would have associated with at this time were John Donne, John Marston, Francis Bacon and Southampton.[12]

It is worth noting that Barnfield was also a friend of John Marston, who was later (with Thomas Middleton) associated with Derby in the revival of the Children of Paul's acting troupe in 1599. It only remains to mention that three of Barnfield's poems were printed together with five of Shakespeare's in *The Passionate Pilgrim*, a piratical publication first issued by William Jaggard in 1599 under the name of William Shakespeare.[13] Barnfield's style was on occasion so similar to Shakespeare's that the authorship of several of the other poems still remains in doubt, and some of them may be either Barnfield's or Shakespeare's.

We next look into those plays of Shakespeare which have links with Stanley, in particular with his travels on the continent of Europe.

Annex: Barnfield's Epistle Prefaced to Cynthia, Etc.

To the Right Honorable, and most noble-minded Lorde, William Stanley, Earle of Darby, &c.

Right Honorable, the dutifull affection I beare to your manie vertues, is cause, that to manifest my loue to your Lordship, I am constrained to shew my simplenes to the world. Many are they that admire your worth, of the which number, I (though the meanest in abilitie, yet with the formost in affection) am one that most desire to serue, and onely to serue your Honour.

Small is the gift, but great is my good-will; the which, by how much the lesse I am able to expresse it, by so much the more it is infinite. Liue long: and inherit your Predecessors vertues, as you doe their dignitie and estate. This is my wish: the which your honorable excellent giftes doe promise me to obtaine: and whereof these few rude and vnpollished lines, are a true (though an vndeseruing) testimony. If my ability were better, the signes should be greater; but being as it is, your honour must take me as I am, not as I should be. My yeares being so young, my perfection cannot be great: But howsoeuer it is, yours it is; and I myselfe am yours; in all humble seruice, most ready to be commaunded.

Richard Barnefeilde.

27. Plays Linked with Stanley

A number of Shakespeare's plays can be linked with William Stanley, some with greater confidence than others.

Love's Labour's Lost

We shall start by considering *Love's Labour's Lost*, which was published in 1598, the first of the plays to have the author's name attached to it (in the form "William Shakespere").[1] Because of the large number of rhyming couplets, and also a perfect sonnet, it was thought by early commentators to be Shakespeare's first play, written before 1590; it offers a dazzling display of his exuberant poetical skills. Modern commentators now date the composition to around 1593–1594 based on historical considerations, and a first printing in 1596 or 1597, no copy of which has survived.[2] The edition of 1598 is described as "newly corrected and augmented," which while a stock phrase may well record what actually happened. The play is full of clever wordplay, puns, and literary allusions, and is filled with witty pastiches of contemporary poetic forms. It is often assumed that it was written for performance at the Inns of Court, whose students would have been well able to appreciate its sophisticated and artificial style.[3]

The play's characters and some of its plot are based on people and events associated with the Court of Henri Bourbon (later Henri IV of France) at Nérac, in Navarre, between 1578 and 1582. For example the names Berowne, Longaville and Dumain are taken from those of le baron de Biron, le duc de Longueville and le duc du Maine, all prominent at that period. Professor Abel Lefranc stated that the play is a "reflection of a scintillating episode in our [France's] history.... The very substance of the play ... is impregnated with quite recognizable French elements."[4] He was confident that the author Shakespeare must have had "virtually impeccable and absolutely amazing acquaintance with aspects of France and Navarre of the period that could have been known only to a very limited number of people."

William Stanley set out for the Continent with his tutor Richard Lloyd in 1582, and traveling south from Paris towards Spain it is likely that they spent some weeks at Nérac in 1583, although there is no record of such a stay (there were other Englishmen resident there at the time, including Anthony Bacon, Francis Bacon's elder brother). What links the play with Stanley is the character of Holofernes, who appears to be modeled on that of his tutor (15 years his senior); for a start, "Holofernes" was the name of the tutor of Rabelais's Gargantua.[5] In *Love's Labour's Lost* a masque is performed of "The Nine Worthies," and James Greenstreet[6] identified two sources of this masque as *The Nine Worthies* performed at the annual Chester festivities and a poem written by Richard Lloyd, published in 1584, with the title *A brief discourse of the most renowned actes and right valiant conquests of these puisant Princes, called the Nine Worthies.*[7] There are a number of similarities between Lloyd's verse and the masque in Shakespeare's play. As an example, in Lloyd's *Nine Worthies* we find the following description of one of the worthies, Alexander the Great:

> This puissant prince [Alexander] and conqueror bare in his shield a Lyon or,
> Wich sitting in a chaire hent a battel axe in his paw argent.[8]

In the masque, Act V, scene ii, lines 569ff, appears the following repartee from Costard to Sir Nathaniel, interrupting the declarations of Alexander.

> O, Sir, you have overthrown Alisander the conqueror!... Your lion, that holds his poleaxe sitting on a close-stool, will be given to Ajax. He will be the ninth Worthy. A conqueror and afeard to speak! Run away for shame, Alisander.

A poleaxe is a battle axe but, instead of a chair, Shakespeare substitutes a close-stool, that is a commode (a stool containing a chamber pot). It seems highly likely that Stanley is here poking fun at his humorless tutor and his long poem. And here is what John Raithel writes about the influence of the Chester entertainments.[9]

> As for *The Nine Worthies* produced at Chester, the influence is more structural as, for example, in the conclusions of both the Chester performance and the performance in *Love's Labour's Lost* where declarations are made by the seasons of the year. In the Chester pageant they are *Ver*, *OEstas*, *Autum*, and *Hiems*, while *Love's Labour's Lost* includes just two, "Hiems, Winter; Ver, Spring."

A further link between Lloyd and Holofernes is that Holofernes frequently inserts Latin phrases in his speeches, just as Lloyd did in his writings.

Another of the characters is Armado, a self-important and grandiloquent Spaniard. Several commentators identify him with one Antonio Perez, a Spanish exile who frequented Court circles in the 1590s.[10] At one point he is called "peregrinate," which seems clearly to point to his surname. It so happened that he was present at the wedding of William Stanley (by now Sixth Earl of Derby) with Lady Elizabeth Vere in January 1595, so Stanley would have encountered him here if not earlier. I believe it was Frances Yates who first noticed that the point of the dialogue between Moth and Armado in Act I, scene ii, lines 34 to 51, is the pageboy Moth's gently teasing Armado by trying to get him to say "three," a word which he avoids as (being Spanish) he is unable to pronounce "thr."[11] He gets to say (or try to say) the word twice in the first scene of Act III in conversation with Moth, and then right at the end of the play (V. ii. 867) he has to attempt it again in front of the King and Court, and doubtless the actor originally playing him displayed all sorts of facial contortions in the effort to get the word out, to general hilarity.[12]

Just to substantiate this point, line 34 of Act I, scene ii, reads as follows in the Quarto:

> *Armado.* I have promised to studie three yeeres with the duke.

while in the Folio it reads:

I have promis'd to study iij. yeres with the Duke.

So at this point Armado *holds up three fingers*, to avoid having to say the word "three." This might be regarded as further evidence that the author himself revised the copy for the First Folio. Who else, thirty years after it was written and twenty years after the last recorded performance, would remember this detail?

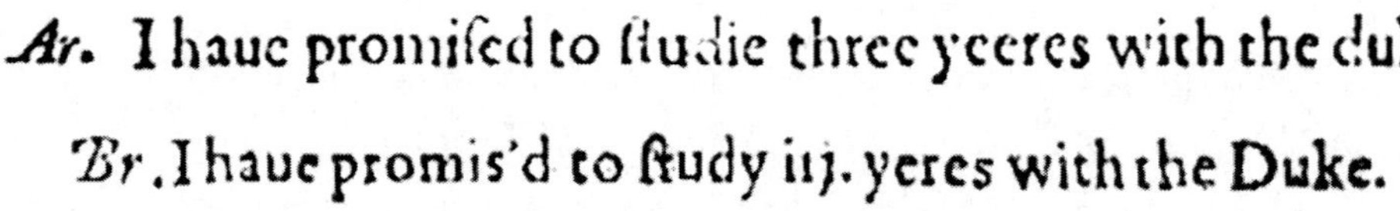

Ar. I haue promiſed to ſtudie three yeeres with the duke,

Br. I haue promis'd to ſtudy iij. yeres with the Duke.

Figure 27.1 *Love's Labour's Lost*, Act I, scene ii, line 34: upper, from Quarto; lower, from Folio. "*Br.*" is short for "Braggart," i.e., Armado.

As an aside, most commentators believe that Moth is a playful picture of Thomas Nashe, Moth being Thom backwards (approximately) and portrayed as a youth ("boy") rather than at his real age. Nashe was more than once dubbed "Juvenal"[13] because of the caustic tone of his pamphlets, and Moth is called "juvenile" in the play; he is of diminutive stature, as was Nashe. This might be seen as Stanley getting his own back on Nashe (but in an affectionate way) for his insulting epistle to *Strange News*. It has also been shown by Robert Gittings that Berowne's speech at the end of Act III borrows heavily from *The Unfortunate Traveller* by Nashe; it is almost as if Shakespeare happened to reread this work when writing (or rewriting) the play.[14] In addition, the King in the play is given the name "Ferdinand," which seems like a bow in the direction of William's elder brother Ferdinando; it may be that the play was originally intended as a kind of courtly gift towards the man who was in line for the throne.

There is one more passage in the play which finds a deep resonance elsewhere. In Act V, scene ii, Rosaline says to Katherine:

You'll ne'er be friends with him [*Cupid*]: he killed your sister.
He made her melancholy, sad, and heavy:
And so she died.

This is thought to be a reference to Hélène de Tournon, who became enamored of a young lord. He was forced by his family to ignore her as beneath him in rank, and as a result she pined away and died of love. The story (which will be told more fully when we consider *Hamlet*) was not written down and published until 1624, but it was a favorite story of Queen Marguerite of Navarre.[15] Hélène was the daughter of one of her ladies in waiting and she was very fond of her. Only someone who had met the Queen and got to know her personally would be likely to have heard it, and we may imagine Stanley storing it up during his time at Nérac (though it must be borne in mind that there is no record of his staying there).

Hamlet

There is one episode concerning the death of Ophelia in *Hamlet* that reflects even more strongly the story just outlined above about Hélène de Tournon. The full account of what occurred on Queen Marguerite's visit to Brabant in June and July 1577 is given in her 1624 *Mémoires*.[16] Hélène was a young girl of noble birth, loving and beloved by the Marquis de Varembon, when suddenly (and to her inexplicably) she was treated by her lover with disdain. The motive for the simulated contempt is (as may appear to be the case with Hamlet and Ophelia) a difference in rank, preventing marriage. The young girl is distraught by the coldness of the Marquis, who has left town, and eventually dies for love ten days later. While her funeral is in progress the Marquis returns to Brabant and inquires who has died and is informed who it is. Filled with remorse, he goes down to the grave into which Hélène's coffin has been placed, and, so says Marguerite de Valois, "son ame, que je crois, allant dans le tombeau (his soul ... going into the grave) requetir pardon a celle que son desdaigneux oubly y avoit mise."

In the play, Hamlet, returning from England, finds himself in a graveyard where a grave is being dug for someone, who turns out to be Ophelia. The funeral procession arrives, and Laertes jumps into the grave first, followed by Hamlet. They grapple, and Hamlet says

> I loved Ophelia. Forty thousand brothers [V.i.265–7
> Could not with all their quantity of love
> Make up my sum.

This is the first and only time he admits to his love for her (apart from their first encounter, where he immediately contradicts himself). The similarity between the two stories suggests that in writing about Ophelia's death, Shakespeare, whom we think was Stanley, having heard Marguerite's story of Hélène de Tournon from her own lips, made stark use of it in this tragic scene.

I now want to embark on a discussion of the plot of *Hamlet*, so well known to every theater-goer the world over.[18] Or is it? Like many people I had seen the play and read the text several times, and thought I knew (in so far as anyone can) what it was all about. But then I read a book by Beryl Hughes which shone a completely new light on all the scenes which involve Ophelia, and made (and still makes) me feel that an essential thread running through the whole work has been overlooked for centuries.[19]

Here is the gist of her assessment. Hamlet returns to Elsinore after hearing about the death of his father, and finds that not only has he lost his father, killed by poison, he has lost the crown (to which he might have expected to have been elected), he has lost the inheritance of his father's wealth and lands, and he has lost his mother, now married to his uncle, the new King. But this is not enough; he has still more to lose: *he must lose everything*.

In Act II, scene 1, we find Ophelia describing to her father, Polonius, how Hamlet visited her in her room.

> *Ophelia.* My lord, as I was sewing in my closet, [lines 77–83
> Lord Hamlet, with his doublet all unbraced,
> No hat upon his head, his stockings fouled,
> Ungartered, and down-gyved to his ankle,
> Pale as his shirt, his knees knocking each other,
> And with a look so piteous in purport
> As if he had been loosed out of hell
> To speak of horrors—he comes before me.
> *Polonius.* Mad for thy love?

Ophelia. My lord, I do not know,
But truly I do fear it.

But this is not, as Polonius surmises later, "the very ecstasy [madness] of love." No commentator I have read suggests any other interpretation for Hamlet's behavior, but in the light of Beryl Hughes's insight I offer the following. What has happened is that Hamlet has just been told by the servant waiting on him as he is dressing the shattering news that the king early in his reign, before marrying Gertrude, had been seen visiting Ophelia[20] in her chamber and is suspected of having slept with her. He is appalled, and immediately rushes to her room to see whether there can be any truth in what he has been told. He gazes intently at her face, and while his nodding three times may suggest that he fears the worst, he can no more be certain of Ophelia's guilt than he can be certain of Claudius's over his father's death. His doubts remain and surface several times later in the play. The scene continues:

Polonius. What said he? [lines 84–96
Ophelia. He took me by the wrist and held me hard,
Then goes he to the length of all his arm
And with his other hand thus o'er his brow
He falls to such perusal of my face
As a' would draw it. Long stayed he so;
At last, a little shaking of my arm
And thrice his head thus waving up and down,
He raised a sigh so piteous and profound
As it did seem to shatter all his bulk
And end his being. That done, he lets me go
And with his head over his shoulder turned
He seemed to find his way without his eyes
(For out o' doors he went without their helps)
And to the last bended their light on me.
Polonius. Come, go with me: I will go seek the King.
This is the very ecstasy of love.

Many things in the play contribute to this interpretation of events, although Shakespeare is careful only to provide hints. For example, in II.ii.174 Hamlet calls Polonius a "fishmonger," a slang term for a procurer or brothel-keeper—he is accusing him (but only in jest—or perhaps disdain) of having provided Ophelia for the king's pleasure. Shortly after, he says, "Conception is a blessing, but not as your daughter may conceive—friend, look to't."[21] But Polonius is unaware of what Hamlet is hinting at, which will become only too evident later in the play, when in the mad scene (IV.v.63–64) Ophelia addresses Claudius directly: "Before you tumbled me, you promised me to wed."[22] So now, Hamlet has lost his father, the crown, his inheritance, his mother, and faith in the girl he loved. He has indeed lost everything, all down to the machinations of Claudius.

What is so remarkable about Hamlet's situation is the way it parallels William Stanley's situation in 1600–1601, at around the time that the version of Hamlet entered in Stationer's Hall in July 1602 and published the next year was probably being written (or perhaps revised and rewritten). William has lost his elder brother Ferdinando, also killed by poison, he has lost his ancestral lands, willed to his sister-in-law and her daughters, he has lost confidence in the virtue of his wife, rumored to have slept with Essex, just as Hamlet lost confidence in the virtue of Ophelia, and like Hamlet, William was also heir-apparent to a throne (which by now was more than likely to be offered to King James of Scotland). William too has lost everything[23] (although he has inherited the earldom, for all that his sister-in-law Alice would have denied it to him by pretending to be pregnant).

The similarity does not end there. While Ferdinando was on his sickbed a tall man "with a ghastly and threatening countenance" entered his bedroom and "crossed him" two or three times—but to his utter astonishment no one else in the room saw the man, evidently a ghost.[24] William of course was aware of this apparition, and it is not difficult to surmise that this may be the origin of the ghost of Hamlet's father, who sets Hamlet on the path of determining his uncle's guilt; no ghost appears in any of the sources for *Hamlet*—this is one of Shakespeare's original additions to the story.[25] It is universally agreed that Hamlet's character has much in common with the author's character. It now seems that there is a hitherto unsuspected concordance between events in William Stanley's life and events in the play.

A Midsummer Night's Dream

This play has often thought to have been performed as part of the festivities celebrating the marriage of William Stanley, now Earl of Derby, with Lady Elizabeth Vere on 30 January 1595,[26] in the presence of Queen Elizabeth. It contains what is supposed to be a graceful reference to the Queen as "the imperial votaress ... in maiden meditation, fancy-free." A good case can also be made for supposing that "the much-traveled Theseus might have been thought appropriate to William Stanley, whose own travels are said to have taken him as far as the Holy Land and Russia" (E. K. Chambers).[27] Ernst Honigmann adduces several other reasons for this identification.[28] The play within the play, organized by Bottom the weaver, is regarded by several commentators as being modeled on the midsummer festival of plays held at Chester every year, unique to that town. The guilds of tradesmen organized pieces for performance "with great zest, and the list of trades who participated in these crude representations included tanners, tailors, barbers, tinkers, masons, carpenters, butchers, saddlers and so forth."[29] We are also told that "the night was given up to frivolity and license, in which amorous couples wandered into the woods then adjoining Chester (like the couples in *MND*) and Lefranc has traced records of paternity cases which came before the Bench as a sequel." There is a further connection between *Midsummer Night's Dream* and the Chester representations, in that the only known play where a man is transformed into an ass is in the Chester play *Balaam and His Ass*, put on by "the Chappers and Lynnan Drapers."

These tradesmen's performances were frequently patronized by Henry Stanley, father of Ferdinando and William, and it is recorded that on one occasion Ferdinando accompanied him. It is more than likely that all his sons accompanied him at other times.

Measure for Measure

The play *Measure for Measure* derives from *The Right Excellent and Famous Historye of Promos and Cassandra*, by George Whetstone, published in 1578 (or perhaps from his later prose version of the story, published in 1582). Whetstone had derived his plot from one of the Italian author Cinthio's collection of stories called *Gli Hecatommithi*, written in 1565. Shakespeare's play is set in Vienna, but Georges Lambin discovered that the plot of *MM* is so very similar to events that occurred in Paris in 1582 that *only someone present at the time* could have written it.[30]

In August of this year King Henry III of France, preparing for one of his occasional monastic retreats, appointed a deputy as governor in his place. Less than a month later an individual called Tonart was charged with fornication and condemned to death, just as Claudio is in the play. Tonart was accused of seducing the daughter of the President of the Parliament of Paris (although they had in fact married secretly), and like Claudio he was eventually pardoned. Many details of Whetstone's story are changed to correspond to the real-life events which occurred in Paris in these months, to such an extent that Lambin's conclusion seems inescapable. Here are two examples. The name of the condemned man in Cinthio is "Vico," in Whetstone he is "Andrugio," while Shakespeare calls him "Claudio": Tonart's first name was "Claude"; and the vows made by Isabella correspond closely to those laid down for the nuns of Sainte Clare, which would only be known to someone in Paris at this time.[31]

Here are the names of the main characters as given by Whetstone, names of people prominent in Paris in 1582, and the names Shakespeare gives to his characters.

Whetstone	*People in Paris involved in the Tonart affair*	*Shakespeare MM*
King	Henri III, whose favourite chateau was at Vincennes	Duke Vincentio
Promos	Jerome Angenouste, Councilor in the Paris Parliament and one of Tonart's judges	Angelo
Cassandra	Sainte Isabelle of France, founder of the Convent of Nuns of Sainte Clare at Longchamp, Paris	Isabella
Andrugio	Claude Tonart, secretly married to the daughter of the President of the Parliament of Paris	Claudio
—	Guillaume du Vair, Councilor in the Paris Parliament	Varrius
—	La Roche Flavin, another Councilor	Flavius
—	Saint-Luc (François d'Espinay), favourite of Henri III	Lucio
—	Bernadino de Mendoza, Spanish ambassador	Barnadine
—	Ragasoni, a legate of the Pope	Ragozine

Georges Lambin points out that Shakespeare assigns names to his characters derived from names of people who were prominent in Paris during the months William Stanley spent there with his tutor. He also finds that Shakespeare must have consulted the rules for aspiring nuns to the order of St. Clare, since several of the lines of dialogue quote them almost verbatim. Lambin notes that the only English convents of Nuns devoted to St. Clare had disbanded by 1539, so it is unlikely that Shakespeare could have had knowledge of the rules from an English source. William Stanley visited Paris again in 1585, as a member of his father's grand embassy to confer the Order of the Garter on Henri III, and would have been able to refresh his memory about the events of two years earlier.

The Merry Wives of Windsor

The author of *Merry Wives* had a precise knowledge of all the accouterments of a Knight of the Garter. The "Queen of the Fairies" speech to the elves and fairies in *The*

Merry Wives of Windsor directly concerns heraldic aspects of the Knights of the Garter, as described by John Raithel.[32]

> About, about: [V.v.55ff
> Search Windsor Castle (Elues) within, and out.
> Strew good lucke (Ouphes) on euery sacred roome, [children of elves
> That it may stand till the perpetuall doome,
> In state as wholsome, as in state 'tis fit,
> Worthy the Owner, and the Owner it.
> The seuerall Chaires of Order, looke you scowre
> With iuyce of Balme; and euery precious flowre,
> Each faire Instalment, Coate, and seu'rall Crest,
> With loyall Blazon, euermore be blest.
> And Nightly-meadow-Fairies, looke you sing
> Like to the *Garters*-Compasse, in a ring
> Th' expressure that it beares: Greene let it be,
> More fertile-fresh then all the Field to see:
> And, *Hony Soit Qui Mal-y-Pence*, write
> In Emrold-tuffes, Flowres purple, blew, and white,
> Like Saphire-pearle, and rich embroiderie,
> Buckled below faire Knight-hoods bending knee;
> Fairies vse Flowres for their characterie.

> The fairies and elves are consecrating Windsor Castle and, in particular, St. George's Chapel, for this is the part of Windsor Castle concerned with the Knights of the Garter ceremonial. In the chapel, each Knight of the Garter is allotted a stall ("faire Instalment") in which is displayed his banner ("loyal blazon") bearing his coat of arms ("Coate"), and his helmet sporting his distinctive crest ("Crest"). The French phrase *Hony Soit Qui Mal-y-Pense* is on the garter itself ("Buckled below faire Knight-hoods bending knee"). (The French *Hony Soit Qui Mal-y-Pense* means roughly "evil be to whom who thinks bad of it" or "Evil to him who thinks evil," a saying with no clear traditional source.) In addition, much of the action in *The Merry Wives of Windsor* takes place in a tavern called "The Garter."

While it is true that Derby was appointed KG in May 1601, and would therefore have become very familiar with all these minutiae (if he was not familiar with them before), there is nothing in this passage which specifically relates to him; many other people would have been similarly informed. There is, however, one scene of the play which does present a connection. We turn again to John Raithel for this account.[33]

> The play opens with a pompous and enraged Justice Shallow promising to bring a "riot" (an illegal act of multiple individuals) to the attention of the council of the Star Chamber (I.i.32ff):
>
> **Shal**: Sir Hugh, perswade me not: I will make a Star-Chamber matter of it,
> if hee were twenty Sir Iohn Falstoffs, he shall not abuse Robert
> Shallow Esquire.
>
> ...
>
> **Shal**: The Councell shall heare it, it is a Riot.
>
> ...
>
> **Shal**: The Councell shall know this.
>
> ...

Shal: Knight, you haue beaten my men, kill'd my deere, and broke open my Lodge.

About the time this play was first performed and published, in fact in 1602, an action that had been pending for some years was brought before the Star Chamber by one Justice of the Peace Stephen Proctor against officers of Will Derby. Proctor was a neighbor to Derby's Yorkshire estate, and in the surviving records of the action we read that Derby's side refers to Proctor as "puffed up with vain glory." Proctor, for his part, claims that the Earl of Derby's men performed many of those actions attributed by Justice Shallow to Falstaff, including assaulting his men and killing his deer.

In addition to both the association of the play with a legal action involving the Earl of Derby, and his investiture as a Knight of the Garter, there is a final suggestive note to add concerning *The Merry Wives of Windsor*. The quarto edition seems to refer to Derby's neighbor Proctor himself in a wordplay with a reference to "Proctors," a word for attorneys. The following line disappeared when the play was published in the First Folio (and the suit had been long resolved):

Sir Hugh Goe laie the Proctors in the street [scene 18

The quarto of *MWW* was a very inferior publication, and the play was thoroughly revised and greatly increased in length for the First Folio. We may again suppose that the revision, and the omission of the line mentioning the Proctors, was carried out by Derby in the years leading up to 1623.

Edward III

The play *The Raigne of King Edward III* was published anonymously in 1596. It was not included in the First Folio, but is now generally regarded as being written either wholly or in part by Shakespeare; in 1998 Cambridge University Press published an edition of the play under Shakespeare's name. In the early 1990s Roger Prior claimed that the copy of Froissart's *Croniques* [*sic*] held in the British Library, once owned by and annotated by Henry Carey, Lord Hunsdon, was studied and used by the author of *Edward III*. So the author of the play "must have known Hunsdon personally, had access to his library, and used his privileged knowledge in the writing of the play," which furthermore "contains specific references to Hunsdon's interests; it flatters him by referring more or less directly to his achievements and by providing support for his views."[34] Now Hunsdon was the Lord Chamberlain in charge of the troupe of players which was formed from the remnants of Lord Strange's players when it was broken up after the death of Ferdinando, Fifth Earl of Derby, in April 1594, and his son George was William Stanley's brother-in-law (Ferdinando's wife was a sister of George's wife). It would seem natural then that the chief playwright of the Lord Chamberlain's Men (if he was Stanley) would have associated with him and made use of his library, especially given the close relationship between him and his son, who in 1597 himself became the Lord Chamberlain in charge of the leading Court acting troupe.

Coauthored Plays

A number of Shakespeare's plays are thought to have been coauthored, including the early plays *Titus Andronicus* with Peele,[35] *Henry VI, part 1*, coauthored with Nashe[36] and

Marlowe, *Henry VI, part 2*, coauthored with Marlowe,[37] and *Edward III* (discussed above) perhaps coauthored with Kyd.[38] Shakespeare is also thought to have contributed the 1602 additions to Kyd's *The Spanish Tragedy*, and the quarrel scene in *Arden of Faversham*,[39] such as might be expected from someone closely connected with a theatrical troupe, as Derby was with his own players at the Boar's Head Theatre in 1599. (One could envisage Derby putting on *The Spanish Tragedy* at the Boar's Head and writing additional lines to enhance the play's impact.) Moreover, Thomas Merriam has concluded that the verse in *Henry V* was written by Marlowe; all Shakespeare did was to write the prose parts, having come across an uncompleted play by Marlowe.[40] It would be fair to say that many of these findings are open to revision, as the techniques of stylometry are continually being refined and improved, but it is interesting that both Nashe and Marlowe have been suggested as coauthors as they are both known to have been associated with Ferdinando and hence William Stanley.

Other plays believed to have been coauthored are *All's Well that Ends Well*[41] and *Timon of Athens*, both with Thomas Middleton,[42] who was linked with Derby (together with John Marston) in the revival of the Boar's Head Theatre in 1599.[43] Middleton is also thought to have updated *Macbeth* in 1616, and made alterations to *Measure for Measure*[44] in 1621 (*ODNB*). Further, *Henry VIII* and *The Two Noble Kinsmen* are generally thought to have been coauthored with John Fletcher. I take "coauthorship" to be a neutral term, which might involve two people planning in advance to write a play together, or one person writing part of a play and handing it to someone else to co-write or to complete alone, or someone years later finding an old play parts of which need finishing or rewriting, and so on.

Other Plays

There are other plays that have been linked with Stanley. For example, it has been claimed that Malvolio in *Twelfth Night* is based on the Fourth Earl's servant, William Farington (or ffarington), who served as Henry's secretary from 1561, and from 1586 to 1591 as his comptroller or steward; he displayed marked puritanical tendencies. In this capacity he kept detailed household accounts and occasionally noted down the visits of troupes of actors and the comings and goings of the members of the family (he also noted down an occasion when William and Ferdinando went hawking together). But Farington had independent means, having inherited a wealthy estate, and similarities between his character and that of Malvolio are largely conjecture, so the link is faint.

More relevant is *The Tempest*, since Frances Yates's study of this play has shown that the character of Prospero is probably based on that of John Dee, who was the inheritor in England of the occult tradition in its Rosicrucian form.[45] It is well established that William Stanley frequently visited Dee[46] at his Mortlake home, which possessed one of the largest libraries in the country. Writers and philosophers abroad often donated copies of their books to him, and it is easy to suppose that William occasionally borrowed books from him. Once again, one of the main characters is called Ferdinand, presumably with a nod in the direction of his deceased elder brother. Although supporters of Derby are very ready to see his hand in this play, it does not seem to me that there is anything *specific* which points directly to Stanley, so again I regard this link as faint.

The links between William Stanley and *Love's Labour's Lost*, however, are very strong. It is barely credible that any other playwright would have known Richard Lloyd's obscure poem about the Nine Worthies which is parodied in its final act. The links with *Hamlet* and *Midsummer Night's Dream* are not as strong, but highly suggestive. *Merry Wives* deals with festivities associated with Windsor and the Knights of the Garter, which are particularly relevant to Derby, installed KG in May 1601. Of *Measure for Measure* one can perhaps say no more than that Stanley was in Paris when the real-life events which colored the play were actually happening; it may be that other people were there and reported their recollections to some other playwright. Nevertheless, Stanley stands out as someone with the special knowledge that informs all these plays.

We next look into various miscellaneous items of evidence, each of which tends to point towards the destination to which our journey was directed from the very beginning.

28. Pointers to Stanley

There are a number of items in the documentary record not so far discussed which either point to Stanley, or are at least clearly consistent with his authorship of the canon. I shall look at them in no particular order.

Place-Names

Most of the places mentioned in the plays are easy to identify, but some are obscure—Wincot, Burton Heath, Cotsall.[1] Orthodox biographers claim to locate these close to Stratford-upon-Avon, but A. J. Pointon[2] has recently shown that all three are located on Watling Street, the ancient highway that links North Wales to Canterbury in Kent. It is significant that Watling Street would have been the route that the Stanleys would have taken to get to London. They would pick it up somewhere near Shrewsbury, and then travel through Cotsall (now spelled Codsall), Sutton Coldfield, Wincot (now spelled Wilnecote but still pronounced Wincot), Tamworth, Hinckley, Stony Stratford, Burton Heath (actually Barton-on-the-Heath), Dunsmere Heath, St. Albans and thence to London; all these places are mentioned in the plays. Derby would have traveled via Watling Street many times to and from Lancashire.

Thomas Edwards's L'Envoy

"L'Envoy" appended to Thomas Edwards's 1595 poem *Cephalus and Procris. Narcissus* has already been mentioned (Chapter 4) in connection with uncertainty over the authorship of *Venus and Adonis*.[3] It consists of 15 six-line stanzas which refer to each of six poets by a name taken from one of their best-known poems. Shakespeare is alluded to as "Adon," short for "Adonis," in this stanza:

> *Adon* deftly masking through
> Stately tropes rich conceited
> Showed he well deserved to,
>   Loves delight on him to gaze,
> And had not love her selfe intreated,
>   Other nymphs had sent him bays.

The next stanza portrays him

Eke in purple robes distained
Amidst the Centre of this clime
I have heard say doth remaine,
 One whose power floweth far,
That should have been of our rime,
 The onely object and the star.

The word "masking" perhaps indicates a pen name, as already suggested, and "purple robes" and "one whose power floweth far" suggest someone of noble birth and a wealthy landowner (if he was "the star," had he already proved himself a "star of poets"?). Charlotte Carmichael Stopes[4] thought that "the Centre of this clime" referred to Liverpool and its environs, and opted for Ferdinando Stanley, Fifth Earl of Derby, as the poet hinted at; the poem had been entered on the Stationers' Register in October 1593, which was the month after Ferdinando inherited the earldom. But by 1595 William had inherited the earldom in turn, and it is just as likely that Edwards was covertly indicating that William Stanley was the poet behind the mask William Shakespeare; the second stanza above may have been added to the poem after William became earl in 1594, between the date of the Register entry and the publication date. However, there is no way of knowing which of the brothers Edwards had in mind; after all, Ferdinando was known to his contemporaries as a fine poet. It so happens that Ferdinando and William spent some of their childhood years in Meriden Manor, a property of their father's, and William is thought to have occasionally used the manor as a retreat later in life.[5] Meriden, in the Warwickshire Forest of Arden, is traditionally known as "the centre of England."[6]

The Dedications to Venus and Adonis *and* Lucrece

The first words of Shakespeare that any reader in the 1590s would have read would have been the dedication to Henry Wriothesley, Third Earl of Southampton and Baron Titchfield, prefaced to *Venus and Adonis*, published in 1593.

> *RIght Honourable, I know not how I shall offend in dedicating my vnpolisht lines to your Lordship, nor how the worlde vvill censure mee for choosing so strong a proppe to support so vveake a burthen, onelye if your Honour seeme but pleased, I account my selfe highly praised, and vowe to take aduantage of all idle houres, till I haue honoured you vvith some grauer labour. But if the first heire of my inuention proue deformed, I shall be sorie it had so noble a god-father: and neuer after eare so barren a land, for feare it yeeld me still so bad a haruest, I leaue it to your Honourable suruey, and your Honor to your hearts content, vvhich I wish may alvvaies ansvvere your ovvne vvish, and the vvorlds hopefull expectation.*
>
> Your Honors in all dutie,
> William Shakespeare.

The tone is deferential and dignified. One has a distinct sense of someone of lower status addressing someone of superior status. The dedication prefaced to *Lucrece* the following year is markedly different.

> THE loue I dedicate to your Lordship is without end; whereof this Pamphlet without beginning is but a superfluous Moity. The warrant I haue of your Honourable disposition, not the worth of my vntutored Lines makes it assured of acceptance. VVhat I haue done is yours, what I haue

> to doe is yours, being part in all I haue, deuoted yours. VVere my worth greater, my duety would shew greater, meane time, as it is, it is bound to your Lordship; To whom I wish long life, still lengthned with all happinesse.
>
> Your Lordships in all duety,
> William Shakespeare.

Many people have commented on the much greater warmth and self-confidence displayed by the later dedication. The poet seems not only to have gained in assurance but also gained in status. In *V&A* he dedicates his lines; in *Lucrece* he dedicates his love. Something momentous has happened to change the relationship between the two men.

When *Venus and Adonis* was published in 1593, Stanley was a commoner, a younger son (granted, a son of an earl), and although he and Southampton were both studying law at the Inns of Court the social difference between them was immense. They may have been friends, but the niceties of deference had to be observed, at least in print. But when it came to the publication of *Lucrece*, entered in the Stationers' Register on 9 May 1594, Stanley had been Sixth Earl of Derby for three weeks, and was now of equal status with Southampton. There is also perhaps a hint of the exaggerated affection later to be exhibited in some of the sonnets, several of which had probably already been written.

Francis Beaumont's The Woman Hater

Beaumont, in his play *The Woman Hater*, written for the Children of Paul's acting troupe sometime before 1606, mocked Shakspere (the Stratford man) in a speech in Act 1, scene 3 as "another pair of legs," according to Andrew Gurr[7]:

> And you shall see many legs too; [*cut*] another pair you shall see, that were heir-apparent legs to a glover, these legs hope shortly to be honourable, when they pass by they will bow, and the mouth to these legs will seem to offer you some Courtship; it will swear but it will lye, hear it not.

"Legs" seems (in this context) to refer to a courtier; to "make legs" was to make an elaborate bow involving drawing back one leg and bending the other, while doffing one's hat in a sweeping gesture (only seen nowadays in pantomimes, I would guess). Shakspere's father had died in September 1601, his trade was that of glover, and that the passage refers to Shakspere seems plausible, especially as he was now officially a "Groom of the Chamber" (along with a hundred or more others); we may perhaps choose to overlook the implication of mendacity. The excised text reads:

> amongst the rest you shall behold one pair, the feet of which were in times past sockless, but are now, through the change of time (that alters all things) very strangely become the legs of a Knight and a Courtier[.]

William Stanley became the Sixth Earl of Derby (with subsidiary title Lord Strange) through the sudden death of his elder brother Ferdinando, the Fifth Earl, the previous Lord Strange. He was appointed Knight of the Garter in April 1601, and these events may have motivated the use of the words "alters," "strange," "Knight" and "Courtier" in this passage; "sockless" maybe implies that he was not a professional actor (or that he never took comedy roles, with perhaps an implication that in his youth he had acted on the stage, whether private or public). If Beaumont had Derby in mind—he was "heir-apparent" to the throne up until James succeeded, which may have prompted the curiously inappropriate use of this term for the Stratford man in this passage—then, as Julia Cleave[8] has surmised, he may here be dropping a subtle hint that the Stratford man had already been assigned the role that was later to be thrust upon him.

"My Name Is Will*"*

In the last line of sonnet 136 the poet writes, "And then thou lovest me for my name is *Will*." For the orthodox, this is simply an abbreviation of the name "William." But it so happens that William Stanley, Lord Derby, always signed himself "Will: Derby," never William.

Sonnets 135, 136 and 143 all make use of the author's name, as the following excerpts show (italics in original):

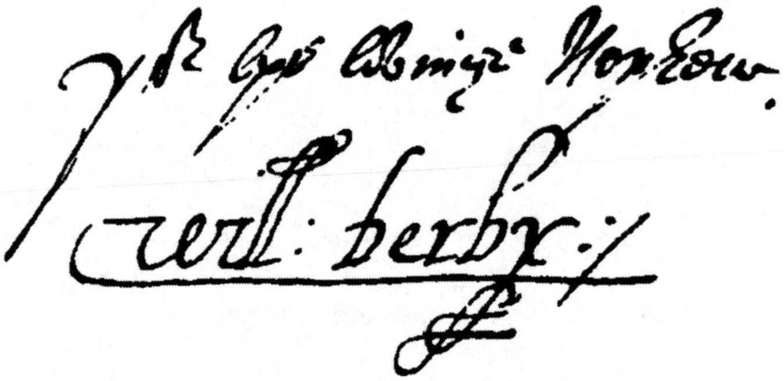

Figure 28.1 "Yo[u]r l[ordshi]p's lovinge Nephew Will: Derby:/"

Who ever hath her wish, thou hast thy *Will*, [#135.1–2
And *Will* do boote, and *Will* in overplus,

If thy soule check thee that I come so neere, [#136.1–2
Sweare to thy blind soule that I was thy *Will*,

So will I pray that thou maist have thy *Will*, [#143.13–14
If thou turn back and my loude crying still.

The word "Will" occurs nine times in these sonnets. Commentators make much of the ambiguity occasioned by a secondary use of the word on occasion to mean genitalia. But the primary sense of the word in these sonnets (leaving aside Shakespeare's bawdy tendencies) is that of the poet's name, Will.

John Marston's Histrio-Mastix

In *Histrio-mastix*, published in 1610 and probably by John Marston,[9] occurs a scene headed "Enter Troilus and Cressida."

Troilus Come Cressida, my cresset light, [lantern
Thy face doth shine both day and night,
Behold, Behold thy garter blue
[*line missing*]
Thy Knight his Valiant elboe wears,
That When he Shakes his furious Speare
The foe in shivering fearfull sort
May lie him down in death to snort.

This passage, with "Shakes" and "Spear" both capitalized, apparently associates Shakespeare with Troilus, a deceived husband, and with the blue garter as worn by the Knights of the Garter. Only Derby among authorship candidates was a Knight of the Garter, and his wife's alleged infidelity (recalling Cressida in Shakespeare's play) would have been known to Marston, not backward when it came to mocking jibes. Marston was associated with Derby (and Thomas Middleton) in the revival of the Children of Paul's acting company, but perhaps they had fallen out.

John Davies of Hereford's Epigram on "Will: Shake-speare"

John Davies of Hereford's 1610 epigram with the heading *To Our English Terence, Mr. Will: Shake-speare* [*sic*][10] applies well to Derby; the two men knew each other, since at one time his patron was Derby's father and he may have been Derby's writing master. Notice that "Will": has a colon, exactly as Derby always signed his name (see above). The poem begins:

Some say good *Will* (which I in sport do sing)
Had'st thou not plaid some Kingly parts in sport
Thou had'st bin a companion for a *King* [might have been
And beene a King among the meaner sort.

The hyphenated name is thought by authorship doubters to indicate a made-up name, that is a pseudonym, and as Terence in classical Roman times was accused of taking credit for the plays of aristocrats, there is an implication that Shakespeare's plays were also written by an aristocrat. Terence's reputation was familiar to Elizabethan authors, and Roger Ascham writes (1570): "It is well known by good record of learning, and that by Cicero's own witness, that some Comedies bearing Terence's name were written by worthy Scipio and wise Laelius."[11]

Derby is believed to have taken parts in plays in the family's Lancashire mansions and elsewhere, and Davies is perhaps hinting that he might have been chosen by Queen Elizabeth as her consort but for this.[12] His great-grandmother was Henry VIII's younger sister, and Derby had been heir-apparent to the throne since April 1594; "a King among the meaner sort" may possibly indicate descent through the female ("meaner"—lesser) line. He was in any case hereditary king of the Isle of Man, and this title had recently been restored to him by an Act of Parliament of July 1609, having been removed while his inheritance was in dispute; this event may have prompted Davies's poem. Davies has been identified as the author of *A Lover's Complaint*, printed at the end of *Shake-speare's Sonnets*.[13]

The rest of the epigram is as follows.

Some others rail, but rail as they think fit,
Thou hast no railing, but, a raigning Wit.
And honesty *thou sowest, which they do reap,*
So to increase their Stock, *which they do keep.*

The next sentence of the poem claims "Thou hast ... a raigning wit," and the word "raigning" seems to resonate with Derby's one-time heir-apparent status, and he was still in line for the throne if James and his three children died without issue (a circumstance necessitating the continuation of the deception; he was a king-in-waiting up until Charles I became king). The last sentence may perhaps refer to stationers printing his plays and profiting from them.

John Davies of Hereford's Microcosmos

In an earlier poem of 1603, *Microcosmos*, Davies wrote as follows, apparently referring to Shakespeare.[14]

Players, I love yee, and your *Qualitie*,
As ye are Men, *that* pass time not abus'd:
W. S. R. B. And some I love for *painting, poesie*,
And say fell *Fortune* cannot be excus'd
That hath for better *uses* you refus'd:
Wit, Courage, good shape, good partes, and all *good*,
As long as al these *goods* are no *worse* us'd,
And though the *stage* doth staine pure gentle *bloud*,
Yet generous yee are in *minde* and *moode*

The *Shakespeare Allusion Book* confidently assumes the initials in the margin stand for William Shakespeare (i.e., Shakspere) and Richard Burbage. But while John Raithel agrees that Davies is talking about Shakespeare, he doesn't believe he is talking about Shakspere. He goes on to say:

> Stanley's writing teacher is here referring to William Stanley ("W. S.") and the manager/lead actor of Derby's Men, Robert Browne ("R. B."). Davies' entry is published in 1603, the year that Robert Browne died, having led Derby's Men from approximately 1598–1603. Any doubt about this is removed by the penultimate line:
>
> And though the *stage* doth staine pure gentle *bloud*
>
> Shakspere had no gentle blood, and Stanley did. That the stage stained gentle blood is the whole idea of why he is hidden, referred to, for example, as "W. S." and not by his name. If he was Shakspere, Davies would have simply used his name explicitly, and he would have never mentioned "gentle bloud."

The word "generous" in the last line is also highly inappropriate if applied to Shakspere, since at this period the word meant "of noble or aristocratic lineage" (*Oxford English Dictionary*). This passage seems to be another hint that in his youth Derby had occasionally taken part in stage plays, whether privately or publicly we do not know.

The same initials occur in the margin against another line of poetry, published two years later.

W. S. R. B. Yet some she guerdond not, to their desarts;

John Raithel suggests that this refers to Robert Browne, who had just "dyed very pore," and "If William Stanley was writing the works of Shakespeare, he was certainly not getting his just deserts for it."[15]

"The Phoenix and Turtle"

Shakespeare's poem "The Phoenix and Turtle" was published in 1601 in Robert Chester's *Love's Martyr*,[16] dedicated to Sir John Salusbury, whose wife was Derby's half-sister. His name subscribed to the poem is spelled "Shake-speare," the hyphen perhaps suggesting that the name was known to be a pen name.

John Donne Addresses the "E. of D."

Sometime, probably in the mid–1590s, John Donne wrote the following lines, adopting according to Dennis Flynn "the pose of a poetic neophyte," as if submitting his work "for approval as to a master."[17]

> See, Sir, how as the Suns hot Masculine flame
> Begets strange creatures on Niles durty slime,
> In me, your fatherly yet lusty Ryme
> (For, these songs are their fruits) have wrought the same.

These lines are addressed "To E. of D. with six holy Sonnets," and there has been much speculation about who "E. of D." might have been. Flynn considers that "E. of D." could refer to Ferdinando Stanley as Fifth Earl of Derby, but then goes on to say that the evidence suggests rather that "E. of D." was Ferdinando's brother William. Further evidence for this identification comes from the last two lines of Donne's poem, which read:

> You are that Alchimist which always had
> Wit, whose one spark could make good things of bad.

Flynn goes on to say

> At about the time of Ferdinando's death, George Chapman named "ingenious *Darbie*" along with "deepe searching *Northumberland*, and skill-imbracing *Heire of Hunsdon*" as associates in what has become known as "the School of the Night," a group of students of alchemy and allied disciplines.

The *"Heire of Hunsdon"* was Sir George Carey, married to the sister of Ferdinando's wife, and "*Northumberland*" was the Ninth Earl of Northumberland, whose interest in alchemy is well established. While there is uncertainty about which Earl of Derby Chapman is referring to, Flynn points out that William Stanley's name frequently occurs in the diaries of John Dee, the savant and alchemist, while Ferdinando is nowhere mentioned. To sum up, it seems likely that Donne is addressing his friend William Stanley, whose "fatherly"—he was ten years older than Donne—"yet lusty Ryme" has begotten (by example) Donne's own six poems. The Nile's engendering powers turn up again in *Antony and Cleopatra*.[18]

North's Plutarch

One copy of the translation by Thomas North of Plutarch's *Lives of the Noble Grecians and Romans*, published in 1579, is now owned by the Shakespeare Birthplace Trust.[19] An inscription on the title page records that the book was given to Henry Stanley, Fourth Earl of Derby, by William Chaderton, who became bishop of Chester in 1579; the book then supposedly passed to the Fifth Earl, Ferdinando. A second inscription, also in Latin, later scribbled over and partially obscured, is difficult to make out, but appears to record that the volume was presented by "Alisia Comitessa," Ferdinando's widow, to "Wilhelm[us]" almost certainly her brother-in-law William Stanley. A third inscription "Edw: Stanley 1611" near the bottom right of the page indicates that the book remained in the Stanley family for some years.

Shakespeare based his Roman and Greek plays, including *Antony and Cleopatra*, *Julius Caesar*, *Coriolanus* and *Timon of Athens*, on the stories in this book (at times quoting the wording almost verbatim), and if William was Shakespeare it is likely that this was the copy he used. Edward Stanley was William's first cousin, and we can readily imagine William passing the book on to his cousin in 1611, having no further use for it. The epitaph for Edward on his monument in Tong Church, Shropshire, is thought to have been written by Shakespeare, as described below.

Peacham's Omission

In *The Compleat Gentleman* of 1622 Henry Peacham included a list of the seven greatest deceased poets of the Elizabethan era.[20] Remarkably, he does not include Shakespeare, which suggests that he knew that *the author was still alive*. Recall also Ben Jonson's words in the First Folio of 1623: "Thou art a Monument without a tomb"—no tomb because no corpse. The next words are: "And art alive still ... ," ostensibly referring to his works, but perhaps with a second implication.[21]

The 1632 Second Folio

The text of the Second Folio of 1632 was printed from a marked-up copy of the First Folio, with thousands of amendments and improvements,[22] including correctly printing "u"s and "v"s, which up till then had been used interchangeably in most publications.[23] Several errors were corrected in such a way as to suggest that the original author was at work.[24] For example *Romeo and Juliet*, Act 1, scene 5, 44–46:

F1. O, she doth teach the torches to burn bright!
It seems she hangs upon the cheek of night
Like a rich jewel in an Ethiop's ear

F2. O, she doth teach the torches to burn bright!
Her beauty hangs upon the cheek of night
Like a rich jewel in an Ethiop's ear

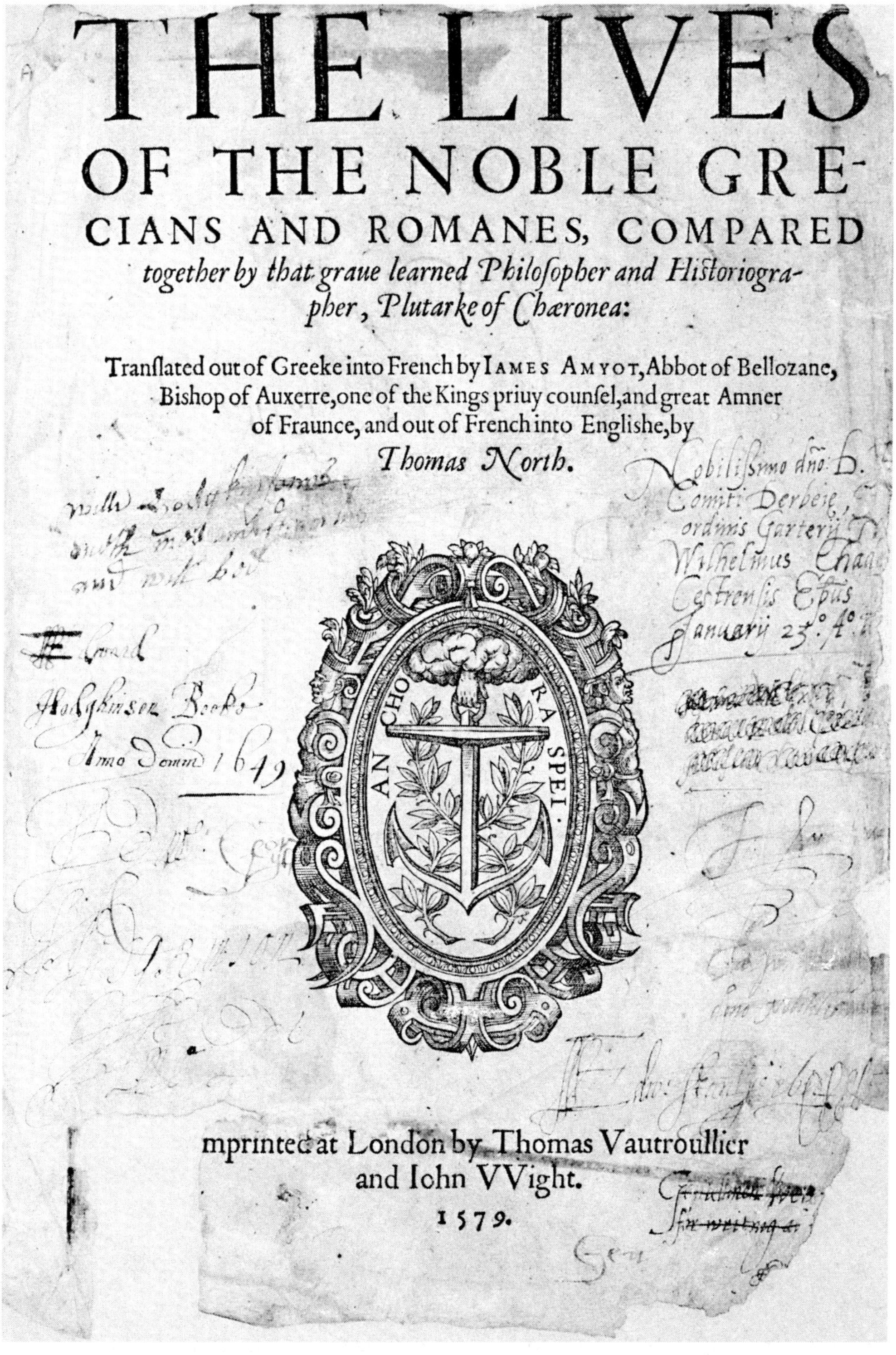
THE LIVES
OF THE NOBLE GRE-
CIANS AND ROMANES, COMPARED
together by that graue learned Philosopher and Historiogra-
pher, Plutarke of Chæronea:
Translated out of Greeke into French by JAMES AMYOT, Abbot of Bellozane,
Bishop of Auxerre, one of the Kings priuy counsel, and great Amner
of Fraunce, and out of French into Englishe, by
Thomas North.
ANCHORA SPEI
mprinted at London by Thomas Vautroullier
and Iohn VVight.
1579.

Figure 28.2 Title page of the copy of *North's Plutarch* once owned by Derby (by permission of Shakespeare Birthplace Trust).

Also *1 Henry VI*, Act 1 scene 4, 95–6:

F1. I will, and like thee,
Play on the Lute, beholding the Townes burne:
F2. I will, and **Nero**-like will
Play on the Lute, beholding the Townes burne.

Also *Henry V*, Act 3, scene 7, 11–12:

F1. What a long night is this! I will not change my
horse with any that treads but on four **postures**.
F2. What a long night is this! I will not change my
horse with any that treads but on four **pasterns**. [hocks instead of hooves

There are many other examples. Paul Werstine estimates that early 20th-century editions of Shakespeare took over some 600 of the improvements found in the Second Folio. More recently, according to Werstine, editors avoid doing so, on the grounds that the Second Folio has "no authorial authority."[25] Looking at the first example above, it seems extraordinary that modern editors should prefer the F1 reading over the F2, which seems (to this untutored ear) so quintessentially Shakespearean. But so it is.

The Second Folio was "sumptuously printed on the best paper available, and provoked from the Puritan William Prynne the complaint that 'Shakespeare's plays are printed on the best crown paper, far better than most Bibles.'"[26] No independent publisher in the whole history of publishing has ever published a second edition on better paper than the first, so this suggests that it was financed by someone wealthy and with a special interest in the plays. Derby's wealth at his death ten years later was "incalculably vast" (*ODNB*).

The Stanley Epitaphs

There are three epitaphs to members of William Stanley's family which have all been ascribed to Shakespeare. In 1633 Sir William Dugdale visited Tong Church in Shropshire and made notes of two inscriptions on a monumental tomb to Sir Thomas Stanley and his son Sir Edward Stanley, adding that they were by William Shakespeare.[27] On one end of the tomb appears the following (these exact transcriptions were made by Helen Moorwood[28]):

ASK WHO LYES HEARE, BVT DO NOT WEEP,
HE IS NOT DEAD, HE DOOTH BVT SLEEP
THIS STONY REGISTER IS FOR HIS BONES
HIS FAME IS MORE PERPETVALL THEN THEISE STONES
AND HIS OWNE GOODNES WT HIM SELF BEING GON
SHALL LYVE WHEN EARTHLIE MONAMENT IS NONE

On the other end:

NOT MONVENTALL STONE PRESERVES OVR FAME
NOR SKY ASPYRING PIRAMIDS OVR NAME,
THE MEMORY OF HIM FOR WHOM THIS STANDS
SHALL OVTLYVE MARBL, AND DEFACERS HANDS

WHEN ALL TO TYMES CONSVMPTION SHALL BE GEAVEN
STANDLY FOR WHOM THIS STANDS SHALL STAND IN HEAVEN

Thomas Stanley, William's uncle and governor of the Isle of Man, died in 1576 and Edward Stanley, William's cousin, in 1632. Helen Moorwood deduces that the tomb may have been erected soon after the death of Margaret, Thomas's wife, in around 1601–1603. The epitaphs may have been added either then or after the death of Edward. Ernst Honigmann floats the possibility that Shakespeare could have been asked to write the epitaphs around 1600, and the one for Edward could have been kept "in storage" until 1632.[29] While the first epitaph above is not particularly distinguished, the second one has a real Shakespearean ring to it.

The third epitaph is on a monument in Chelsea Old Church, London. According to the inscription, the Knight of the Order of Bath, Sir Robert Stanley, who died on January 3 "Anno Domini 1632" (i.e., 1633), is buried under the monument. Sir Robert was the second son of William Stanley. He would have been about 25 years old when he died. Here is the poem.

To say a STANLEY lyes here, that a lone
Were Epitaph enough noe brass noe stone
Noe glorious Tombe, noe monumentall Hearse,
Noe guilded Trophy or lamp labourd Verse
Can dignifie his Graue or sett it forth
Like the Immortal fame of his owne Worth
Then reader fixe not here but quitt this Roome
And flye to Abram's bossome theres his Tombe
There rests his Soule & for his other parts
They are imbalm'd & lodg'd in good mens harts
A brauer monument of Stone or Lyme,
Noe Arte can rayse for this shall out last tyme

Carl Nordling writes as follows about these epitaphs[30]:

> It is obvious that the poems in the two churches cannot have been written by two different authors. The reason for this is that the similarities are so many and so conspicuous. In both cases the buried men are close relatives to the 6th Earl of Derby (William Stanley)—son, uncle and cousin. In both cases one of the buried persons died in 1632(-33). Both epitaphs are written in English on the same metre and with the same rhyme pattern.... We also notice the words *monument* (Chelsea) and *monament* (Tong). Neither epitaph contains any biographical information, not even any Christian name. Instead, the family name, *Stanley*, is included in both.... Both poems contain the concepts of "eternal," "outlive" and "fame." The theme is exactly the same in both cases: The fame and the memory of the deceased shall live much longer than sarcophagi and monuments.

Nordling then goes on to say these poems remind one very much of the following lines in sonnets by Shakespeare.

Not marble, nor the gilded monuments [#55
Of princes, shall outlive this powerful rhyme

Your name from hence immortal life shall have [#81
Though I once gone, to all the world must die;
The earth can yield me but a common grave,
When you entombed in men's eyes shall lie.

To make him much outlive a gilded tomb [#101

And thou in this shalt find thy monument. [#107
When tyrants' crests and tombs of brass are spent.

The wording in the epitaphs can be correlated with lines from the plays, as follows.

Epitaphs:	*Shakespeare:*	
Immortal fame	immortal fame	[H5 III.ii.10
noe brass, noe stone	nor brass, nor stone	[WT I.ii.360
noe glorious tombe	a glorious tomb	[3H6 I.iv.16
noe guilded trophy	... than gilt his trophy	[Cor I.iii.41
quitt this roome	quit the house	[Per III.ii.17
Abram's bossome theres his tombe	... sleep in Abraham's bosom	[R3 IV.iii.38
lodg'd in good mens harts	lodged in my heart	[LLL II.i.174
this shall out last tyme	outlive the age	[Per V.i.14

A good case can be made for the view that the three epitaphs were all written by William Stanley in 1632 or 1633 to commemorate three close relatives, his uncle, his cousin, and his second son. That their wording has strong Shakespearean echoes helps to support the case for him as their author, or at the least is not inconsistent with it.

These somewhat miscellaneous items might be regarded as collateral evidence supporting Derby's authorship of the canon. It seems worth pointing out in particular that item 4, the extract from Francis Beaumont's *Woman Hater*, is the only place where a (supposed) reference to the Stratford man is juxtaposed to a (supposed) reference to Derby. If these references have been correctly interpreted we might be excused for wondering what Beaumont had in mind. Was he perhaps hinting that the actor was allowing people to think he was the author with a similar name (whose identity Beaumont would surely have known)? Alternatively, as suggested by Julia Cleave (see above), it may be that he had wind of a plan to offload the authorship onto the Stratford man in due course. His play was put on by the Paul's Boys acting troupe which had been revived by Derby in 1599 (see Chapter 24), and it is likely the two men knew each other. On the other hand, we may be straying too far from the path of our journey, and should perhaps stick to the main highway and avoid such entertaining digressions.

We next look at some of the surviving letters of Derby, to see whether his writing is consistent with the wording found in the plays.

29. Derby's Letters

For all that William Stanley was described as a "copious carminist" and (supposedly) bracketed with three poets and playwrights (as described in Chapter 7), no poems or plays with his name attached to them have come to light, nothing was ever printed over his name, and all that survives of his handwriting are some fifty letters written after he inherited the earldom. They are mostly short and deal with the administration of his estate and with duties arising from the offices he held under the Crown. Nevertheless enough material exists to enable his writing and spelling habits to be analyzed, so that they can be compared with what can be deduced about Shakespeare's writing and spelling habits, in so far as these can be extracted from the printed texts. To begin with we look at Shakespeare's idiosyncrasies, and then see how many (if any) can be found in Derby's letters.

Shakespeare's Writing Idiosyncrasies

Legibility

Ernst Honigmann has made a detailed study of Shakespeare's handwriting, presented in his analysis of *Othello*,[1] and he frequently remarks how copyists or compositors made many errors in trying to read the text in front of them. He writes, "Graphically related variants are so numerous that misreading must account for most if not all of them." He goes on to quote J. Dover Wilson,

> ... minim letters, ie letters formed of more or less straight strokes, are m, n, u, i, c, r, w; and the large number of compositor's errors in words containing such letters prove that he [Shakespeare] must have been more than ordinarily careless in the formation of them, that he did not properly distinguish between the convex and concave forms, and that he often kept no count of his strokes, especially when writing two or more minim-letters in combination.[2]

Honigmann continues by enumerating 17 different classes of misreading errors commonly committed by compositors, occupying three pages of his text, as for example "for" for "forth," or "with" for "which" and vice versa. Later he writes:

> ... one is driven to the conclusion that Shakespeare, when he wrote at speed, did not form every letter clearly—indeed scrawled, rather than wrote, and not infrequently left word endings as one or more illegible pen strokes.[3]

It is evident that Shakespeare's penmanship was difficult to read and that many individual letters were imperfectly formed.

"Their" for "Thy"

In the sonnets of 1609 there are fifteen instances where the word "their" has been set into type when the word "thy" was clearly the word the poet intended. Here are a few examples.[4]

To show me worthy of *their* [thy] sweet respect [#26.12
Excusing *their* [thy] sins more than *their* [thy] sins are [#35.8
Intitled in *their* [thy] parts, do crowned sit [#37.7
As thus, mine eyes due is *their* [thy] outward part [#46.13
And my heart's right, *their* [thy] inward love of heart [#46.14

The remaining examples are to be found in #27.10, #31.8, #43.11, #45.12, #46.3, #46.8, #69.5, #70.6, #128.11 and #128.14. It has been suggested that the explanation for these peculiarities is that the writer (assumed to be the poet) used an abbreviation for "thy" which was misread as an abbreviation for "their." The following is an extract from an article (unsigned) published in 1931.[5]

> Now there is a very rare abbreviation for thy, namely y^{y}, and a fairly common abbreviation for their, namely y^{r}, and unless the former was made very distinctly, it would almost invariably be misread as the latter. And it is very difficult to see how else the confusion could come about.

Here the "y" in "y^{y}" and "y^{r}" is the Elizabethan form of the old English letter "þ" called "thorn" and sounding "th"; this was written identically with "y" by writers at the time. It can still be found today in phrases such as "Ye Olde Curiositie Shoppe" and so on (this should be pronounced "The," but is often pronounced "Ye," either jokily or from ignorance). If this was characteristic of the poet then it is easy to see how confusion could have occurred, though one might be surprised at how often the compositor failed to try to make sense of what he was putting into type.

Spelling Habits

Ernst Honigmann has summarized Shakespeare's characteristic spelling habits in his analysis of *Othello*, with examples from many other plays. His assumption is that several of the plays were set into print (the "good quartos") from texts in Shakespeare's own handwriting (or if the copytext had been written out by someone else, then at least some of his characteristic spellings would have been reproduced precisely).[6] Leaving aside for the moment Shakespeare's spelling of individual words, Honigmann gives the following as habitual traits.

(a) Use of "y" for modern "i," e.g., ayme, ayre, choyce, dye, flye, lye, etc.
(b) Use of "-oo-" for "-o-," e.g., approoue, (a)boord, moouing, prooue.
(c) Doubling of consonants, e.g., abhorre, Citadell, Citty, comming, parallell.
(d) Initial "in-" for "en-," e.g., inchanted, indured, infetter"d, inforce, ingender"d.
(e) Final "-full" for "-ful," e.g., faithfull, fearfull, lawfull, lustfull, pitifull, powerfull.

In addition to these, Eric Sams has noticed a preference for final "-ll" over "-l," whether in words ending in "-ful" or otherwise, and also for final "-ie" over "-y." He finds that Shakespeare often added "u" to "a," e.g., in a word such as "graunt," and "c" to "nk," e.g., "thanck," and frequently employed terminal "-nes" for "-ness" or "-nesse."[7]

Spelling of Individual Words

There are a number of words in the canon with odd spellings which Honigmann calls "Shakespearian," in the sense that they occur several times in different plays and poems. Here is a list of the ones that were used most often.[8] A full list of all the words is given in the annex to this chapter.

> beleeue, Citty, Countrey, Kitchin, lowd, mistris, peece, pitty, prooue, shew(es), Souldier, tearme, vertue.

Derby's Letters

We now reproduce some of Derby's letters and observe how many of Shakespeare's oddities turn up in them.

Letter from October 1607

The following is a transcription of a letter written to his uncle, Robert Cecil, Secretary of State and by now Lord Salisbury, dated the last of October 1607.[9]

> My very good Lo:[rd] I understand by this berer, M^{r}
> Gamull Recorder of ye Cytty of Chester, that
> he entendeth to become an humble petic[i]oner to
> his Ma[jes]^{tie} aswell on the behalf of him self as
> of ye said Cytty, and lykewise to preferr a
> petic[i]on to ye l[or]ds of ye Councell for ye hearinge
> of a Cawse before yo[u]^{r} l[ordshi]ps touchinge a stone
> wall or Cawsey erected uppon ye ryver of Dee
> nere to ye said Cytty, And forsomuch as he is
> one who hath geven good testimony of his love[10]
> towardes me I Could do no less then at his request
> make bold to Commend hym to yo[u]^{r} l[ordshi]ps
> ho[noura]^{ble} Considerac[i]on And this beinge all his request
> to me at this tyme I humbly Commend me to yo[u]^{r}
> l[ordshi]p: and so take my leave. Knowsley ye last
> of Octob[e]r 1607
> Yo[u]^{r} l[ordshi]ps lovinge Nephew
> and assured frend
> Will: Derby: /

It is apparent that Derby regularly used a number of abbreviations, in particular "y^{e}" for "the" (eight times in this letter). He might well therefore have written "y^{y}" and "y^{r}" for "thy" and "their," as discussed above, although no example of either of these has come to light so far. The large number of "y"s in place of modern "i"s accords with Shakespeare's habitual trait (a), and the doubled consonants in Cytty, preferr, Councell, uppon, accord with trait (c). A feature of Derby's handwriting is that initial lowercase "c"s are written somewhat larger than other lowercase letters, so that it is often difficult to know whether or not he intended them to be read as capitals. For example, in the letter above the capital "C" of

"Could" must surely have been meant to be read as lowercase, and probably also those of "Commend" and "Consideracon," and perhaps those of "Cawse" and "Cawsey" as well (the capital "C" of "Cytty" may be an acknowledgment of its importance). We shall return to this feature later on.

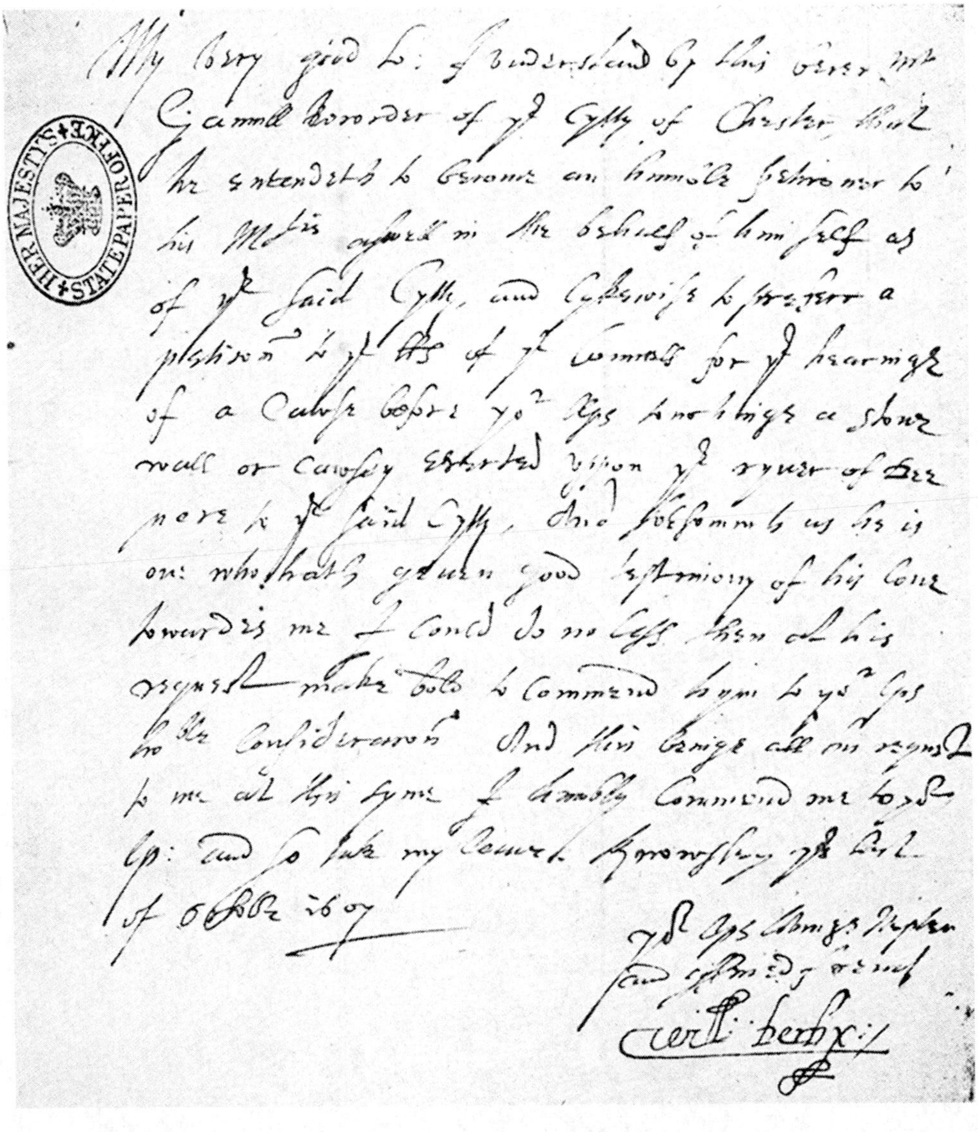
My verry good Lo: I understand by this berer mr Gamull Recorder of ye Cytty of Chester that he entendeth to become an humble petitioner to his Matis aswell in the behalf of himself as of ye said Cytty, and lykewise to prefer a petition to yor LLs of ye Counsell for ye hearinge of a Cawse before yor Lps touchinge a stone wall or Cawsey erected vpon ye ryuer of Dee nere to ye said Cytty. And forsomuch as he is on: who hath gyuen good testimony of his love towardes me I could do no less then at his request make bold to Commend hym to yor Lps honble Consideracon And this beinge all my request to me at this tyme I humbly Commend me to yor Lp: and so take my leave [illegible] of October 1607

Yor Lps [illegible]
[illegible]
Will: Derby

Figure 29.1 Derby's letter to Lord Salisbury, 31 October 1607, copyright © The National Archives, CSP-Dom.

Letter from December 1605

Here is another letter dated 16 December 1605, also addressed to Robert Cecil.[11]

> My verie good Lo:[rd] I am loath to troble yo[u]^{r} l[ordshi]p w[i]th many
> Lynes in theis troblesome tymes, but synce I am inforced

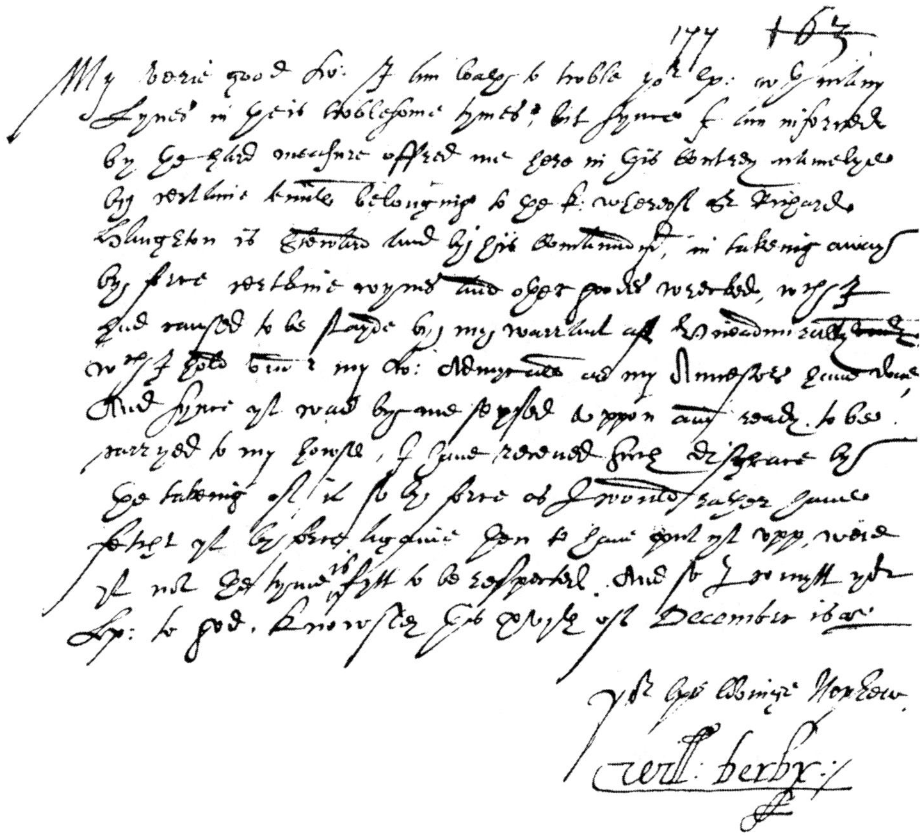

Figure 29.2a Derby's letter to Lord Salisbury, 16 December 1605, copyright © The British Library Board, BL Add. MS 12506, f. 207.

by the hard measure offred me here in this Contrey namelye
by certain ten[a]ňtes belonging to the k:[ing] whereof S[i]r Richard
Haughton is Steward and by his Comaundm[e]ňt in takeing away
by force certain wynes and other goods wrecked, w[hi]ch I
had caused to be stayde by my warrant of viceadmiralty
w[hi]ch I hold und[e]r my Lo:[rd] Admyrall as my Ancestors have done,
And synce yt was by me seysed uppon and ready to bee
carryed to my howse I have receved such disgrace by
the takeing of it so by force as I would rather have
fetcht yt by force againe then to have put yt upp, were
it not the tyme is fytt to be respected, And so I comytt yo[u]r
L[ordshi]p to god. Knowsley this xvjth of December 1605
Yo[u]r l[ordshi]ps lovinge Nephew
Will: Derby:/

The letter has a postscript offset to the left-hand side.

My lo:[rd] I pray yo[u]r l[ordshi]p move my lo:[rd]
Admyrall that I may know his l[ordshi]ps
pleasure herein, for I wrot post

to his l[ordshi]p vppon y^{e} first notice of y^{e}
wrack, and had not my care ben the
greater all o[u]^{r} ten[a]n̆tes and frendes on both
sides had byn at Jarre, er this.

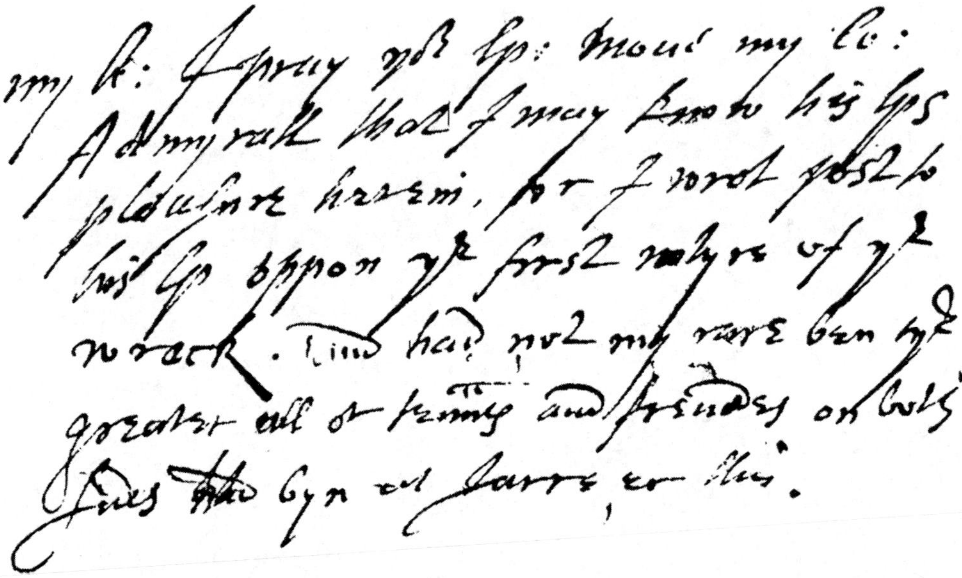

Figure 29.2b Postscript to Derby's letter to Lord Salisbury, 16 December 1605, copyright © The British Library Board, BL Add. MS 12506, f. 207.

Here again there are a number of abbreviations and a large number of "y"s instead of modern "i"s, habitual trait above. There are doubled consonants in Admyrall, upp, fytt, comytt, as in trait (c), and "inforced" replaces "enforced" in accord with (d). And both "Contrey" and "Commaundm[en]t" exhibit the large initial lower-case "c"s, which are such a feature of Derby's handwriting.

Commentary

I have drawn attention to the oversized initial "c"s in both letters because in several of the sonnets words are also spelled with a capital "C" for no discernible reason, for example:

Vttring bare truth, euen so as foes Commend. [#69.4
For Canker vice the sweetest buds doth loue, [#70.7
Reserue their Character with goulden quill, [#85.3
When in the Chronicle of wasted time, [#106.1

It seems likely that in these lines the compositor mistook what was intended to be a lower-case "c" for a capital; elsewhere in the sonnets "character" is spelled with a small "c" (twice) and so also is "canker" (three times). While nouns are occasionally capitalized if they have some special significance, the capital "C" of the verb "Commend" is unique (see the first letter above, where it occurs twice). It is noteworthy also that in the quarto of *Love's Labour's Lost* there are some 20 words with unnecessary capital "C"s, in that of *Merchant of Venice* about 7, in *Midsummer Night's Dream* about 6, in *Richard II* about 7, in *Richard III* about 5, in *1 Henry IV* about 15, in *Othello* about 30 and in *Troilus and Cressida* around 15; these are all "good" first quartos, thought by all commentators to have been printed directly from Shakespeare's manuscripts.

Another feature observable in both letters is the use of a colon to signify an abbreviation, e.g., "Lo:" for Lord and "k:" for King; it is also found in the abbreviated form "Will:" of his signature. The same use of colons with abbreviations occurs in the spoken text (not speech headings) of some of the quartos, e.g., "Lo:" 12 times in *Richard II*, II.iii.30, 31, 37, 41, 76 (twice), III.ii.33, 63, 64, 67, III.iii.101, 131; twice in *1 Henry IV*, I.iii.289, IV.iv.30; in *Richard III*, around 50 times in the first three Acts; "L:" is used for Lord in *Hamlet Q1*, III.ii.109. In addition the abbreviation "Ric:" for Richard occurs in the text of *Richard II*, III.ii.60. These line references are to the equivalent lines in the Folio (Riverside edition). It is worth adding that all the speech prefixes in *Romeo and Juliet*, Q1, are abbreviated using colons, but it is impossible to know whether these colons were present in the compositor's copy or were his own personal preference.

Honigmann makes an important point about the words he regards as particularly "Shakespearian."[12]

> Even though several of the "Shakespearian" spellings listed above were not uncommon, the stock of spellings shared by Q *Othello* with other Shakespeare texts (notably with *Hamlet* Q2) cannot be ascribed to sheer coincidence. To put it another way: a decided preference for *shew* (instead of *show*), or for *vertue* (instead of *virtue*), or for *sence* (instead of *sense*), was not unusual, taking each word individually. But how many other writers shared Shakespeare's preference for *shew* and *vertue* and *sence* and all the other strong or occasional preferences listed above?

Honigmann is making a strong case for *Othello* Q having been printed from Shakespeare's manuscript ("foul papers"), since it exhibits the same spelling preferences found in other Shakespeare quartos. Inadvertently he is also making a strong case for identifying someone with the same spelling preferences as the real author of Shakespeare's works. The similarity between Derby's writing habits and Shakespeare's is astonishing and truly remarkable. It is the last of the building blocks which form the edifice which supports the contention expressed in the title of this book, and one of the most compelling.

Annex

The following is a list of all the words in *Othello* with odd spellings which Honigmann regards as "Shakespearian," since they are found in three or more other plays. Those marked with an asterisk are those which occur most frequently.

> accumilate (4 times), affoordeth, ake, approoued, atchieu'd, attone (attonement), battaile, Battell, be(a)stiall, beleeue*, boord (aboord), boulster, cald (= called), catieffe (= caitiff) [Catiffe, 14 times elsewhere], cease (= seize), Cittadell (7 times), Citty*, clime (= climb), Coffe, coming, controule, coppied, Countrey*, Crocadile (5 times), dam (= damn), demy (= demi), desteny, Deuesting (3 times), deuided, ecchoes, Epithites (6 times), extacy [extac(s)ie elsewhere], extreame, eyd (= eyed), (vn)fould, ghesse (= guess), grones, groser (= grosser), herraldry, Honny, humaine, hye (= high) ['hie' is more common], Iland(ers), Intirely, Isebrookes (= ice brooks), ise [Isacles, ysicles, Isyckles], Kitchin*, Lethergie(s) (7 times), lyer (= liar), lowd*, Lyon, mandat, mannage, mary (=

marry, exclamatory), meerly, merrits, mistris*, moouing, musique, musition, peece* (= piece), Physition, pitty*, politique, prooue*, prophane, Qu. (= cue), rellish, roule (= roll), rore, sayd, sed (= said), sence (= sense), shew(es)*, sillable, Souldier*, stroake, subborn'd/ed (14 times), suddain, Sy/ibell (= sibyl), sy/ien(s) (= scion), tearme*, tirran(o)us, vertue*, Warriour, Wensday.

Honigmann takes these words from the earliest "good" texts of the following plays, which he regards as having been printed from Shakespeare's manuscript, or something very close to it.

1H4, 2H4, 3H6, AC, AW, CE, Cor, Ham, H5, JC, LLL, Luc, MA, Mac, MND, MV, RJ, Oth, R2, R3(F), Son, STM, TA, TC, Tim, Tit, TS, VA, WT

Two of these words appear in the two Derby letters reproduced above, i.e., "Cytty" and "Contrey." While they are not spelled identically as shown there, i.e., "Citty" and "Countrey," they do share peculiarities in each case, a capital "C" and "tt," for "Cytty," and a capital "C" and "-ey" for "Contrey." Furthermore the double "l" spelling of "Admyrall" is also to be found in *Henry VI part 3*, III.iii.252, *Richard III*, IV.iv.437, *Henry V*, IV.viii.92 and *Edward III*, III.i.73,148,149. Notice also that half the words starting with "c" were regularly spelled by compositors with a capital "C," such capitalization being so distinctive a feature of Derby's handwriting.

Conclusion

It is now time to review the evidence presented in the preceding chapters and come to some kind of conclusion. Put simply, we have eliminated the actor from Stratford-upon-Avon, and in his place found a man of good family, well educated, who traveled on the Continent for several years, studied law, mixed with poets and playwrights, and was in the right place at the right time to have written the works of Shakespeare. But did he do so? In 1599 he was recorded as "busied only in penning comedies for the common players." Were these the plays we now know as William Shakespeare's, or were they other plays now lost or misattributed?

We found at the beginning of our investigation that Derby was in line to hold the canopy over King James at his coronation anointing in 1603, making him the authorship candidate most likely to have written sonnet 125 ("Wer't ought to me I bore the canopy?"); no other candidate so far proposed was likely to bear the canopy on any occasion. Two years earlier he had been appointed a Knight of the Garter, which (as it happened) rendered him eligible for that role—the Queen had "graced [*Shakespeare's*] desert," wrote Henry Chettle shortly after her death, and membership of the Order of the Garter was the highest honor she could bestow. These were the first two pointers towards Derby as Shakespeare.

In the following chapters we deduced that Spenser's "gentle Willy," who had written several plays by 1592, was also called by him "Aetion," man of the eagle, almost certainly a reference to the Derby crest of an eagle and child. We found that Nashe's "gentle M. William Apis lapis" (lazy bee) can be identified with Spenser's "gentle Willy" (honey-flowing and resting in idle cell), and that Nashe regarded him as a friend—and then proceeded to insult him viciously, revealing among other libels that he was a heavy drinker (a trait not altogether unknown among the writing fraternity). His portrait of William (portrait of Shakespeare?) is given in Appendix B. We also noted that Gabriel Harvey bracketed "M. Apis Lapis" with three poets who also wrote plays, Greene, Marlowe and Chettle. There can be little doubt that these Williams, all styled "gentle" (well-born), are William Stanley, still at this time a commoner with no expectations and few responsibilities. But since his elder brother was likely to succeed Queen Elizabeth, as a great-great-grandson of Henry VII, one of those responsibilities would have been to refrain from publishing poems and plays under his own name; it was essential to use a pseudonym to avoid bringing disparagement on to the family name, so close to the throne.

The gross exaggerations and outright fictions with which Shakespeare invested the Stanley ancestors in two of the *Henry VI* plays and in *Richard III* (three of the earliest plays, the last written before 1592 and printed in 1597) might well have been perpetrated by

William Stanley, in order to play up the notion that the Tudors owed the success of their campaign against Richard III to those ancestors; perhaps this was done partly in order to mollify his family who appear to have disapproved of him—why, we do not know, but it may well have been because of his play-writing activities. We have also found reasons for supposing that several of the plays were revised and lengthened in the years leading up to 1623, when the First Folio was printed, indicating that the poet was alive at that date. Furthermore, some of the many revisions found in the Second Folio of 1632 are such as might well have been made by the author himself.

We next embarked on an analysis of the sonnets, which have intrigued and baffled so many commentators down the years. The Fair Youth was identified beyond reasonable doubt as Henry Wriothesley, Third Earl of Southampton, whom the poet regarded as "royal" in some sense. Investigation of his early life showed that his contemporaries also accorded him the kind of respect and adulation which might be considered appropriate to someone of royal blood.

The urgency with which the poet begs Southampton to have a son can be explained on the view that a potential heir with a son would be far more acceptable as a successor to the Queen than a potential heir who had no son, such as William Stanley, who reveals himself in several of the sonnets—if he was their author—as someone both unwilling and unsuited to occupying such a position; he had become heir-apparent to the throne on the death of his brother in 1594. The likelihood of the Queen's nominating Southampton as her heir (if he was her son) was remote (*very* remote), but had a precedent in the form of the illegitimate Henry Fitzroy ("son of the king"), created Duke of Richmond, who was about to be named his heir by Henry VIII when he fell ill and died. It seems possible that some courtiers at least would have been happy had she followed this example, though we cannot know whether the populace would have accepted him. I must again stress that the whole of this particular detour away from the main path of our journey is highly speculative. Nevertheless, the fact remains that the key to the truth or otherwise of Southampton's royalty lies encased in lead in the vault underneath a Hampshire parish church.[1]

So far we have outlined a plausible narrative of William Stanley's life. Brought up in the household of one of the very richest earls in the country, entertained from childhood by visiting players and by his father's own troupe, we can imagine him as a young boy following the players around and absorbing unconsciously all the tricks of the trade that make a play successful. Educated at St. John's College Oxford from age 12 to 15 or 16, at a time when the students of his college frequently put on plays, he later embarks on a lengthy continental tour (although we know very little of his itinerary). He is then mentioned as writing poetry and plays and mixing with other poets and playwrights. His friendship with Dr. John Dee would have given him access to his library, the largest in the country, where he would have found many of the books which are drawn upon in the plays. But nothing we have outlined so far comes anywhere close to identifying him with Shakespeare. The most we can say at this point is that we have found nothing that might rule him out.

The first hard evidence that serves to identify Derby with Shakespeare is the acrostic "Stenley" or "St(e)anley" defined by the final letters of seven of the actors' names printed in a list in the First Folio. One of these letters, "t," was tacked on to the end of the name William Kemp to give "Kempt," the only occurrence of his name spelled in this way; this pretty much proves that the acrostic was no accident of chance but deliberately contrived to record his name—it is a neat touch, to have the players' names spell out the name of the playwright. As we have seen, several of the plays can be directly linked with Derby, notably *Love's Labour's Lost*, with its parody of lines from his tutor Richard Lloyd's obscure poem on the Nine Worthies, and *Midsummer Night's Dream*, drawing on plays written for the Chester festivals attended by Derby in his youth and probably later in life as well. On a personal level, his rage and fury on hearing rumors of his newly married wife's infidelity may have found catharsis in the writing of *Othello*. In addition, he financed the revival of the Paul's Children acting troupe "to his great pains and charge" in 1599, and also supported his own company's residence at the Boar's Head Theatre in Aldgate. This company, Derby's Men, was summoned to perform two plays at Court for each of the Christmas festivities of 1599 and 1600 (though the names of the plays were not recorded). No other member of the upper classes was so involved in everything theatrical. Various other pieces of evidence also point more or less directly to Derby, or at least are consistent with his authorship of the canon. Lastly we found that the handwriting of Derby's letters bears a striking resemblance to what has been deduced about Shakespeare's handwriting, a remarkable discovery.

There rests the case for William Stanley. Many hitherto unexplained circumstances surrounding the Shakespeare canon find simple explanation with this attribution. Why the obsession with kingship and its problems, as exhibited in the history plays ("*uneasy lies the head that wears a crown*")? Because he and his brother were descended from Henry VII, and his brother was in line to succeed Elizabeth.[2] Why the pseudonym? The closeness of his brother to the throne would have demanded such a ruse to avoid besmirching the family name by linking it with the public theaters, universally regarded as disreputable or worse. Why continue the deception long after the accession of King James? Because if James's three children died young, Derby would have become the next heir as the remaining great-great-grandson of Henry VII; he was a kind of king-in-waiting, and it was unthinkable that his association with players and the theater should become common knowledge (in any event, it seems likely that remaining unidentified had become congenial to him, perhaps even a social and psychological necessity).

Where did he learn the craft of writing plays? Firstly from attending performances at his father's grand mansions and while at Oxford, and secondly by collaborating in the early plays—*Titus Andronicus, Henry VI, Parts 1* and *2, Edward III*—with Peele, Marlowe and Kyd, all experienced playwrights. How to account for the dramatic change in tone from the deference of the dedication to *Venus and Adonis* to the love and lifelong devotion promised in that to *Lucrece?* Because twenty-three days before *Lucrece* was registered in Stationers' Hall, William had inherited the earldom, and was now of equal status with Southampton. By now, 1594, somewhere between ten and twenty of the plays had been written or coauthored, displaying increasing mastery of the art, and with some of the masterpieces already completed—*Richard III, Love's Labour's Lost, Romeo and Juliet*. Why did no one reveal the true name of the man behind the pseudonym? Because by the time the name "Shakespeare" was first attached to a printed play, 1598, Derby had already inherited the earldom and become the prospective heir to Queen Elizabeth, and no one would be foolish enough to offend the next monarch by revealing his secret.[3]

Why was the authorship off-loaded onto the actor and businessman William Shakspere when the First Folio was put together in 1623? The similarity of the names might suggest that Stanley had knowledge of the existence of the Stratford man, perhaps because the actor had joined Lord Strange's Men, his brother's troupe, sometime in the period 1590–93. Stanley might have thought that the longer and more up-market version of the name would suit a poet and playwright, with its nod in the direction of Minerva, who brandished a spear and was the Roman goddess of poetry and theater. The idea of casting the actor as the writer would probably never have arisen if Stanley had not unexpectedly inherited the earldom and become Queen Elizabeth's potential successor and also King James's, if his three children had died young.[4]

Derby is an attractive character and the case for him is strong, but is it strong enough for him to be finally recognized as the real Shakespeare? Would he ever have been considered as an authorship candidate if George Fenner's two letters had not been intercepted and preserved in the State Papers Domestic? This is a tough question, and the answer might well be "no"; certainly the outcome would have been doubtful. We should indeed be thankful that they did survive.

At this point, now that we have reached the end of our journey of exploration, I shall invite the reader to form his or her own conclusion, based on what has been set out in this book. It will come as no surprise if I say that in so far as a scientist is ever certain of anything, I am certain that the evidence converges on William Stanley as the man who wrote under the pen name William Shakespeare. Does it matter who wrote the canon? Of course it does—the British sense of fair play would insist upon it. Will it affect the way the plays are perceived? Broadly speaking, probably not; perhaps the greatest bonus is that we now have a life of a playwright which resonates with the plays, unlike the life of the actor and businessman from Stratford-upon-Avon.[5]

It is my hope that this book will inspire further research, and my expectation is that new findings will endorse its conclusion—that the works of William Shakespeare were written by William Stanley.

Appendix A. Oxford Eliminated

Edward de Vere, 17th Earl of Oxford, has by far the greatest number of supporters among those looking today for the real Shakespeare. We here give six reasons for eliminating him from the authorship, three concerned with writing habits, and three cases where the sonnets do not match up with details of Oxford's life.

"Earnestly desire"

This phrase, with several variants, was frequently used by Oxford when writing to Lord Burghley, since he was in a position to accord Oxford favors, or to seek approval from the Queen for Oxford's endeavors. I give below the phrases which include these words; the numbers refer to Oxford's letters as given on Nina Green's website[1] (a modern spelling version of the letters posted on Professor Alan Nelson's website[2]). The letters are numbered in both collections as #02, etc.

1569:	#02	earnestly desiring
1572:	#03	affectiously and heartily desire
	"	humbly desire
	#05	most earnestly desire
1575:	#06	earnestly hath desired
	#08	gladly hath desired
1576:	#09	most earnestly I shall desire
1581:	#13	earnest desire
1584:	#16	most earnestly desire
1590:	#17	most earnestly desire
	#18	most earnestly desire
1593:	#21	most earnestly to desire
1594:	#22	most heartily desire
	"	most earnestly desire
1595:	#23	most heartily desire
1596:	#27	most earnestly to desire
1600:	#30	most heartily desire
1601:	#31	most earnestly desiring
	#33	most earnestly desire
	#36	most earnest desire
1603:	#39	most earnestly desire
	#40	most earnestly desire
	#42	most earnestly therefore desire

	#43	most earnestly desire
1595:	#51	earnestly and heartily desire
	#56	most earnestly desiring
	#61	earnestly in HM's service desire
	#65	most earnestly at this time desired
1599:	#66	most earnestly desire
	"	earnest desire

The phrase "most earnestly desire" occurs 17 times (including slight variants) in Oxford's letters. There are 7 other phrases which use the words "earnest" and "desire" ("earnestly desiring," "earnestly hath desired," "earnest desire" [twice], "most earnest desire," "earnestly ... desire" [twice]), bringing the total of times that Oxford associated the two words in his ms letters to 24; he also used the phrase "earnestly desiring" in his prefatory letter to Bedingfield's *Cardanus Comfort*, making a grand total of 25. In addition, Oxford used 8 other adverbs to qualify "desire" on 7 occasions ("affectiously and heartily," "humbly," "gladly," "heartily" [4 times]).

In contrast, while Shakespeare uses the verb "desire" around 247 times, he *never* uses the phrase "earnestly desire" (or any variants thereof). On only *four* occasions does he use an adverb to qualify "desire," i.e., "fehemently" (*sic*—Welsh dialect in *MWW*), "humbly" (*T&C*, twice), and "most heartily" (*HVIII*). He uses the word "earnestly" only 8 times, as against Oxford's 35. In contrast, Oxford uses the verb "desire" 76 times, and qualifies it 29 times. At the same rate, Shakespeare should have qualified "desire" 94 times, rather than just 4, and should have qualified it with "earnestly" 81 times, rather than never.

Thus a combination of two words which Oxford uses 25 times is *not once* used by Shakespeare, and the verb "desire," which Oxford couples with an adverb 29 times (i.e., 38 percent), is only 4 times coupled with an adverb by Shakespeare (i.e., 1.6 percent). In view of the fact that Shakespeare's output of words is roughly 20 times that found in Oxford's surviving papers, one would expect that some traces at least of Oxford's fingerprints would appear somewhere in the canon, if he were the real Bard. Instead, the complete absence of these particular characteristic writing habits of Oxford's from Shakespeare's works suggests strongly that Oxford was not Shakespeare, and would seem to be on its own almost sufficient to rule him out.

It has been suggested that letter-writing is substantially different from play-writing, and that this might account for such a discrepancy (and also for those described below). But I do not think this argument holds. Writing a letter involves one person speaking to another by means of the written word, while play-writing involves writing words that the actors speak. The similarity is far stronger than the difference.

"To Do or Not to Do"

A book by Jonathan Hope, *The Authorship of Shakespeare's Plays*, is not about the Authorship Question, but about distinguishing scenes written by Shakespeare from those written by Fletcher in, e.g., *Henry VIII*, or *The Two Noble Kinsmen*, and also testing which of the apocrypha he might perhaps have written. One technique Hope describes concerns the use of the verb "to do" as an auxiliary.[3] He distinguishes between four "unregulated" usages (obsolete) and four "regulated" usages (modern), and he assumes that the proportion of "regulated" usage to total usage (which he calls "regulation rate") is typical of each writer. An additional supposition (for which there is evidence) is that the usage of "to do" is

TABLE OF "TO DO" USAGE

Unregulated	*Regulated*
(no longer in use)	(in use today)
I did go home (unemphatic)	I went home
I went not home	I did not (didn't) go home
Went you home?	Did you go home?
Went you not home?	Did you not (didn't you) go home?

essentially unthinking, and largely fixed early in life, so that those born earlier are likely to employ regulated usages less often than those born later. These ideas are broadly borne out by his statistics. The writers whose plays he has studied are Shakespeare, Marlowe, Dekker, Fletcher, Middleton and Massinger.

Hope is immediately faced with a problem, since while the regulation rates for Marlowe through to Massinger roughly correlate with their birth dates, Shakespeare's ratio is significantly lower than expected. Thus for Marlowe (b. 1564) the average figure is 88 percent, Dekker (1572) 89 percent, Fletcher (1579) 93 percent, Middleton (1580) 91 percent and Massinger (1583) 91 percent. But Shakespeare (who is assumed to be the actor Shakspere), born in the same year as Marlowe, comes in at 83 percent, way below what might have been expected. For Hope's purposes, this is a bonus, as it allows him to distinguish quite readily between scenes in *Henry VIII* written by Shakespeare and those written by Fletcher. And he has a ready explanation for Shakespeare's old-fashioned "to do" usage—for was he not born in darkest Warwickshire, where they might well be expected to be years behind the rest of the country? (But Fletcher and Massinger were also born in the provinces.) However, if one extrapolates backwards in time very roughly, which is all the figures allow one to do, one finds that "Shakespeare" was probably born some years before Marlowe, i.e., before 1564. Not surprisingly, Hope does not explore this avenue.

In his analyses Hope did not distinguish between verse and prose in Shakespeare's plays, and so I set myself the task of doing this for many of them. It turns out that the average regulation rate for Shakespeare's verse is 81.5 percent, while the figure for prose is 86 percent, and 90 percent when interrogatives are omitted. In contrast, the figure for all of Oxford's letters (which contain no interrogatives) is 81.4 percent, *very significantly different* from Shakespeare's declarative prose (90 percent). This difference is the more obvious if one compares the percentages of unregulated usage: 18.6 percent for Oxford, and 10 percent for Shakespeare. Thus Oxford employs old-fashioned usages *nearly twice as often* as Shakespeare does in his declarative prose passages, suggesting strongly that Oxford was not Shakespeare.

"Sith—Sithence—Since"

The three words "sith," "sithence" and "since" were all used by both Oxford and Shakespeare. As all three words can mean either "because" or "after that time" (*OED*), it is interesting to compare Oxford's usage with Shakespeare's. This table shows the number of times each word was used in the sense "because."

		Oxford's Poems	*Oxford's Letters*	*Shakespeare's Plays*	*Shakespeare's Poems*
"BECAUSE"	Sith:	2	48	21	2
	Sithence:	0	2	1	0
	Since:	1	0	231	33

The pattern of use of these words in Oxford's works is clearly a bad match to the pattern in Shakespeare's works. Thus, to convey the sense "because," Oxford almost invariably uses "sith" (94 percent of the time), while Shakespeare uses "sith" infrequently (8 percent), much preferring "since" (92 percent). Thus Oxford is 12 times more likely to use "sith" than Shakespeare, while Shakespeare was 46 times more likely to use "since" than Oxford. These results suggest strongly that Oxford did not write Shakespeare. The next table shows the number of times each word was used in the sense "after that time."

		Oxford's Poems	*Oxford's Letters*	*Shakespeare's Plays*	*Shakespeare's Poems*
"AFTER THAT TIME"	Sith:	0	1	1	0
	Sithence:	0	15	1	0
	Since:	0	9	192	6

To convey the sense "after that time," Oxford was twice as likely to employ "sithence" as "since," and employed "sithence" 60 percent of the time, while Shakespeare almost invariably employed "since," only once using "sithence," a ratio of about 200 to 1. Again the discrepancies are so great as to make it likely that Oxford and Shakespeare were two different writers, assuming that most of the canon represents most of what Shakespeare wrote.

It has been claimed that editors and compositors would have had a tendency to change the words "sith" and "sithence" to "since," on the assumption that the modern form was gradually superseding the older forms. But there is no evidence for this—rather the reverse. Terry Ross[4] has found that comparing the First Folio with the early quartos that two "siths" were changed to "sinces," whereas five "sinces" were changed to "siths," the opposite of what has been claimed. No changes from "sith" to "since" or vice versa occurred in any of the subsequent reprintings of the Folio in 1632, 1663/4 and 1685.

There are other discrepancies between Oxford's and Shakespeare's writing habits, in particular the use of "has" and "hath." Shakespeare's ratio of "has" to "hath" is 1 to 5 (around 400 to 2000); Oxford's is zero, since he never wrote "has" (he used "hath" over 100 times). As Shakespeare's output of words was about 20 times Oxford's, it is odd, to say the least, that several of Oxford's preferences are not reflected in the canon, if he was the true Shakespeare. But in any case, the relative usage rates of "sith," "sithence" and "since" are such as to throw very strong doubts on the credibility of the hypothesis that Oxford wrote Shakespeare.

The First 17 Sonnets

Many Oxfordians believe that the first 17 sonnets were written by Oxford to encourage the "Fair Youth" (Southampton) to marry his daughter Elizabeth. But the text suggests otherwise. If one looks at the way the Fair Youth is addressed in the first 17 sonnets, it contrasts strongly with the way his potential bride is referred to. The poet starts off with "From fairest creatures...," who evidently include the young man as one of their number. Then, leaving aside some 100 pronouns etc. referring to a particular person, the young man is addressed in various ways, all clearly referring to one specific individual:

#1 "the world's fresh ornament"; "only herald"; "tender churl"
#2 "If thou couldst answer, This fair child..."
#3 "Thou art thy mother's glass"
#4 "beauteous niggard"; "profitless usurer"
" "What acceptable audit canst thou leave?"
#6 "That's for thyself to breed an other thee."
#9 "That thou consum'st thyself in single life?"
#11 "As fast as thou shalt wane, so fast thou grow'st"
#13 "You had a father: let your son say so."
#17 "But were some child of yours alive that time,
" You should live twice—in it, and in my rhyme."

The above are just a small selection of quotations which make it clear that Shakespeare is addressing one specific individual, the Fair Youth. He is seeing a particular person in his mind's eye with great clarity.

In contrast, when he is thinking of the young man's future bride, here is a *complete* list of the terms in which he refers to her:

#3 "some mother"; "where is she?"
#6 "some vial"; "some place"; "those"
#9 "a widow"
#16 "many maiden gardens"

It could hardly be clearer that he has no particular girl in mind: he hasn't the least idea who the young man's potential wife might be, he has no clear picture of her in his mind's eye, and she could be anyone from a large number of suitable young ladies.

To sum up, reading these sonnets shows that Shakespeare knows exactly who the young man is (even though he doesn't tell us his name), and further that he has *no* prospective bride in mind (and couldn't produce a name even if pressed). My target is those many Oxfordians (Looney, Sobran, Dickinson, Holmes, to name just authors of books) who assert that these 17 sonnets were written to persuade Southampton to marry *specifically* Oxford's own daughter Elizabeth, the implication being that this is (yet more) circumstantial evidence that Oxford wrote the sonnets, and hence the canon. In my view, a close reading of these sonnets does not support this interpretation, and hence these sonnets do not provide any circumstantial evidence pointing to Oxford as the poet. If Oxford were urging the young man to marry his own daughter Elizabeth, it is pretty odd, not to say incomprehensible, that he should refer to her in such vague terms as those above. He has no difficulty in letting us know that he has a specific young man in mind, so why not a specific girl? Either he had forgotten he had a daughter, or he didn't think she was a suitable bride for Southampton, or he wasn't addressing Southampton, or these sonnets were written by someone else.

Sonnet 125

I believe there is a flaw in the usual Oxfordian reading of sonnet 125, which I will try to explain here. These are the first four lines (the sonnet was discussed earlier in Chapter 5).

Wer't ought to me I bore the canopy,
With my extern the outward honoring,
Or layd great bases for eternity,
Which proves more short than wast or ruining?

The majority of Oxfordians believe that Oxford's high status as Lord Great Chamberlain gave him the privilege of acting as one of the bearers of the canopy (a richly embroidered cloth held up on four poles by four bearers) over Queen Elizabeth. But in fact the reverse is the case: he was *of far too high a status* ever to have done so. Chapter 5 shows that noblemen only ever carried the canopy either at a coronation (when traditionally they were also Knights of the Garter) or at the christening of the monarch's child. There were no such christenings during Elizabeth's reign, and since Oxford was not a Knight of the Garter he would not have been eligible to carry the canopy over the anointing of the sovereign James I—but in any case he was otherwise fully occupied with far more important duties during this ceremony. He is in charge of all the items of the regalia, he attends the King as he makes his vow at the altar, he removes the outer robes of the King before the anointing, and after it he touches the King's heels with the spurs. Towards the end of the ceremony, the highest nobility swear allegiance directly to the Sovereign, but the LGC does homage to the King on behalf of himself *and all the rest of the earls*, "who attend upon the LGC to signify their consents."[5]

Thus Oxford had many important and highly visible duties during the coronation, but they did not include bearing the canopy. To sum up, I would say it is inconceivable that Oxford ever carried or would have carried or would have aspired to carry the canopy over Queen Elizabeth or King James, on any occasion. At public ceremonies, apart from a coronation, he would have carried his six-foot white wand of office, just as his successor does today at the State Opening of Parliament.

Sonnet 126

Sonnet 126 is so placed as to bring the sequence of sonnets to the "Fair Youth" to some kind of conclusion, yet it does not seem to relate well with the sonnets that immediately precede it. Here it is, with certain key words emphasized.

O thou my lovely Boy who in thy power,
Dost hold Time's fickle glass, his tickle hour:
Who hast by **waning grown**, and therein show'st,
Thy lovers **withering**, as thy sweet self **grow'st**.
If **Nature** (sovereign mistress over wrack)

As thou goest onwards still will pluck thee back,
She keeps thee to this purpose, that her skill
May time disgrace, and wretched minutes kill.
Yet fear her O thou minion of her pleasure,
She may detain, but not still keep her **treasure**!
Her ***Audit*** (though delayed) answered must be,
And her *Quietus* is to render thee.

The only commentator known to me who has made a determined attempt to relate the sonnets to contemporary events is R. J. C. Wait, in *The Background to Shakespeare's Sonnets.*[6] He makes a number of connections between particular sonnets and actual events which are very plausible, and some of them seem incontrovertible. Since he is not part of the Shakespeare establishment (although an orthodox Stratfordian) his findings have been almost universally ignored by the experts. He connects this sonnet convincingly (in my view) with the theme of the first 17, though in the final analysis this must remain a matter of opinion. These urge the young man to marry and have a son, and in sonnet 126 *the poet's wish has been fulfilled.* The "lovely boy" is the young man's son and heir, who is addressed (so to speak) in the hearing of the young man, and the "lovers" of line 4 are the poet, the young man and his wife, and maybe other well-wishers. Just as they wither as the baby grows, so in turn the baby too must wither, and Nature's ***Audit***—accounting, summing up—however reluctant, is to claim the offspring as well as the parents, in due course. Thus the whole sequence returns to its starting point, and the cycle of life and death comes full circle.

The first clue is in the opening lines of sonnet 11:

As fast as thou [*the young man*] shalt **wane** [*decay, grow old*], so fast thou **grow'st**
In one of thine [*your son, growing up*], from that which thou departest;
And that fresh blood which youngly [*in your youth*] thou bestow'st [*on your son*]
Thou mayst call thine, when thou from youth convertest. [*grow old*]

Compare lines 3–4 of sonnet 126:

Who [*the young man's son*] hast by [*others'*] **waning grown**, and therein show'st
Thy lovers [*parents, friends*] **withering** [*waning, ageing*], as thy sweet self **grow'st**.

The idea that one person's growth is accompanied by others waning is expressed elsewhere in the prose and verse of the period.[7] Compare also sonnet 12, lines 11–12:

Since sweets and beauties do them-selves forsake,
And <u>die</u> [*wane*] as fast as they see others **grow**;

Sonnet 15 also plays on the same theme. Other clues suggesting that the young man's son is being addressed in sonnet 126 can be found in sonnet 4, lines 11–12:

Then how when **Nature** calls thee [*the young man*] to be gone [*die*],
What acceptable ***Audit*** [*other than a son and heir*] canst thou leave?

Compare lines 5 and 13–14 of sonnet 126:

If **Nature** (sovereign mistress over <u>wrack</u> [*the result of waning*])
... ...
Her [*Nature's*] ***Audit*** (though delayed) answered must be,
And her *Quietus* [*discharge from debt*] is to render thee [*the young man's son, i.e., claim his life at the end*].

the son being the greatly desired "acceptable ***Audit***" or final accounting, as in sonnet 2, lines 10–11:

> If thou couldst answer, "This fair child of mine
> Shall sum my count [*audit*]

There are more clues in sonnet 2:

> Then being asked, where all thy beautie lies,
> Where all the **treasure** [*which you have amassed or begotten*] of thy lusty daies,
> To say within thine own deepe sunken eyes [*a wasted life, rather than in a son*],
> Were an all-eating shame and thriftlesse praise.

Compare line 12 of sonnet 126:

> She [*Nature*] may detain, but not still keep her **treasure** [*the young man's son*]**!**

The ***Audit*** is to be fulfilled in the young man's son and heir. Southampton's eldest son, James, was born on 1 March 1605, some months after Oxford's death in June 1604. Thus on Wait's interpretation here is another sonnet, besides the first 17 and sonnet 125, that does not fit well with Oxford.

While it is true that this sonnet is usually regarded as having been addressed to the young man, Wait rejects this idea, since (among other reasons) as he says of the opening words *"O thou my lovely boy":* "There is no other line addressed to the young man which carries such a sickly flavour." (Other commentators have found the word "too mawkish."[8]) His arguments for believing the sonnet to be addressed to the young man's infant son are too long to summarize here (only some of them are given above), and are well worth reading. And as Nina Green has said, to address a 30-year-old married man, already father of a daughter, who had recently been released from two years in the Tower after a conviction for treason, as *"my lovely boy,"* would be incongruous to the point of absurdity.[9]

Appendix B. Portrait of William Stanley (Portrait of Shakespeare?). Nashe's Epistle to "Strange News"

This is a modern spelling version, based on Nina Green's modern spelling version,[1] which I have altered here and there. The words underlined are discussed in Chapter 7.

STRANGE NEWS

of the intercepting certain letters and a convoy of verses
as they were going privily to victual the Low Countries.

Unda impellitur unda
By Thomas Nashe, gentleman
Printed 1592.

To the most copious Carminist
of our time, and famous persecutor of Priscian, his
very friend, Master Apis lapis, Tho. Nashe wisheth new strings to his old tawny Purse, and
all honourable increase of acquaintance in the Cellar.

Gentle Master William, that learned writer, Rhenish wine & sugar, in the first book of his Comment upon Red-noses, hath this saying, *veterem ferendo iniuriam inuitas nouam*, which is as much in English as, one Cup of nipitaty pulls on another. In moist consideration whereof, as also in zealous regard of that high countenance you show unto Scholars, I am bold, instead of new Wine, to carouse to you a cup of news, Which, if your Worship (according to your wonted Chaucerism) shall accept in good part, I'll be your daily Orator to pray that that pure sanguine complexion of yours may never be famished with pot-luck, that you may taste till your last gasp, and live to see the confusion of both your special enemies, Small Beer and Grammar rules.

It is not unknown to report what a famous pottle-pot Patron you have been to old Poets in your days, & how many pounds you have spent (and, as it were, thrown into the fire) upon the dirt of wisdom called Alchemy. # Yea, you have been such an infinite Maecenas to learned men that not any that belong to them (as Sumners, and who not) but have tasted of the cool streams of your liberality.

I would speak in commendation of your hospitality likewise, but that it is chronicled in the Archdeacon's Court, and the fruits it brought forth (as I guess) are of age to speak for themselves. Why should virtue be smothered by blind circumstance? An honest man of

Saffron Walden kept three sons at the University together a long time,[2] and you kept three maids together in your house a long time. A charitable deed, & worthy to be registered in red letters.##[3]

Shall I presume to dilate of the gravity of your round cap and your dudgeon-dagger? It is thought they will make you be called upon shortly to be Alderman of the Steelyard. And that's well remembered; I heard say, when this last Term was removed to Hertford, you fell into a great study and care by yourself to what place the Steelyard should be removed. I promise you truly, it was a deep meditation, and such as might well have beseemed Elderton's parliament of noses to have sit upon. A Tavern in London, only upon the motion, mourned all in black, and forbare to girt her temples with ivy because the grandam of good-fellowship was like to depart from amongst them.

And I wonder very much that you samsownd not yourself into a consumption with the profound cogitation of it.

Diu viuas in amore iocisque, whatsoever you do, beware of keeping diet. Sloth is a sin, and one sin (as one poison) must be expelled with another. What can he do better that hath nothing to do, than fall a-drinking to keep him from idleness?

Faugh! Methinks my jests begin already to smell of the cask, with talking so much of this liquid provender.

In earnest thus: there is a *Doctor and His Fart*[4] that have kept a foul stinking stir in Paul's Churchyard. I cry him mercy. I slandered him; he is scarce a Doctor till he hath done his Acts. This doddypoll, this didapper, this professed political braggart, hath railed upon me without wit or art in certain four pennyworth of Letters and three farthingworth of sonnets. Now do I mean to present him and Shakerley to the Queen's fool-taker for coach-horses, for two that draw more equally in one oratorial yoke of vainglory there is not under heaven.

What say you, Master Apis lapis, will you, with your eloquence and credit, shield me from carpers? Have you any odd shreds of Latin to make this letter-monger a coxcomb of?

It stands you in hand to arm yourself against him, for he speaks against Cony-catchers, and you are a Cony-catcher, as Cony-catching is divided into three parts: the Verser, the Setter, and the Barnacle.[5]

A Setter I am sure you are not, for you are no Musician, nor a barnacle, for you never were of the order of the Barnardines, but the Verser I cannot acquit you of, for Master Vaux of Lambeth brings in sore evidence of a breakfast you won of him one morning at an unlawful game called rhyming. What lies not in you to amend, play the Doctor and defend. A fellow that I am to talk with by and by, being told that his Father was a Rope-maker,[6] excused the matter after this sort: *And hath never saint had reprobate to his father?* They are his own words; he cannot go from them. You see here he makes a Reprobate and a Rope-maker *voces conuertibiles.* Go to, take example by him to wash out dirt with ink, and run up to the knees in the channel if you be once wet-shod. You are amongst grave Doctors and men of judgment in both Laws every day; I pray, ask them the question in my absence, whether such a man as I have described this Epistler to be, one that hath a good handsome picke-devant, and a pretty leg to study the Civil Law with, that hath made many proper rimes of the old cut in his day, and deserved infinitely of the state by extolling himself and his two brothers in every book he writes, whether (I say) such a famous pillar of the Press, now in the fourteenth or fifteenth year of the reign of his Rhetoric, giving money to have this illiterate Pamphlet of Letters printed (whereas others have money given them to suffer themselves to come in Print), it is not to be counted as flat simony, and be liable to one and the same penalty?

I tell you, I mean to trounce him after twenty in the hundred, and have a bout with him with two staves and a pike for this gear.

If he get anything by the bargain, let whatsoever I write henceforward be condemned to wrap bombast in.

Carouse to me good luck, for I am resolutely bent; the best blood of the brothers shall pledge me in vinegar. O, would thou hadst a quaffing-bowl which, like Gawain's skull, should contain a peck, that thou might'st swap off a hearty draught to the success of this voyage.

By whatsoever thy visage holdeth most precious I beseech thee, by John Davies' soul and the blue Boar in the Spittle I conjure thee, to draw out thy purse and give me nothing for the dedication of my Pamphlet.

Thou art a good-fellow, I know, and hadst rather spend jests than money. Let it be the task of thy best terms to safe-conduct this book through the enemy's country.

Proceed to cherish thy surpassing carminical art of memory with full cups (as thou dost); let Chaucer be new scoured against the day of battle, and Terence come but in now and then with the snuff of a sentence, and *Dictum puta*, We'll strike it as dead as a door-nail; *Haud teruntij estimo*, we have cat's-meat and dog's-meat enough for these mongrels. However I write merrily, I love and admire thy pleasant witty humour, which no care or cross can make unconversable. Still be constant to thy content, love poetry, hate pedantism. *Vade, vale, caue ne titubes, mandataq{ue}; frangas.*

Thine entirely,
Tho. Nashe

Appendix C. The Odds That Chance Produced "Henry Wr-ioth-esley"

It is a difficult matter to try to ascertain the odds that the name "Henry Wriothesley" might have occurred accidentally in the Dedication to the Sonnets, when it is treated as a transposition cipher. There are a number of methods that could be used, and the one chosen here is as follows. We shall consider first the name HENRY, and it will be assumed that a reasonably good estimate of the odds that it might appear in any 5-letter vertical site in any array can be assessed by imagining 5 letters picked one by one at random out of a notional "black bag" containing all the letters of the Dedication.

There are 144 letters in the text (disregarding Thomas Thorpe's initials, "T. T.," printed in larger type and offset to one side at the end); the number of "H"s is 10, "E"s 23, "N"s 13, "R"s 9, and there is just one "Y." The probability that an H is picked first from the bag is thus 10 out of 144, i.e., 10 ÷ 144, and the probability that E is the next letter picked is 23 out of 143 (since there are now only 143 letters left in the bag). The fractional likelihood of the name "Henry" being drawn from the bag is therefore the product of these five probabilities, i.e.,

$$(10 \div 144) \times (23 \div 143) \times (13 \div 142) \times (9 \div 141) \times (1 \div 140)$$

If we take 30 as the maximum array row size, and 6 as the minimum, the total number of possible vertical sites for a 5-letter word in any of these 25 arrays is 1,800. In terms of picking letters out of an imaginary black bag, this means that we may make 1,800 trials of extracting 5 letters, since it is immaterial in which site the word is found. Thus the probability that one of these sites might contain the name HENRY is (replacing "×" by "." to save space):

$$1800 \,.\, (10.23.13.9.1) \div (144.143.142.141.140) \simeq 1 \text{ in } 1192$$

That is, there is one chance in about 1192 that the name HENRY appears by accident anywhere in the Dedication, when it is regarded as a simple transposition cipher.

In a similar way we find that for the segment ESLEY of the name "Wr-ioth-esley" the probability is:

$$1800 \,.\, (23.10.6.22.1) \div (144 \,.143 \,.142 \,.141 \,.140) \simeq 1 \text{ in } 1056$$

Thus there is one chance in about 1056 that the segment ESLEY appears by accident anywhere in the Dedication. The segment IOTH lies adjacent to ESLEY (something it is reasonable to believe was deliberately contrived by the cryptographer), so that there are only 16 possible sites for it to occupy in the same array. The probability that it is found in one of them is:

$$16 \,.\, (14.8.17.10) \div (139\,.138\,.137\,.136) \simeq 1 \text{ in } 1173$$

A similar argument for the segment WR, which can be located anywhere in the remaining vacant sites in the same array, a total of 116, yields:

$$116 \,.\, (4.9) \div (135\,.134) \simeq 1 \text{ in } 4.33$$

To find the overall odds that the name "Wr-ioth-esley" might appear by chance in the Dedication, the separate odds are multiplied together giving (roughly) one in 5.4 million. However, since (as we have seen) it would be acceptable if one or two of these segments had to be read upwards (but hardly all three, as the decipherer might then never spot the name), it is appropriate to divide this figure by 4, to give odds of roughly one in 1.35 million.

The joint probability of finding the full name "Henry Wriothesley" in the Dedication can thus be assessed as the product of the probabilities of the separate names, resulting in odds of one in about 1.6 thousand million (i.e., one in 1.35 million times one in 1192).

These odds would be much the same for finding any name consisting of a 5-letter first name and an 11-letter last name (similarly split into three segments). If then we also take into account the fact that this man was already regarded as one of the most likely candidates[1] for "Mr. W. H." and the "Fair Youth," the probability that his name turns up in the Dedication by chance is considerably reduced, though by how much it is virtually impossible to estimate. It is therefore reasonable to conclude that there is a very high probability indeed that the name was deliberately encoded into the Dedication by someone wishing to preserve it for posterity.

Appendix D. More Letters by Derby

Here are a few more letters, either written by Derby or dictated by him to a secretary.

A Letter in His Own Hand to Sir Julius Caesar Dated 25 March 1606.[1]

S[i]^{r}, I have here inclosed sent unto you accordinge
to his Ma[jes]$^{t[y]s}$ pleasure to me signifyed by yo[u]^{r} let[ter]^{s} thee
Deputac[i]on under my hand and seale to be disposed
according to yo[u]^{r} dyrec[t]ions from his highnes. So
w[i]th my harty Commendacions I bydd you
farewell. Lathome this xxvth of March 1606

Y[ou]^{r} loving ffrend,
Will: Derby:/

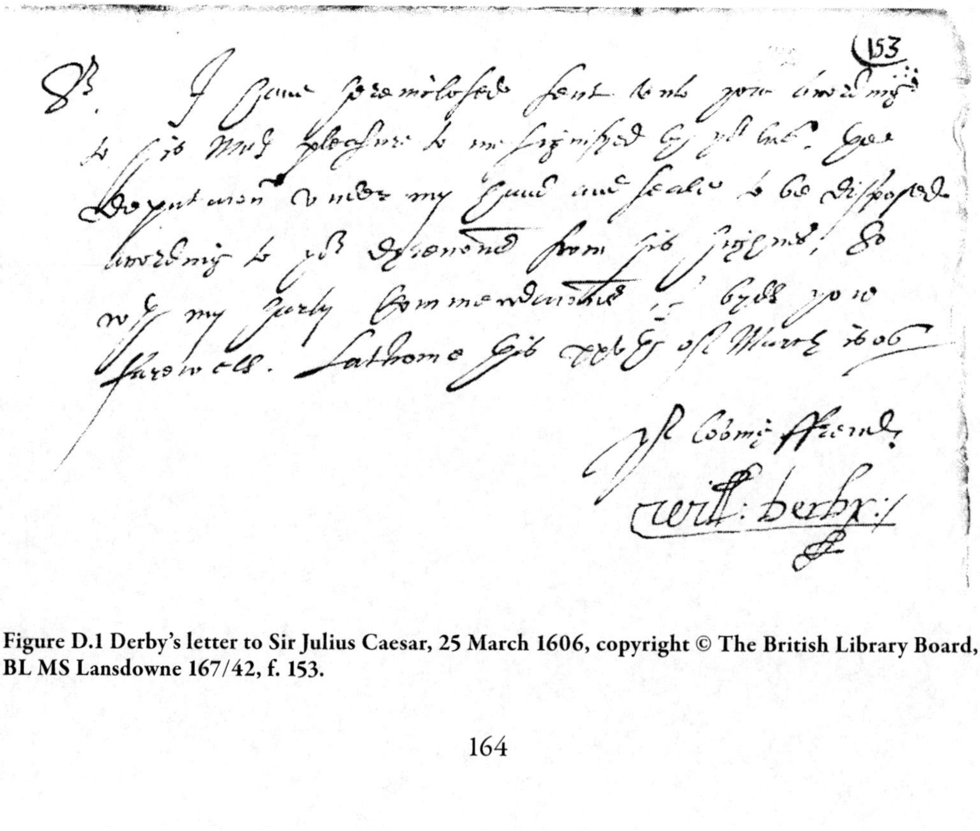

Figure D.1 Derby's letter to Sir Julius Caesar, 25 March 1606, copyright © The British Library Board, BL MS Lansdowne 167/42, f. 153.

As with the other letters reproduced in Chapter 29 there are a number of "y"s where at the time it was normal to use "i"s. There are doubled consonants in "bydd" and "ffrend," and also "inclosed" for "enclosed," initial "in-" for "en-" being Shakespeare's habitual trait (d) from Chapter 29. Note also the capital "C" in "Commendations," such capital "C"s being typical of both Shakespeare's and Derby's hands. A "deputation" in this context is a legal document appointing one person to act on behalf of another (as in "depute"), and Derby is here appointing three vice-chamberlains to act on his behalf following his own appointment as High Chamberlain of the County of Chester.

The document (full of ponderous legal phraseology) is included with the letter; it is carefully written in his own handwriting but in Court Hand rather than in his usual secretary or italic hand so as to be very legible, since it had the force of law. Several words display typical Shakespearean characteristics, including doubled letters in naturall, yett, Margarett, finall, lett, especiall, and one word "tearme" which was a spelling frequently used by Shakespeare (see Chapter 29). In addition the word "Palatine" (as in "County Palatine") is spelled 11 times with an "n" before the "t," e.g., "Palentine" and variations. This was an obsolete spelling by that time, but turns up twice in Shakespeare's *Merchant of Venice*, I.ii.45 "Countie Palentine," and I.ii.57, "Why hee hath ... a better bad habite of frowning then the Count Palentine."

A Letter Written to His Brother-in-Law Sir John Salusbury, Dated 27 November 1598.[2]

Sir John Salusbury married Derby's (illegitimate) half-sister Ursula, whose mother was his father Henry's partner after he had banished his wife.

> To my lovinge brother
> John Salusburie Esqr. These
>
> Sr. you shall understande, that my Lorde of Essex is to make speedy repayre intoe Irelande, myself accompanyinge him. To whiche servyce, if you have any inclynation, I would gladly heare from you, with all convenient speede, that you may be remembred as ys fytt, whčh yf you undertake, wee shalbe partakers of all fortunes, and so expectinge yor answere, do very lovinglye commende mee to yor selfe and my good sister.

Note the "y"s in "repayre," "inclynation," "ys," "yf," and both the "y" and the doubled "t" in "fytt." All these spellings are consistent with Shakespeare's spellings, as described in Chapter 29. In the event Derby did not join Essex, and it may be hypothesized that the Queen forbade him to go as he was her heir-apparent.

A Letter Written to His Uncle Robert Cecil Dated 4 January 1596.[3]

> Thanks good Uncle for your kind remmembrance and accordinge to your postscript I will cum to be A suter to her Majē myselfe who am not a little Joyfull to understand of her gratyousnes so hyghely to highly [crossed out] favor my wyff and me and thus though satisfyed yet not without salutinge you with these few unworthy hasty lynes do cease[,] restinge always
>
> Your lovinge Nephew
> And trew frend
> Will: Derby:

Again there are numerous "y"s where even at the time "i" would be the usual spelling. Doubled consonants also occur in "remmembrance" and "wyff."

A Letter Written to Sir Robert Cecil Dated the Last of November 1599.[4]

My verie good Uncle, I geve yow harty thanks
for yor kind paynes taken in my Cause wherof
I pray yor Contynuance, and what so ever yow
shall think fitt to be done by me for ye further
effecting and Conclusion of ye agrem^{t} and peace
betwene me and my Neeces, I wilbe ready to Confirm.
I would have ben there my self, but for seinge my
wife at Hackney, and therefore do eftsoons pray
yow undertak for me. And so wth my lovinge
Commendacons do betak yow to Gods favo^{r} this last
of Novemb^{r} 1599.
Yo^{r} lovinge nephew
Will: Derby:/

Apart from "y"s for "i"s, there are two examples of "y^{e}" for "the," "fitt" for "fit," and several initial capital "C"s where lowercase would be normal.

A Letter Written to Sir William More, Dictated to a Secretary on 6 January 1599.[5]

Good Sir William More, I understand that Henry Woods of Chobham, a servant of mine is pressed for a soldier within Surrey. And for that I hear that you are a Justice of the Peace thereabouts, and intending to go for Ireland myself I shall in kindness desire you that he may be released, seeing it is more fit, he being my man, attend me than be under the command of any other. If you afford me this favour I shall take it very thankfully. And so do commit you to God, this vjth of January 1598.

Your loving friend
Will: Derby:/ [Derby's signature

A Letter to "Sir G. M." Dictated by Derby to a Secretary on 6 May 1619.[6]

Sir, I received a letter from you the 6th of this instant May of his Majesty's pleasure to have the Companions of the Order of the Garter to attend his Majesty the 25th of this month for the celebration of St. George's feast. For as much as I am altogether unable to travel by reason of an ague wherewith I have been troubled this [paper torn] weeks. I pray you therefore to excuse me to his Majesty to spare my attendance at this time. I have also written to my Lord Chamberlain [to] the same effect. So with my hearty commendations I rest,

Lathom this vjth of May 1619

Your loving friend
Will: Derby: [Derby's signature

The above letters are typical of those that survive. It can be seen that Derby often signs off as "loving friend" or "loving nephew." The sense perhaps implies "true and faithful" rather than anything more affectionate, though he was clearly on good terms with his uncle Robert Cecil (who was actually two years younger than he was).

Other Derby Letters

In other letters[7] written by Derby to Robert Cecil occur the following spellings.

accquainted, att, beeinge, behaulfe, berer, busines, byn, Caracter, Cause, Circumstances, Comitt, Commendations, Conclusion, Confirme, Consequence, Conveniente, delyver, desyringe, deteynethe, fayll, faythfull, fitt, frend, goodds, greatt, Highnes, howse, hyly, intreate, itt, joyfull, kynd, kyndely, Lo:, Lp^{s}, lyfe, lyff, lyttle, markett, monethe, neereste, nott, occations, owtt, parcells, perceyve, petytyon, playne, quietnes, receyved, redy, referre, remembred, royall, seinge, semes, severall, speches, spediest, suter, sutor, thankfull, thankfulnes, thatt, therfor, trew, troble, troblsome, uppon, verie, viceadmirall, waytt, w^{ch}, wiffe, wrytten, wyff, y^{e}, yf, ymploy, y^{or}, ys, ytt.

These exhibit frequent use of "y" for "i," doubled letters, "intreate" for "entreat," final "-full" for "-ful," initial capital "C"s and frequent use of "Lo:", all previously found by Honigmann to be typical of Shakespeare's spelling habits (as described in Chapter 29). The words "busines," "Highnes" and "quietnes" exhibit Shakespeare's preference for this termination over "-ness" or "-nesse," as found by Eric Sams (also discussed in Chapter 29), together with other preferences such as "behaulfe" over "behalf(e)" and for "verie" over "very," and several examples of final "-ll" rather than "-l" in words other than those ending in "-ful."

Derby's letters show that he had four styles of handwriting, a secretary hand, a cursive mixed hand when he was writing in a hurry, a Court hand in a document with legal force, and a well-formed italic hand often used when he was writing formally to his uncle Robert Cecil, who was Secretary of State and to whom it might have been inappropriate to use his hurried hand. His skill at writing both italic and Court hands suggests that he was taught by a writing-master such as John Davies of Hereford, one of his father's protégés.

Appendix E. Postscript: Henry Heir?

In the analysis of the Dedication to the Sonnets given earlier, there was something I omitted to mention, a puzzle which nagged away at me for some time until I arrived at the explanation I am about to propose, mind-blowing though it may appear to be.

The Dedication was considered in some detail in Chapters 18 and 19, where it was revealed that it was carefully designed to preserve the name "Henry Wriothesley." The name is found in four segments, HENRY, WR, IOTH, ESLEY, when the 144 letters of the Dedication are written out in perfect rectangles. HENRY is found (diagonally) in a rectangle with 9 rows of 16 letters, and the segments of WR-IOTH-ESLEY are found (vertically) in a rectangle with 8 rows of 18 letters, with IOTH adjacent to ESLEY, a circumstance which seems to have been deliberately contrived to reassure the decoder that he has found the correct solution to the cipher.

T	O	T	H	E	O	N	L	I	**E**	B	E	G	E	T	T	E	R
O	F	T	H	E	S	E	I	N	**S**	V	I	N	G	S	O	N	N
E	T	S	M	r	W	H	A	L	**L**	**H**	A	P	P	I	N	E	S
S	E	A	N	D	T	H	A	T	**E**	**T**	E	R	N	I	T	I	E
P	R	O	M	I	S	E	D	B	**Y**	**O**	V	R	E	V	E	R-	L
I	V	I	N	G	P	O	E	T	W	**I**	S	H	E	T	H	T	H
E	**W**	E	L	L-	W	I	S	H	I	N	G	A	D	V	E	N	T
V	**R**	E	R	I	N	S	E	T	T	I	N	G	F	O	R	T	H

Figure E.1 The Dedication as an array having 8 rows of 18 letters.

The puzzle is this: why didn't the creator of the cipher encode the name Wriothesley in just *two* segments, WRIOTH and ESLEY rather than three? Here is the 8 by 18 rectangle again from Chapter 18. It can be seen that there is space for the letters WR, reading upwards, below the segment IOTH; they would replace the letters IN. The cryptographer only needed to change the last seven words to achieve this (and it can be seen that the word HENRY would not be affected). Someone clever enough to have devised the dedication as it stands would surely have been clever enough to find words which supplied WR in place of IN. My own feeble attempt is shown below: "the adventurer in setting forth his writings."

T	O	T	H	E	O	N	L	I	**E**	B	E	G	E	T	T	E	R
O	F	T	H	E	S	E	I	N	**S**	V	I	N	G	S	O	N	N
E	T	S	M	r	W	H	A	L	**L**	**H**	A	P	P	I	N	E	S
S	E	A	N	D	T	H	A	T	**E**	**T**	E	R	N	I	T	I	E
P	R	O	M	I	S	E	D	B	**Y**	**O**	V	R	E	V	E	R-L
I	V	I	N	G	P	O	E	T	W	**I**	S	H	E	T	H	T	H
E	A	D	V	E	N	T	V	R	E	**R**	I	N	S	E	T	T	I
N	G	F	O	R	T	H	H	I	S	**W**	R	I	T	I	N	G	S

Figure E.2 The Dedication with the last few words changed.

Sadly, the words I came up with have nothing of the style and panache of the original, but at least they achieve the desired objective of encoding the name in only two chunks. Our cryptographer was obviously clever enough to do something similar or better, so why didn't he? Eventually it dawned on me that a possible reason was that *there might be another word* hidden in the Dedication, which made the cryptographer content to settle for three segments rather than two to supply the name "Wriothesley." It was a hard enough task to encode two words; to encode three in the neatest possible way would truly be a *tour de force*, apparently beyond the cryptographer's skill, and doubtless he was content to settle for something less than perfect.

At the start of our analysis of the Dedication as a transposition cipher we counted the number of letters, hoping to find that it would have factors which would suggest one or more perfect rectangles in which to arrange them, and came up with 144 (suggesting several rectangles of different sizes). But if we go back to the Dedication as printed (Chapter 18), it can be seen that while the main body of the text has 144 letters, there are two more, off to one side, T. T., bringing the total up to 146. If we disregard the lower-case "r" of "Mr" the total is 145; keeping the "r" but dropping T. T. gives 144 letters, while dropping both T. T. and the "r" gives 143 letters. All of these numbers, 146, 145, 144 and 143, have factors, so all suggest different rectangles which need to be examined. The number 146 has factors 2 and 73, and the number 143 has factors 11 and 13, and it doesn't take long to establish that nothing is hidden in the four corresponding rectangles; the number 144 has already led to the two words HENRY and WR-IOTH-ESLEY.

We are therefore left with 145, the total number of capital letters, with factors 5 and 29, suggesting two rectangles which should be investigated. And here something very remarkable emerges. If we write out the capital letters of the Dedication in 5 rows, each of 29 letters, this is what we get.

T O T H E O N L I E B E G E T T E R O F T H E S E I N S V

I N G S O N N E T S Mr W **H** A L L H A P P I N E S S E A N D

T H A T E T E R N I T I **E** P R O M I S E D T O O V R E V E

R-L I V I N G P O E T W **I** S H E T H T H E W E L L-W I S H

I N G A D V E N T V R E **R** I N S E T T I N G F O R T H T T

Figure E.3 The Dedication as an array with 5 rows of 29 letters.

If "Mr. W. H." after reversing the initials, is "Mr. Henry Wriothesley," then this third word seems to be telling us that Henry is an "HEIR," since the "H" of "Henry" is the first letter of "HEIR."[1] And if he is an heir, who is he heir to?

We discovered in Chapter 14 that two distinguished orthodox commentators had found that the poet of the sonnets believed that the Fair Youth was royal, in some sense, or wrote about him as if he did indeed partake of royalty. We deduced in Chapter 18 from the Dedication that the Fair Youth was Henry Wriothesley, Third Earl of Southampton, and in Chapter 20 we deduced from remarks made by his contemporaries that he was thought to have some special relationship with Queen Elizabeth, perhaps even to be her son: *"Bright may he shine immortally ... in* [the Queen's] *fair firmament."* Now, amazingly enough, we appear to have this view confirmed by a third word hidden in the Dedication.

At this point I am inclined to advise the reader to lie down quietly in a darkened room, to try and absorb the implications of this momentous revelation, which had already become gradually apparent in earlier chapters. Can it possibly be true? Or would it be more correct to say that the poet, William Stanley, Sixth Earl of Derby and a member of the aristocratic establishment, thought it to be true? Were he and his contemporaries mistaken, or were he and they privy to a state secret of such stupendous magnitude that hardly any hint or whisper of it has been picked up by any historian of the period?

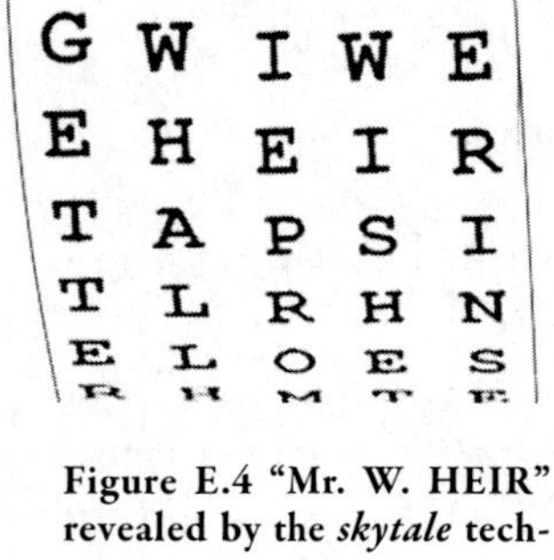

Figure E.4 "Mr. W. HEIR" revealed by the *skytale* technique.

I have to confess that when I first became aware of the enormity of this discovery—the discovery that this was what many people in high places thought at the time, whether or not it was biological fact—I was utterly amazed. I repeat: Can it possibly be true? I hardly know how to answer my own question. What I will say is that everything now seems to hang together in a remarkably consistent manner.

Why does the poet of the sonnets urge with such desperate intensity the Fair Youth to have a son? Because he himself, the heir-apparent, does not wish to inherit the throne, and a potential heir—even an illegitimate one—who already has a son is far more likely to be chosen to succeed Queen Elizabeth than one who is childless. The love for the Fair Youth (Southampton) expressed by the poet (William Stanley) can now be seen as a complex mixture of loyalty to the Tudor dynasty, admiration for a charming well-brought-up young nobleman, friendship for a fellow student first encountered studying at the Inns of

Court, and a kind of dazzlement at his strikingly handsome mien. His "beauty," so frequently extolled throughout the sonnets, encompasses not only his physical beauty (captured in the many portraits of him that survive), but also the beauty inherited from his mother, the Queen—his beauty of descent: his Tudor blood (ready to pass on to his son).

The poet of the sonnets asserts several times (see Chapter 13) that his verse will make the Fair Youth immortal—"*Your name from hence immortall life shall have*"—and he also writes "*Thou in this shalt find thy monument.*" In our first discussion of the Dedication it was noted that the full stops after every word gave it the character of a Roman Latin inscription, where words were conventionally separated by stops rather than spaces. So perhaps the line may be amplified to read "Thou in this [*publication*] shalt find thy monument [*with a memorial inscription that will record for all time your name and the fact that you were the heir to the throne through your mother Queen Elizabeth*]." Have we at last divined the underlying mission (the "second intention") of the first 127 sonnets, to record a state secret of such appalling magnitude that no one dared to do more than hint at it during the Queen's lifetime, but which was so colossally important that it was unthinkable that it should be lost to posterity? *Veritas filia temporis*—time will tell.

TO•THE•ONLIE•BEGETTER•OF•
THESE•INSVING•SONNETS•
Mr•W•H•ALL•HAPPINESSE•AND•
THAT•ETERNITIE•PROMIS
ED•BY•OVR•EVER-LIVING•PO
ET•WISHETH•THE•WELL-WISH
ING•ADVENTVRER•IN•SETT
ING•FORTH• **T•T•**

Figure E.5 The Dedication as a Roman monumental inscription.

Chapter Notes

Introduction

1. The two letters were written by the Catholic George Fenner, both dated 30 June 1599, and were found in the State Papers, Domestic, by James Greenstreet in 1891. They had been intercepted and never reached their intended recipients, who were Catholics living abroad hoping to establish a Catholic-friendly regime following the demise of Queen Elizabeth. William Stanley was descended from Henry VII and had a strong claim to succeed to the throne after Elizabeth's death, but his views on Catholics are not known. James Greenstreet, "A Hitherto Unknown Noble Writer of Elizabethan Comedies," *The Genealogist*, New Series, vol. 7 (London: 1891), 205–08; "Further Notices of William Stanley, 6th Earl of Derby, K. G., as Poet and Dramatist," *The Genealogist*, New Series, vol. 8 (London: 1892), 8–15; "Testimonies against the Accepted Authorship of Shakespear's Plays," *The Genealogist*, New Series, vol. 8, (London: 1892), 137–146.

Fenner's letter to Balthazar Gybels, Antwerp, contains the sentence "Therle of Darby is busyed only in penning comedies for the commoun players." His letter to Sire Humfredo Galdelli or to Giuseppe Tusinger contains the sentence "Our Earle of Darby is busye in penning commodyes for the commoun players." The implication seems to be that he was perceived as being uninterested in having Catholic support for his claim to the throne. *State Papers, Domestic, Elizabeth*, vol. 271, nos. 34 and 35, per A. W. Titherley, *Shakespeare's Identity: William Stanley 6th Earl of Derby* (Winchester: Warren and Son, 1952), 30.

2. John Harris, http://www.forumgarden.com/forums/members/spot.html.

3. Figure 1.1 consists of reproductions (perhaps tracings) of the signatures on the original documents. http://images.search.yahoo.com/search/images?_adv_prop=image&fr=ytff1-yma3&va=Shakespeare%27s+signatures. Photographs of the six signatures are given in E. K. Chambers, *William Shakespeare: A Study of Facts and Problems*, vol. 1 (Oxford at the Clarendon Press, 1930), facing 507.

4. Charlton Ogburn, *The Mysterious William Shakespeare* (McLean, VA: EPM Publications, 1984).

5. The stylistic incompatibilities between Oxford's and Shakespeare's writing habits are discussed in Appendix A, together with problems connected with the sonnets.

6. John Michell, *Who Wrote Shakespeare?* (London: Thames & Hudson, 1996). A major difficulty with William Stanley as an authorship candidate derives from the fact that he left no poetry signed with his name; only a few short letters survive, some of which are discussed in Chapter 29 and Appendix D.

Chapter 1

1. William Shakespeare, *Comedies, Histories, & Tragedies* (London: Isaac Jaggard and Ed. Blount, 1623). "Folio" refers to the size of the paper, close to American legal; "First" because there were three subsequent similar publications, the Second Folio in 1632, the Third in 1663–1664, and the Fourth in 1685.

2. A. J. Pointon, *The Man Who Was Never Shakespeare: The Theft of William Shakspere's Identity* (Tunbridge Wells, U.K.: Parapress, 2011), 24. The entries in the Church Register would have been made by someone local who knew the family and knew how they pronounced their name. Besides "Shakspere" (18 times, plus two "Shakspeares" and one "Shaksper"), the name is also spelled "Shaxpere" (twice) and "Shagspere" (once) in the Church Register. These last two spellings tend to confirm that the name was pronounced with a short "a." (It may be relevant to add that there was a word in common use in the countryside, "shack," meaning grains of corn fallen on the ground during harvest, and used to feed chickens and pigs, which may have influenced the pronunciation.)

It must be emphasized that we cannot really be sure *how* the name sounded when it was pronounced. The fact remains that the actor's name (and that of family members) was never spelled with an "e" after the "k" in the Church records, while the dramatist's was always spelled with an "e" after the "k" on editions of the poems and plays, with two exceptions (more if spurious plays are included). The poet's name was spelled on title pages with a hyphen—"Shake-speare"—17 times, and once without the "e"—"Shak-speare." The use of a hyphen is often claimed to indicate a made-up name or pen name. The first instance of the hyphenated spelling occurs in a footnote to the second poem in Henry Willoughby's *Willobie his Avisa* (1594), four months after the publication of *Lucrece*.

Yet Tarquyne pluckt his glistering grape,
And Shake-speare paints poore Lucrece rape.

This may hint that the author's name was already recognized as a pen name. The name was spelled with a hyphen on several other occasions when the poet was being referred to.

The entry in the Parish Register for Shakspere's burial is reproduced in Chapter 4, where the name is spelled "Shakspere." It is interesting to note that the Christian name of the son of Shakspere's friend Richard Quiney was spelled "Shaksper" and "Shakspere" in the Register; he died in May 1617, aged six months.

3. *Oxford Dictionary of National Biography* (abbreviated *ODNB* throughout this book).

4. "...to ourselues wee ioyned those deserueing men, Shakspere, Hemings, Condall, Philips and others partners in the profittes..."; "...and placed men Players, which were Hemings, Condall, Shakspeare, &c." E. K. Chambers, *William Shakespeare: A Study of Facts and Problems*, vol. 2 (Oxford at the Clarendon Press, 1930), 66.

5. Kenneth Muir, *Shakespeare's Sources* (London: Methuen, 1957).

6. Henry Chettle, *England's Mourning Garment* (London: Thomas Millington, 1603), f. D3 (reprint, Amsterdam: Da Capo Press, 1973).

7. Leslie Hotson, *Mr. W. H.* (London: Hart-Davis, 1964), 38–39.

8. The vague idea that something was amiss was articulated by the eminent American scholar Dr. W. H. Furness, who wrote in 1866, "I am one of the many who have never been able to bring the life of William Shakespeare [i.e., *the actor William Shakspere*] and the plays of Shakespeare within planetary space of each other. Are there any two things in the world more incongruous?" He went on to say that if the plays had been published anonymously, they would "by now" have been attributed to Francis Bacon. Letter to Nathaniel Holmes, 29 October 1866. Nathaniel Holmes, *The Authorship of Shakespeare* (New York: Hurd and Houghton, 1875).

Just over a hundred years later, Samuel Schoenbaum wrote: "Perhaps we should despair of ever bridging the vertiginous expanse between the sublimity of the subject [*the poetry and plays*] and the mundane inconsequence of the documentary record [*of the actor from Stratford-upon-Avon*]. What would we not give for a single personal letter, one page of diary!" *Shakespeare's Lives* (Oxford: Clarendon Press, 1970), 767.

Earlier, John Dover Wilson had written of *Love's Labour's Lost*: "To credit that amazing piece of virtuosity to a butcher-boy who left school at thirteen, or even to one whose education was nothing more than what a grammar school and residence in a little provincial borough could provide, is to invite one either to believe in miracles or to disbelieve in 'the man of Stratford.'" *The Essential Shakespeare: A Biographical Adventure* (Cambridge: Cambridge University Press, 1932), 41–42.

But it seems that these three distinguished scholars were well able to suppress any doubts they may have had about "the man of Stratford," and had no qualms about supporting the received view of the authorship.

Chapter 2

The material in this chapter and the next is largely drawn from my paper "Shakespeare's Impossible Doublet: Droeshout's Engraving Anatomized," *Brief Chronicles*, vol. 2 (2010), 9–24. http://www.briefchronicles.com/. This was later republished in John Shahan and Alexander Waugh, eds., *Shakespeare Beyond Doubt?* (Tamarac, FL: Llumina, 2013).

1. William Shakespeare, *Comedies, Histories, & Tragedies* (London: Isaac Jaggard and Ed. Blount, 1623).

2. A doublet was a close-fitting upper-body garment, with or without sleeves, made from a double thickness of cloth, sometimes with padding or stiffening between the layers depending upon the fashion of the day.

3. June Schlueter, "Martin Droeshout *Redivivus*: Reassessing the Folio Engraving of Shakespeare," *Shakespeare Survey*, vol. 60 (2007), 237–251. Droeshout went on to have a successful career as an engraver both in Spain and England, and engraved portraits of many well-known and distinguished people, including John Donne, the Duke of Buckingham, the Bishop of Durham, the Marquis of Hamilton and Lord Coventry. In 1631 he was commissioned to provide numerous illustrations for the second edition of William Crooke's *Mikrokosmographia* (over 1,000 pages long), testifying to an excellent reputation.

4. Sidney Lee, *A Life of William Shakespeare*, 3rd ed. of revised version (London: John Murray, 1922), 529.

5. M. H. Spielmann, *The Title Page of the First Folio of Shakespeare's Plays: A Comparative Study of the Droeshout portrait and the Stratford Bust* (London: H. Milford, 1924), 32.

6. Anon., "A Problem for the Trade," *The Gentleman's Tailor*, vol. 46 (London: 1911), 93.

7. The production costs of the First Folio have been estimated at £250, around £150,000 in today's money—a huge outlay for the three or four stationers involved. This assumes that 750 copies were printed. It is possible that the undertaking was bankrolled by some wealthy person (Derby was one of the richest people in the country). The volume is thought to have cost 15s. unbound. The annual salary of a university-educated schoolmaster was between £10 and £20 a year. http://www.guardian.co.uk/books/2001/nov/08/shakespeare.

Chapter 3

1. William Shake-speare, *Poems: Written by Wil. Shake-speare, Gent.* (London: John Benson, 1640).

2. Samuel Daniel, *The Civil Wars Between the Houses of Lancaster and York* (London: Simon Waterson, 1609), title page.

3. Leah S. Marcus, *Puzzling Shakespeare: Local Reading and Its Discontents* (Berkeley: University of California Press, 1988), 1–30.

4. There is something slightly odd about the wording "*for* Shakespeare." It might suggest various interpretations, e.g., "instead of Shakespeare," or "on behalf of Shakespeare," or "at Shakespeare's request." Moreover, Jonson calls it a "figure" rather than a "portrait," and in the event it does indeed turn out to be not so much a portrait, more of a booby-trap.

5. Dr. Tarnya Cooper of the National Portrait Gallery, private communication.

6. http://elizabethan.org/sumptuary/index.html. There is no other example of a writer or actor being portrayed in upper-class clothing, to the best of my knowledge. Here, as in so many other ways, Shakespeare is the exception.

7. Marcus, *Puzzling Shakespeare*, 1–30.

8. *Searching for Shakespeare*, exhibition curated by Dr. Tarnya Cooper, National Portrait Gallery, London: March to May, 2006, 48, 120.

9. In William Marshall's 1640 version of the engraving, Figure 3.1, the underpropper shows through on both sides of the collar, and the triangular darts on left and right are mirror images of each other. Through restoring symmetry, Marshall acknowledges—by correcting them—two of the more obvious peculiarities of the Droeshout original.

10. It was shown by George Steevens sometime during the period 1775–85 that both the dedicatory letter and the address to the reader were almost certainly written by Ben Jonson, and most subsequent commentators agree with this finding. Steevens' proof can be found in "Boswell's Malone" (The "Third Variorum"), *The Plays and Poems of William Shakespeare*, vol. 2 (London: 1821), 663.

11. It has recently been shown by Alexander Waugh that "Avon" in the phrase "Sweet Swan of Avon" may have another meaning. In the early 16th century Hampton Court was known as "Avon," a shortening of the name "Avondunum," meaning a fortification by a river (the river being the Thames at Hampton Court). "Sweet Swan of Avon" may therefore mean "Sweet Poet of Hampton Court," where plays were regularly performed in the Great Hall before Queen Elizabeth and King James. Ben Jonson appears to have deliberately used a word with two possible implications, either the Avon of Stratford-upon-Avon, or the Avon of Hampton Court, in order to further the deception. Alexander Waugh, *The Oxfordian*, vol. 16 (September 2014), 97–103.

Chapter 4

1. William Shakespeare, *Venus and* Adonis (London: Richard Field, 1593). The poem proved enormously popular and was reprinted six times before 1600; ten more reprints had appeared by 1640. It consists of 199 stanzas of six lines, a total of 1,194 lines.

2. T. H. [Thomas Heywood], *Oenone and Paris* (London: Richard Jones, 1594). Near the beginning of the dedication occurs the sentence "Heare you have the first fruits of my ... Pen; which, how rude and unpolished it maye seeme in your Eagle-sighted eyes, I can not conceive." As an eagle was the main part of the Derby crest, it might almost appear that T.H. knew who had written *Venus and Adonis*, and was twitting him over it.

3. William Shakespeare, *Lucrece* (London: Richard Field, 1594).

4. S. Schoenbaum, *William Shakespeare: A Documentary Life* (Oxford: Clarendon Press, 1975), 136.

5. H. N. Gibson, *The Shakespeare Claimants* (London: Methuen, 1962), 59–65. However, according to Suetonius, another Labeo, Quintus Fabius Labeo, a one-time consul, wrote plays that were ascribed to Terence, a freed Roman slave who supposedly wrote many plays, some of which were thought to have been written by noblemen. The identification of Hall and Marston's "Labeo" remains in doubt. Alexander Waugh, private communication. See also http://www.realshakespeare.com/the-authorship-question/labeo.

6. Diana Price, *Shakespeare's Unorthodox Biography: New Evidence of an Authorship Problem* (Westport, CT: Greenwood Press, 2001), 225. However, recent research by Alexander Waugh suggests that Covell may have been hinting not at Daniel but at Oxford, the compound word "courte-deare-verse" (a pun on "courtier verse") concealing Oxford's family name "de Vere." Either way, it is clear that several people were puzzled by the name "Shakespeare" attached to *Venus and Adonis*. Alexander Waugh, "A Secret Revealed: William Covell and His Polimanteia (1595)," *De Vere Society Newsletter*, October 2013, 7–10.

7. Susanna made one "painfully formed signature, which was probably the most that she was capable of doing with the pen." Edward Maunde Thompson, "Handwriting," in *Shakespeare's England: An Account of the Life and Manners of His Age*, vol. 1 (Oxford: Clarendon Press, 1916), 294. Susanna was unable to recognize her own husband's handwriting; her sister Judith signed with a mark.

8. Charles Nicholl, *The Lodger: Shakespeare on Silver Street* (London: Alan Lane, 2007), illustrations numbers 4 and 25. Originals in TNA Court of Requests, May–June 1612 (TNA REQ 4/1/4/1).

9. R. A. Foakes, ed., *Henslowe's Diary*, 2nd ed. (Cambridge University Press, 2002).

10. Abel Lefranc, *Sous le masque de William Shakespeare, VIe comte de Derby*, vol. 2 (Paris: Payot et cie., 1918), trans. Cecil Cragg (Braunton, Devon, 1988), 57.

11. Richard Grant White, *Memoirs of the Life of William Shakespeare* (New York: Little, Brown, 1866), 146.

12. E. K. Chambers, *William Shakespeare: A Study of Facts and Problems*, vol. 2 (Oxford at the Clarendon Press, 1930), 169–180.

13. I should like to encourage the reader to examine the reproduction of Dugdale's original sketch of the monument on which the engraving in his book is based, to see how radically the present monument differs from it. The sketch is often assumed to date from 1634, and it can be found here, where a picture of the monument in its current state can also be found: http://shaksper.net/scholarly-resources/reference-files.

14. Brian Vickers, "The Face of the Bard?" *Times Literary Supplement*, London: 18 & 26 August 2006, 15–16.

15. It has even been suggested that the first two were chosen precisely *because* they had written nothing, and that "Maro" refers not to the poet Virgil, but to the mediaeval writer Virgilius Maro, known as "Grammaticus," who wrote two works that were parodies of scholarly writings, full of outlandish stories with fake references to invented classical texts. Jack A. Goldstone, "The Latin Inscription on the Stratford Monument Unraveled, and Its Bearing on the Authorship Controversy," *De Vere Society Newsletter*, July 2012, 11–14.

16. A. J. Pointon, "The Rest Is Silence: The Absence of Tributes to the Author Shakespeare at the Time of Shakspere's Death," eds. John Shahan and Alexander Waugh, *Shakespeare Beyond Doubt?* (Tamarac, FL: Llumina, 2013), 69–70.

17. http://special.lib.gla.ac.uk/exhibns/month/july2001.html.

18. Julia Cleave, "More a Player Than a Playwright?" *De Vere Society Newsletter*, March 2008, 17–19.

19. Apart from verifying Shakespeare's exact knowledge of the multifarious canals mentioned in the plays, employed for cross-country journeys (all recorded on ancient maps), here are four specific examples. Firstly, the sycamore trees of *Romeo and Juliet*, Act I scene 1,

on the outskirts of Verona—still there today. Then the "tranect" in *Merchant of Venice*, Act III scene 4, which has baffled every modern commentator, turns out to be a land-crossing for boats connecting a fresh-water canal with the lagoon, where they would be fitted with cart wheels and wheeled across. Thirdly, locating the "Duke's Oak" in *Midsummer Night's Dream*, Act I scene 2, in an area known as "Little Athens," near Mantua, and lastly, identifying Prospero's island in *The Tempest* with the volcanic island Vulcano, one of the Aeolian Islands, 25 miles north of Sicily. (Act I scene 2: "Come unto these yellow sands"—yellow because of the volcanic sulfur. http://en.wikipedia.org/wiki/Vulcano.) These are all identified by Richard Paul Roe in *The Shakespeare Guide to Italy: Retracing the Bard's Unknown Travels* (New York: HarperCollins, 2011), 9–10, 144–50, 183–84, 265–95.

Chapter 5

The material in this chapter is largely drawn from my paper *"Shakespeare's Sonnet 125: Who Bore the Canopy?"* Notes and Queries, vol. 258, no. 3, September 2013; 438–441.

1. *Shake-speares Sonnets: Neuer Before Imprinted* (London: by G. Eld for T. T., 1609).
2. Leslie Hotson, *Mr. W. H.* (London: Hart-Davis, 1964), 38–39.
3. As readers may know, many of the sonnets are addressed to a young friend, often referred to as the "Fair Youth." The sonnets are discussed in the second section of this book, Chapters 13 to 22.
4. In their editions of (or commentaries on) the sonnets, the following make this allowance, or hint at it: A. L. Rowse (1964), John Dover Wilson (1967), Stephen Booth (1977), Robert Giroux (1982), John Kerrigan (1986), Colin Burrow (2002) and Kenneth Muir (2005). While a number of editors consider the canopy to be metaphorical or figurative, others leave the matter open.
5. A search on the word "canopy" (including variant spellings) both in the *ODNB* and via the internet yielded details of more than 30 occasions when canopies were carried, always over royalty. Canopies in public processions were carried by commoners with one exception. At Queen Jane Seymour's funeral on 12 November 1537, Thomas Fiennes, Ninth Baron Dacre (*ODNB*), and Thomas West, Eighth Baron West and ninth Baron de la Warr (*ODNB*), were two of those who bore the canopy over her hearse.
6. College of Arms, MS R.20 Funeral Ceremony (Anstis); f. 296.
7. *Ibid.*, f. 337.
8. Historical Manuscripts Commission, MSS Rye and Herefordshire Corporations (London: 1892), 15 July 1603. http://www.british-history.ac.uk/report.aspx?compid=67148.
9. "The King, richly mounted on a white gennet, under a rich canopie susteind by eyght gentlemen of the Privie Chamber, for [i.e., *in place of*] the Barons of the Cinque Ports, entered the Royal Cittie of London: etc.," 15 March 1603/4. John Nichols, *The Progresses, Processions and Magnificent Festivities of King James the First* (London: J. B. Nichols, 1828), 324. According to Nicolo Molin, the Venetian ambassador, twenty-four gentlemen participated, "splendidly dressed, eight of whom took it turn and turn about." *Calendar of State Papers (Venetian)* (London: 1900), 26 March 1604. http://www.british-history.ac.uk/report.aspx?compid=95611.
10. Roy Strong, *The Cult of Elizabeth* (London: Pimlico, 1999), 17–55. Three of the canopy-bearers are visible, and have been identified as Sir Robert Cecil and two sons of the Earl of Worcester (all commoners).
11. "In which Order Her Majesty proceeded to the North Door of the church of *Westminster*, where the dean there and the Dean of the Chappel met her, and the whole Chappel in Copes; and St *Edward's* staff with the Inlet in the top was delivered unto her, her Arm, for the bearing thereof, assisted by the Baron of Hunsdon; the Canopy born over her by *Charles Howard* Esq.; Sir *George Howard*, Sir *Richard Blunt*, Sir *Ed. Warner*, Sir *John Perrott*, and Sir *William Fitz-Williams*, Knights; her Grace's Train borne up and assisted, for the weight thereof from her arms, by the Lord *Robert Dudley*, Master of the Horse, and Sir *Francis Knollys*, Vice Chamberlain; and so orderly proceeded to the Travers beside the Table of Administration..." Simonds D'Ewes, *The Journals of all the Parliaments during the reign of Queen Elizabeth* (London: 1682), 58. Charles Howard was later knighted.
12. Ralph M. Sargent, *The Life and Lyrics of Sir Edward Dyer* (Oxford: Clarendon Press, 1968), 130.
13. "During the time of unction, a rich pall of cloth of gold (brought from the great wardrobe by Mr. Rumbal) was held over the king's head by the dukes of Buckingham and Albemarle, the earls of Berks and Sandwich, as knights of the most noble Order of the Garter." T. C. Banks, *An Historical and Critical Enquiry into the Nature of the Kingly Office, etc.* (London: Sherwood, Neely and Jones, 1814), 49–50.
14. "Then four Knights of the Garter, appointed by His Majesty, viz. the Duke of Ormond, the Duke of Albemarle, the Duke of Beaufort, and the Earl of Mulgrave held a Pall or Pallet of Cloth of Gold over the KING during the whole Ceremony of the Anointing." Francis Sandford, *The History of the Coronation of James II* (London: 1687), 91.
15. Peter J. Begent and Hubert Chesshyre, *The Most Noble Order of the Garter 650 Years* (London: Spink, 1999).
16. To see the anointing of Queen Elizabeth II at her coronation in 1953, go to http://pirate.shu.edu/~wisterro/coronation.htm, scroll down to the end of the paragraph headed "The Anointing," and click on the word Anointing.
17. Anon., *The ceremonies, form of prayer, and services used in Westminster-Abby at the coronation of King James the First and Queen Ann his consort* (London: Randal Taylor, 1685).
18. Stephen Booth, who also points out that many words in this sonnet come from the service of Holy Communion. *Shakespeare's Sonnets* (New Haven: Yale University Press, 1977), 429–30.
19. Peter Farey, "Sonnet 125," *The Shakespeare Conference,* 17 October 2006. http://shaksper.net/archive/2006/242-october/25009-sonnet-125. He quotes the 1559 Prayer Book, Holy Communion, which can be found on: http://justus.anglican.org/resources/bcp/1559/BCP_1559.htm.
20. The Garter Feast was held on 2 July. John Nichols, *The Progresses, Processions and Magnificent Festivities*

of King James the First (London: J. B. Nichols, 1828), 193.

21. John Nichols, *The Progresses and Public Processions of Queen Elizabeth* (London: John Nichols and Son, 1823), 145.

22. Nor doth the silver tonged *Melicert*
[i.e., Shakespeare, see below
Drop from his honied muse one sable tear
To mourne her death that graced his desert,
And to his laies opened her Royall eare.
Shepheard, remember our *Elizabeth*
And sing her Rape, done by that *Tarquin*,
Death. [ref. to *Lucrece*

Henry Chettle, *England's Mourning Garment* (London: Thomas Millington, 1603), f. D3 (reprint, Amsterdam: Da Capo Press, 1973). "Melicert" means "honeycomb" in Greek, and was also a name assumed *as a disguise* by a character in Greene's *Menaphon*. Robert Greene, *Menaphon, Camila's alarm to slumbering Euphues in his melancholy cell at Silexedra, &c* (London: 1589).

Chapter 6

1. Francis Meres, *Palladis Tamia. Wit's Treasury* (London: P. Short for Cuthbert Burbie, 1598), 281v, 282r. This publication is important in English literary history as it contains the first mention of the poems and early plays of William Shakespeare. It lists twelve plays—six comedies: *Two Gentlemen of Verona, Comedy of Errors, Love's Labors Lost, Love's Labors Won, Midsummer Night's Dream*, and *Merchant of Venice*; and six tragedies: *Richard II, Richard III, Henry the IV, King John, Titus Andronicus*, and *Romeo and Juliet*, thereby establishing their composition before 1598. It is not known whether *Love's Labors Won* is a lost play or an alternative title for a surviving play.

2. "Shakespeare, whose hony-flowing Vaine..."; Richard Barnfeild, *Poems in Divers Humors* (London: 1598). Marlowe was also described as having a "honey-flowing vaine" by Henry Petowe, *Continuation to Hero and Leander*, vol. 2 (London: Andrew Harris, 1598), 59–62, perhaps copying the epithet from Barnfeild whose work was published first.

3. "Honie-tong'd Shakespeare, when I saw thine issue..."; John Weever, *Epigrammes in the Oldest Cut, and Newest Fashion* (London: Thomas Bushell, 1599), 75.

4. See note 22, Chapter 5.

5. "Mellifluous Shake-speare, whose enchanting quill..."; Thomas Heywood, *The Hierarchie of the Blessed Angels* (London: 1635), Lib. 4.

6. Leslie Hotson, *Shakespeare's Motley* (London: Hart-Davis, 1952), 26.

7. Edmund Spenser, *Teares of the Muses, Thalia* (London: William Ponsonbie, 1591).

8. Nicholas Rowe, *The Works of Mr. William Shakespear* (London: Jacob Tonson, 1709), preface.

9. The *Oxford English Dictionary* gives the oldest and primary meaning of "gentle" as follows: "A. adj. 1.a. (a) Of persons: Well-born, belonging to a family of position; originally used synonymously with *noble*, but afterwards distinguished from it, either as a wider term, or as designating a lower degree of rank."

10. Edmund Spenser, *Colin Clouts Come Home Againe* (London: William Ponsonby, 1595).

11. 'ΑΕΤΟΣ, or 'αιετος,..., an eagle. Liddell and Scott, *A Lexicon, etc.* (Oxford: Clarendon Press, 1944).

12. Edmond Malone, "Life of Shakespeare," in *The Plays and Poems of William Shakspeare etc.*, vol. 2 (London: 1821), 273–74.

13. Sidney Lee, *A Life of William Shakespeare*, revised 3rd ed. (London: John Murray, 1922), 150.

Chapter 7

1. Thomas Nashe, *The Apologie of Pierce Pennilesse, or Strange Newes of the Intercepting Certain Letters and a Convoy of Verses as they were going Privily to Victual the Low Countries* (London: John Danter, 1592). A modern-spelling transcript by Nina Green can be found here: http://www.oxford-shakespeare.com/Nashe/Strange_News.pdf. See Appendix B.

2. Nashe extolled Ferdinando in *Pierce Pennilesse his Supplication to the Devil*, writing "But from general fame, let me digres to my private experience, and, with a tongue unworthie to name a name of such worthines, affectionally emblazon, to the eyes of wonder, the matchless image of honor, & magnificent rewarder of vertue, Jove's eagle-borne Ganimede, thrice noble Amintas." London: Richard Ihones, 1592; repr. by J. Payne Collier, 1842; 91. http://books.google.co.uk/books?id=KY9VdGNg4QcC&printsec=titlepage&as_brr=1&redir_esc=y#v=onepage&q&f=true.

3. In a letter to Lord Burghley 26 January 1591, Sir Robert Sidney writes, "The scholer [Christofer Marly] sais himself to be very wel known both to the Earle of Northumberland and my lord Strang." PRO SP 84 / 44 / 60

4. Robert Greene (1558–1592) was a highly successful playwright and pamphleteer, who later fell upon hard times. He is best known today for his pamphlet *Greene's Groatsworth of Wit Bought with a Million of Repentance* (London: William Wright, 1592), which is often supposed (wrongly, in my view, but that is another story) to contain the first reference to Shakspere in London.

5. Gabriel Harvey, *Foure Letters and Certaine Sonnets* (London: John Wolfe, 1592). Harvey had corresponded with Spenser in the 1570s, and (if they kept in touch) would probably have known who he meant by "Our pleasant Willy" in *Teares of the Muses*.

6. Gabriel Harvey, *Pierce's Supererogation, or A New Praise of the Old Ass* (London: John Wolfe, 1593), 209. It is interesting that Harvey is aware that Stanley, M. Apis Lapis, has written plays, but is apparently unaware (*circa* 1598) that he had written *Venus and Adonis* in 1593 (see Chapter 4).

7. All of whom, Harvey says, Nashe has "shamefully and odiously misused." (*Ibid.*)

8. At one point he writes: "Faugh! Methinks my jests begin already to smell of the cask, with talking so much of this liquid provender."

9. One might then perhaps detect a note of autobiography in the words of the Shepherd in *Winter's Tale* (III.iii.58–61) "I would there were no age between ten and three-and-twenty ... for there is nothing in the between but getting wenches with child..." etc.

10. The story was repeated by Francis Meres, as follows: "*Robert Greene* died of a surfet taken at Pickeld Herrings & Rhenish wine, as witnesseth *Thomas Nashe,*

who was at the fatall banquet." Francis Meres, *Palladis Tamia. Wit's Treasury* (London: P. Short for Cuthbert Burbie, 1598), 286^{v}.

11. Thomas Cooper, *Thesaurus linguæ Romanæ & Britannicæ* (London: 1565). I am grateful to the late Andy Hannas for bringing this to my attention.

12. J. M. Tobin refers to "Shakespeare's habitual incorporating of Nashe's prose into his own expressions, whether of prose or verse." J. M. Tobin, "A Touch of Greene, Much Nashe, and All Shakespeare," *"Henry VI": Critical Essays*, ed. T. A. Pendleton (New York: Routledge, 2001), 42. Tobin has written many other papers detailing Shakespeare's apparent recollections of Nashe's writings. Katherine Duncan-Jones notes that Shakespeare borrows from Nashe's *The Unfortunate Traveller* in *Henry IV, part 1*, and Nashe then borrows from Shakespeare's *Lucrece*. Katherine Duncan-Jones, *Ungentle Shakespeare* (London: Arden Shakespeare, 2001), 69–71.

13. Gabriel Harvey, *Foure Letters, v. supra*, 8.

14. Ernst Honigmann argues strongly for identifying both of Spenser's poets with Shakespeare. E. A. J. Honigmann, *Shakespeare: The Lost Years* (Manchester: Manchester University Press, 1998), 71–76. John Payne Collier is another of those who thought "our pleasant Willy" was Shakespeare, though I do not have a citation for this. Perhaps it is to be found in his *The Works of Edmund Spenser* (Bell and Daldy, 1862).

Chapter 8

1. For a discussion of this topic see Stephen Urkowitz, "Good News about 'Bad' Quartos," *"Bad" Shakespeare: Revaluations of the Shakespeare Canon*, ed. Maurice Charney (London and Toronto: Associated University Presses, 1988), 189–206. The orthodox view is championed by Lukas Erne, who maintains that Shakespeare, apart from being a playwright who wrote theatrical texts for the stage, was also "a literary dramatist who produced reading texts for the page." In many cases these were too long (occasionally far too long) for the stage, and needed to be cut down for performance. Lukas Erne, *Shakespeare as Literary Dramatist* (Cambridge: Cambridge University Press, 2003; revised ed. 2013).

2. Alice Walker, "The 1622 Quarto and the First Folio Texts of *Othello*," *Shakespeare Survey*, vol. 5 (Cambridge University Press, 1952), 16–24.

3. W. W. Greg, *The Shakespeare First Folio, Its Bibliographical and Textual History* (Oxford: Clarendon Press, 1955).

4. E. A. J. Honigmann, *The Texts of Othello and Shakespearian Revision* (London: Routledge, 1996).

5. *Ibid.*, 95–96.

6. *Ibid.*, 96.

7. *Ibid.*, 15.

8. Before a compositor can start setting type, the manuscript has to be "cast off," that is the lines of text have to be counted out so that the allocation of text to each printed page can be determined. For example, imagine 240 lines of verse to be allocated to a quire or gathering of three folded double sheets, giving six leaves and 12 pages. Page 1 will be partnered by page 12, that is they will both be printed simultaneously on the same side of one of the three double sheets. Lines 1 to 20 will be set into type on page 1, and lines 221 to 240 on page 12. The compositor therefore has to count through the text to locate lines 221 to 240. If the manuscript has been revised, with inserted lines or additional speeches on extra sheets of paper, mistakes might easily be made when counting out, hence the desirability of a clean, newly written copy of the revised manuscript to obviate errors. See Peter M. Blayney, *The First Folio of Shakespeare* (Folger Library Publications, 1991), 9–12. In practice, as Blayney explains, the middle two pages would be set into type first, i.e., pages 6 and 7 in our example. The necessity for precise counting of lines remains the same.

9. Edwin Reed, *Francis Bacon Our Shakespeare* (London: Gay and Bird, 1902), 118.

10. In the First Folio text of *The Taming of the Shrew,* the hired player John Sincklo, whose name appears in the left margin as the speaker (rather than the name of the part he was playing) reveals that he had played the part of "Soto" on an earlier occasion (Induction, I.86). The first time a character called "Soto" appears in any play of the period is in *Women Pleased* by John Fletcher, written not before 1619. This is another example where the simplest explanation is that the author was still revising his plays in the years immediately preceding 1623. James J. Merino, *Owning William Shakespeare* (Philadelphia: University of Pennsylvania Press, 2011), 50ff.

Chapter 9

1. Ian Wilson, *Shakespeare: The Evidence* (New York: St. Martin's Press, 1993), 102.

2. Edward Halle, *The Union of the Two Noble and Illustrate Families of Lancastre and Yorke,* (London: 1542; later editions 1548 and 1550), commonly called *Halle's Chronicle.*

3. Ian Wilson, *v. supra*, 102–03.

4. John Weever, *Epigrammes in the Oldest Cut, and Newest Fashion* (London: Thomas Bushell, 1599).

5. E. A. J. Honigmann, *John Weever: A Biography of a Literary Associate of Shakespeare and Jonson* (Manchester: Manchester University Press, 1987), 9–10. Honigmann says that Weever "seems to have been interested in writing for the theatre"; it is not known whether he ever actually did so (p. 18).

Chapter 10

1. J. J. Bagley, *The Earls of Derby, 1485–1985* (London: Sidgwick & Jackson, 1985), 57–77.

2. *Ibid.*, 72.

3. Dennis Flynn, "'Awry and Squint': The Dating of Donne's Holy Sonnets," *John Donne Journal,* vol. 7, no. 1 (1988), 35–46.

4. John Finnis and Patrick H. Martin, "An Oxford Play Festival in February 1582," *Notes and Queries*, vol. 248, no. 4 (December 2003), 391–94.

5. Leo Daugherty, *The Assassination of Shakespeare's Patron: Investigating the Death of the Fifth Earl of Derby* (New York: Cambria Press, 2011), *passim.*

6. He was addressed as "Prince Ferdinando" in a contemporary work. Leslie Hotson, *Shakespeare by Hilliard* (London: Chatto & Windus, 1977), 164. The

miniature portrait discussed by Hotson here is almost certainly a portrait of Ferdinando.

7. By this time Robert was assisting his father Lord Burghley, who besides his appointment as Lord Treasurer was also acting as *de facto* Secretary of State, the office of which had fallen vacant.

8. Lawrence Manley, "From Strange's Men to Pembroke's Men: 2 'Henry VI' and 'The First Part of the Contention,'" *Shakespeare Quarterly*, vol. 54, no. 3 (Autumn 2003), 253–87. Leo Daugherty, *v. supra,* 128–29.

9. Leo Daugherty, *v. supra,* 203–216.

10. "What was become of my Lady Strange?" Captain Duffield reporting conversation made by one Bost, letter of 9 November 1593, *Cecil Papers at Hatfield House*, 203. 150. http://www. britishhistory.ac.uk/report. aspx?compid =112054. It is not clear what prompted this question. It sounds as though she had done something unusual and was not living with her husband; on the other hand it may be an entirely neutral inquiry.

11. *Ibid.*

Chapter 11

1. See Chapter 5, note 22.

2. Nashe's epistle to *Strange News* is given in Appendix B.

Chapter 12

1. William Friedman, and Elizebeth Friedman, *The Shakespearean Ciphers Examined* (Cambridge University Press, 1957), 101.

2. Francis Davison, *Anagrammata in Nomina Illustrissimorum Heroum* (London: Simon Stafford, 1603). http://www.philological.bham.ac.uk/anagrams/.

3. William and Elizebeth Friedman, *v. supra*, 96–97.

4. John Davies, *Hymnes of Astraea, in acrosticke verse* (London: I. S., 1599).

5. William and Elizebeth Friedman, *v. supra*, 98.

6. *Ibid.*, 99.

7. This example comes from the book by Richard Deacon (real name Donald McCormick), *John Dee* (London: Frederick Muller, 1969), 290–91. I am inclined to think that this is a made-up example to illustrate Dee's method, not something composed by Dee himself.

8. John Wilkins, *Mercury, or the Secret and Swift Messenger* (London: 1641), 66 (*recte* 50) (reprint Frank Cass, 1970).

9. A similar method, where the message is conveyed through the first word in each chapter, is used in Robert Harris's novel *The Ghost* (London: Arrow Books, 2008), 393–94.

10. Francesco Colonna, *Hypnerotomachia: The Strife of Love in a Dreame*, Translation by R. D., London: 1592. Facsimile ed., introduced by Lucy Gent (Scholars' Facsimiles & Reprints, 1973).

11. William and Elizebeth Friedman, *v. supra*, 100.

Chapter 13

1. *Shake-speares Sonnets* (London: by G. Eld for T. T., 1609).

2. Both these sonnets refer to baths as providing relief from disease—"sovereign cure," "healthful remedy," and it has even been suggested that the poet might have recently visited the hot spring waters at Bath. John Dover Wilson quotes H. C. Beeching (who quotes from George Steevens' *Notes* of 1773/1790):

> "Query, whether we shall read *Bath* (i.e., the city of that name). The following words seem to authorize it" Steevens. There is undoubtedly a reference to the Bath waters, for the Greek original says nothing about curative powers.

H. C. Beeching, *The Sonnets of Shakespeare* (1904), quoted in John Dover Wilson, *The Sonnets* (Cambridge: Cambridge University Press, 1976), 267. It may be no more than coincidence, but it so happens that on 12 April 1606 Derby wrote to his uncle saying that having been in poor health he was finding "greatt ease" in taking to the waters at Bath. Cecil Papers at Hatfield House, http://www.proquest.com/products-services/cecil_papers.html.

The rest of the publication consists of a narrative poem of 47 stanzas, "A Lover's Complaint." The general opinion is that this is also by Shakespeare, but it has recently been suggested by Brian Vickers that it is really by John Davies of Hereford, who (as it happens) was a friend of Derby. Brian Vickers, *Shakespeare: A Lover's Complaint, and John Davies of Hereford* (Cambridge: Cambridge University Press, 2007). "Hereford" is attached to his name to avoid confusion with Sir John Davies, another writer and poet of the period.

3. Saturn feared that his children would overthrow him, and ate each one upon birth.

4. "In order to persuade a friend to marry, many kinds of reasons could profitably be urged: concern for his own moral and material welfare in the founding of a domestic circle or in the respected position of a husband and father; the desirable possession of a feminine personality, distinguished for beauty, wit, birth, or property, which the poet might, with this intention, sketch in the most alluring colors; finally, if the friend were an Earl of Southampton or a Pembroke, a reference to Noblesse oblige,—to the obligation not to let a noble race die out, but to progress its distinction. Of all these and similar grounds with which a man of flesh and blood might persuade a real friend to marriage, we find in all these sonnets not one so much as touched upon, and instead of them only this one argument, discussed even to satiety: You are beautiful, and must therefore care for the preservation of your beauty through reproduction,—an argument which, in Story-land and addressed to the coy Adonis by lovesick Venus, might find some justification, but which could never, in the actual relations of life, have been seriously advanced by a reasonable man such as we take Shakespeare to have been, in order to persuade another—it is to be hoped also reasonable—man, his friend, to marry." Raymond Macdonald Alden, *The Sonnets of Shakespeare* (Boston & New York: Houghton Mifflin, 1916), 17, quoting Nicolaus Delius, *Shakespeare Jahrbuch* 91 (1865?), 36–37 (my thanks to Richard Kennedy for bringing this quotation to my attention).

5. C. S. Lewis, *English Literature in the Sixteenth Century, Excluding Drama* (London: Oxford University Press, 1973), 503–505.

6. A similar love triangle is hinted at in *Willobie his Avisa* by Henry Willoughby (London: John Windet,

1594). "H. W. being suddenly infected with the contagion of a fantastical fit, at the first sight of A, ... bewrayeth the secresy of his disease unto his familiar frend W. S., who not long before had tried the courtesy of the like passion, and was now newly recovered ... he determined to see whether it would sort to a happier end for this new actor, than it did for the old player." A number of people suppose that "H. W." stands for Henry Wriothesley, Earl of Southampton, who is paying suit to Avisa after an earlier attempt by "W. S.," initials which might stand for William Stanley. The book proved very popular, and went through several editions, suggesting that something scandalous in high places was being obliquely referred to. Recent research suggests that Avisa was Lady Penelope Rich, sister to the Earl of Essex who was the Queen's favorite at this time. Penelope had been married young to Lord Rich, whom she detested, and later formed a liaison with Charles Blount, whom she eventually married. She was not thought to have remained entirely faithful to either of these men. Dr. Ian Wilson, http://www.shakespearesdarklady.com/.

7. A sustained attempt to reorder the sonnets has been made by S. C. Campbell, and her "re-paging" (as she calls it) has met with approval from a number of people; *Shake-speare's Sonnets: The Alternative Text* (Cambridge: Cassandra Press, 2009). Nevertheless, there are good reasons for thinking that the sonnets are (mostly) in the order mapped out by the poet. For example, the first 17 sonnets urge the Fair Youth to have a son, while in the final sonnet of the first sequence, #126, his baby son is addressed in the presence of his parents and others, as discussed in Appendix A; R. J. C. Wait, *The Background to Shakespeare's Sonnets* (London: Chatto & Windus, 1972), 14–16, 123, 189–92, 199.

Further reasons are given by Gerard Ledger, who also comments at length on the frequency of biblical references throughout the collection, so marked that he is driven to observe that in each of five sonnets (#37, #53, #101, #105 and #108) the Fair Youth appears to be being likened to Christ himself. He sums this up by saying "the onlie-begetter is an essential part of the dedication of the sonnets, and the link between the fair youth and the only-begotten Son of God is one which I hope I have shown above to be unmistakable." The "onlie begetter" of the Dedication is a reference to Christ as the "only begotten sonne of the father, full of grace and trueth." The Gospel of St. John 1:14 (The Bishops' Bible, 1568). Gerard Ledger, http://www.shakespeares-sonnets.com/; http://www.shakespeares-sonnets.com/Archive/ded2comm.htm.

If we read this comment in the light of another comment by Frances Yates, to the effect that the iconography of the Virgin Queen can be seen as a transformation of the cult of the Virgin Mary, strange thoughts are liable to flit across the mind. Frances M. Yates, *Lull and Bruno: Collected Essays*, vol. 1 (London and Boston: Routledge and Kegan Paul, 1982).

8. Whether or not the sonnets tell us anything about the man who wrote them (and also about people he knew) has puzzled many orthodox Shakespeareans. Joseph Sobran quotes from a few who have pondered this question. A. C. Bradley wrote "No capable poet, much less a Shakespeare, intending to produce a merely 'dramatic' series of poems, would dream of inventing a story like that of these sonnets, or, even if he did, of treating it as they [the sonnets] treat it. The story is very odd and unattractive.... [but] all this is very natural if the story is substantially a real story of Shakespeare himself and of certain other persons." *Oxford Lectures on Poetry* (Bloomington: Indiana University Press, 1961), 331. C. S. Lewis wrote that the sonnets "tell so odd a story that we find a difficulty in regarding it as fiction." *English Literature in the Sixteenth Century: Excluding Drama* (Oxford: Oxford University Press, 1973), 503. Paul Ramsey writes, "The Sonnets have too much jagged specificity to ignore, too little development and completing of events to be an invention." *The Fickle Glass* (New York: AMS Press, 1979). And Philip Edwards says, "[T]hat there is a solid core of autobiography in the Sonnets, in the events referred to, the relationships described, the emotions expressed, seems to me beyond dispute." *Shakespeare, a Writer's Progress* (New York: Oxford University Press, 1986), 13. Joseph Sobran, *Alias Shakespeare* (New York: Free Press, 1997), 84.

However, very few modern orthodox scholars subscribe to the views just quoted. The prevailing opinion is that while a few may touch on real events, the great majority are examples of abstract poetry written for its own sake, or as an expression of the poet's mastery of the form.

Chapter 14

1. Leslie Hotson, *Mr. W. H.* (London: Hart-Davis, 1964), 26–41.

2. G. Wilson Knight, *The Mutual Flame: On Shakespeare's Sonnets & the Phoenix & the Turtle* (London: Methuen, 1955), 6, 59–63. I am indebted to Hank Whittemore for these quotations.

3. See motto, dedication page. The change of "lovely" to "lively" was suggested by John Padel, *New Poems by Shakespeare: Order and Meaning Restored to the Sonnets* (London: Herbert Press, 1981), 207. The change of "darling" to "daring" is my own suggestion. Shakespeare elsewhere never uses "darling" as an adjective, while "the *daring* buds of May" find an echo in *The Winter's Tale,* IV.iv.118–20.

Daffodils,
That come before the swallow dares, and take
The winds of March with beauty.

It will emerge in Chapter 29 that Shakespeare's handwriting was often hard to read, and compositors made numerous mistakes. To my ears, the amended version sounds more characteristically Shakespearean than the 1609 printed version. As for my parents and family—*Their eternal summer shall not fade.*

Chapter 15

1. Charlton Ogburn, *The Mysterious William Shakespeare* (McLean, VA: EPM Publications, 1984), 319.

2. A. L. Rowse, *Shakespeare's Sonnets* (New York: Harper & Row, 1964), vii.

3. Charlton Ogburn, *v. supra*, 345–46.

4. C. S. Lewis, *English Literature in the Sixteenth Century, Excluding Drama* (London: Oxford University Press, 1973), 503–505.

5. The name "Vere" at this time was pronounced "Vair," and it may be that the words "fair" and "fairest" were sometimes intended to hint at the Fair Youth's sup-

posititious father. It has not escaped notice that the Dedication to the Sonnets is arranged in three inverted triangles comprising six, two and four lines. The name "Edward de Vere" is composed of three words of six, two and four letters.

6. Katherine Duncan Jones, *Shakespeare's Sonnets* (London: Arden, 1997), 453–466. The theme of succession is also invoked in the first of the second series of sonnets, sonnet 127. The first quatrain reads:

In the ould age blacke was not counted faire,
Or if it weare it bore not beauties name:
But now is blacke beauties successive heire,
And Beautie slanderd with a bastard shame.

If there is a "second intention" in this quatrain, then the last two lines might be interpreted as follows.

But now is black[*ened, the name of*] beauties [*the Queen's*] successive heire [*her son Southampton*],
And [*also black is*] Beautie [*the Queen,*] slanderd with a bastard [*Southampton*] shame [*her name is also blackened, slandered by the shame of having borne a bastard son*].

The rest of the sonnet moves seamlessly on to the theme of the Dark Lady, the main concern of the poet in the second series, and no hint of succession can be found in the rest of the sonnets. (The reader should need no reminder that I am exploring the above interpretation, not advocating it.)

7. "But writing in the next century, in all the misery entailed by the ruinous incompetence of the Stuarts, Francis Osborne looked back to the days when a political genius occupied the throne, and only wished the rumors had been true, that even a bastard child of that unmatched strain might have done away with the necessity of the Scottish line. 'This I may safely attest,' he wrote, 'the smallest chip off that incomparable instrument of honor, peace and safety to this now unhappy nation, would then have been valued by the people of England above the loftiest branch in the Caledonian grove.'" Elizabeth Jenkins, *Elizabeth and Leicester* (London: V. Gollancz, 1961), 177, quoting Francis Osborne, *Historical Memoires of the Reigns of Queen Elizabeth and King James* (London: 1658). It appears that Francis Osborne had heard rumors of such a bastard child.

8. In her private prayer book Queen Elizabeth wrote: "Preserve Thou then the mother and the children whom Thou hast given her." It is usually supposed that by "the children Thou hast given her" the Queen was referring to the people of England, and by "mother" her role as Queen. Elizabeth I, *Collected Works*, ed. by Leah S. Marcus, Janel Mueller, and Mary Beth Rose (Chicago: University of Chicago Press, 2000).

Chapter 16

1. This story made a big impression on me when I first read it. But I have been unable to find a source for it, so the reader might prefer to take it with a grain of salt.

2. When Elizabeth came to the throne in 1558, the 1543 Act of Succession stated that the Crown, after her death, would go to the "issue of her body lawfully to be begotten." In the 1571 Act of Treasons this phrase was changed, to read "the natural issue of her body." The words "lawfully to be begotten" were omitted; it has been suggested that this phrase seemed to imply the existence or possibility of *unlawfully* begotten issue, and that this was why the Queen wanted it omitted. Article v., *13 Elizabeth, cap. I, i.*, 1571. See G. W. Prothero, ed., *Select Statutes and Other Constitutional Documents,* 4th ed. (Oxford: Clarendon Press, 1913), 60–62. It is interesting to note that when Henry VIII made Anne Boleyn Marquis of Pembroke in 1532 not long before marrying her, the title deeds stated that the Marquisate would pass to the male heirs born "of her body," rather than "of her body lawfully begotten," the normal wording. Henry's motives for this wording are clear; Queen Elizabeth's for the wording in the Act of Treasons less so. *Letters and Papers, Foreign and Domestic, Henry VIII, volume 5, 1531–1532* (1880), 9–66. Per Philippa Jones, *Elizabeth: Virgin Queen?*, New Holland (2010), 20. My thanks to Hank Whittemore for bringing this to my attention.

3. William Camden, *The History Of The Most Renowned And Victorious Princess Elizabeth, Late Queen of England*, a translation of *Annales etc.*, 1615, vol. 2 (London: 1675), 29.

4. On 25 July 1587, one John Poole, held in Newgate Prison on suspicion of "coining," is recorded by John Gunstone (a Crown agent) as saying, "The Earle of Oxford he said the Quene did woe [woo] him but he would not fall in at that tyme." (But at other times?) *Calendar of State Papers Domestic*, 1598-1601, 373 (PRO SP 12/273/103), f. 185v.

5. R. M. Sargent, *The Life and Lyrics of Sir Edward Dyer* (Oxford: Clarendon Press, 1968), 24–25.

6. *Ibid.*, 26.

7. Gilbert Talbot, 11 May 1573, letter from the Court to his father, the Earl of Shrewsbury, quoted in Edmund Lodge, *Illustrations of British History etc.*, vol. 2 (London: 1791), 100.

8. Gregorio Leti, quoted in *A New Biographical Dictionary, etc.* (London: 1798), 314, footnote T.

9. Gregorio Leti, *La Vie d'Elizabeth, reine d'Angleterre*, vol. 1 (Amsterdam: 1704), 489 (translation of suppressed Italian original, published 1682).

10. John Nichols, *The Progresses, and Public Processions, of Queen Elizabeth*, vol. 1 (London: John Nichols, 1788), 34.

11. Sir Harris Nicholas, *Memoirs of the Life and Times of Sir Christopher Hatton KG* (London: R. Bentley, 1847), 15–16. The "courtship" ran from 1579 to 1581.

12. Frederick Chamberlin, *The Private Character of Queen Elizabeth* (London: 1921), 274. But Chamberlin also provides a translation of the notorious "scandal letter" written in French by Mary Queen of Scots to Queen Elizabeth in 1583 (but probably intercepted before she could read it), wherein she wrote: "That even the count of Oxford dared not reconcile himself [some translators say "cohabit"] with his wife for fear of losing the favor which he hoped to receive by becoming your lover." *Ibid.*, 165ff.

13. Martin Hume, ed., *Calendar of State Papers, Spain (Simancas)*, vol. 4 (London: 1899), 101–12.

Chapter 17

1. Martin Hume, ed., "Arthur Dudley's *Relation,*" *Calendar of State Papers, Spain (Simancas)*, vol. 4 (London: 1899), 101–12.

2. The possibility that he later returned to England and assumed an alias is discussed here. http://www.elizabethfiles.com/the-arthur-dudley-myth/3298/comment-page-1/#comment-7698.

3. E. A. B. Bernard, *Evesham and a Reputed Son of Queen Elizabeth* (Old Evesham Pamphlets, 1926).

4. As an aside, I have been collecting recent UK press items about women who gave birth without having any idea that they were pregnant. They include a 12-year-old girl, a supermarket worker who lay down on the supermarket floor to give birth, and a woman whose third child was born when she went to the bathroom for a different purpose. None of these three (nor any of the others in my collection) had the slightest idea that they were pregnant, none had been trying to conceal the fact, and all had been living daily in close proximity with others who noticed nothing; similar stories emerge every few months. A recent case (18 September 2012) is that of a British soldier serving in Afghanistan who gave birth after feeling stomach pains, not knowing that she was pregnant; as a fighting soldier she would have been fit and slim. http://www.bbc.co.uk/news/uk-19657646.

Let us at least agree that if the Queen needed to conceal a pregnancy from the world at large, she was the best-placed woman in the realm to do so.

Chapter 18

The material in this and the following chapter is drawn from my paper "The Dedication to Shakespeare's Sonnets," *The Elizabethan Review,* vol. 5, no. 2 (Autumn 1997), 93–106. This paper had previously been accepted for publication in *Cryptologia*, the leading academic journal on cryptology, but it was subsequently vetoed by a Board member, on the grounds that publishing a paper that linked Shakespeare with cryptography would tarnish the standing of the journal. The paper was revised for *The Oxfordian*, vol. 2 (October 1999), 60–75; the last two pages of this paper show how the spelling and layout of the Dedication have frequently been garbled by scholars, making it impossible to solve the cryptogram. The paper was then republished in Richard Malim, ed. *Great Oxford* (Tunbridge Wells: Parapress, 2004), 253–266, with a postscript. The original paper was the subject of a full-page feature article in *The Times* of 31 December 1997 by the Science Editor, Nigel Hawkes.

1. *Shake-speares Sonnets* (London, by G. Eld for T. T., 1609). Most commentators opt either for William Herbert, Third Earl of Pembroke, or for Henry Wriothesley, Third Earl of Southampton, as the dedicatee Mr. W. H. Other people who have been proposed as a possible Mr. W. H. include William Hall, William Hart, William Harvey, William Hatcliffe, William Haughton, William Hostler (otherwise William Ostler, the actor), Willie Hughes and even William Himself.

2. Hyder Edward Rollins, ed. *A New Variorum Edition of Shakespeare: The Sonnets*, vol. 2 (Philadelphia & London: J. B. Lippincott, 1944), 166–76. Rollins writes, "An entire library has been written on the four opening words, *To the onlie begetter*" (p. 166). In the seventy years since, the library has grown considerably.

3. Clara Gebert, ed., *An Anthology of Elizabethan Dedications & Prefaces* (Philadelphia: University of Philadelphia Press, 1933). Surprisingly, the Dedication to the Sonnets is omitted.

4. Richard Dutton, *William Shakespeare: A Literary Life* (London: Macmillan, 1989), 41. In stark contrast is the view of Ole Franksen, a noted mathematician and cryptologist, that it is "so obviously a cryptogram it can't possibly be one." Private communication.

5. Kenneth Muir, *Shakespeare's Sonnets* (London: George Allen and Unwin, 1982), 152.

6. Stanley Wells, *Shakespeare's Sonnets* (Oxford: Oxford University Press, 1987), 6.

7. S. Schoenbaum, *Shakespeare's Lives* (Oxford: Clarendon Press, 1970), 67.

8. Northrop Frye, "How True a Twain," contribution to Edward Hubler, ed., *The Riddle of Shakespeare's Sonnets* (New York: Basic Books, 1962), 28.

9. Helen Fouché Gaines, *Elementary Cryptanalysis* (London: Chapman and Hall, 1940), 4.

10. Leslie Hotson, *Mr. W. H.* (London: Rupert Hart-Davis, 1964), 145–57.

11. Here Hotson somewhat sneakily quotes from *Love's Labour's Lost*, I.i.55–57.

BEROWNE: What is the end of study, let me know?
KING: Why, that to know which else we should not know.
BEROWNE: Things hid and barr'd, you mean, from common sense?

12. Benjamin Jonson, *Workes of Beniamin Ionson*, vol. 1 (London: 1616, reprint 1640).

13. Edward Dowden, ed., *The Sonnets of William Shakespeare* (London: Kegan Paul, Trench, 1881), 45.

14. Hotson's solution to this puzzle is that Mr. Hatcliffe's election as a *temporary* prince meant that he could be addressed in lofty terms at the time and for some years afterwards.

15. Richard Deacon (Donald McCormick), *John Dee* (London: Frederick Muller, 1969), 290–91.

16. John Wilkins, *Mercury, or the Secret and Swift Messenger* (London: 1641; reprint London: Frank Cass, 1970), 66.

17. This is because one only needs to write out every third array, since words concealed in the intervening arrays can be read out diagonally, as can be seen in Figure 18.2.

18. F. B. Williams, "An Initiation in Initials," *Studies in Bibliography*, vol. 9 (1957), 163–78.

19. Charlotte Carmichael Stopes, *The Life of Henry, Third Earl of Southampton, Shakespeare's Patron* (Cambridge: Cambridge University Press, 1922), 226.

Chapter 19

1. William F. and Elizebeth S. Friedman. *The Shakespearean Ciphers Examined* (Cambridge: Cambridge University Press, 1957), xv–xvi. William Friedman ("The Man Who Broke Purple") is regarded by many as the greatest cryptologist of the past century. For his achievements during World War II he was awarded both presidential decorations, the Medal for Merit and the National Security Medal. His wife was also a distinguished cryptologist in her own right. Their interest in possible Shakespearean ciphers was a hobby which occupied their leisure for several years.

2. *Ibid.*, 21.

3. Strictly, "steganographer," someone intent on

concealing the *existence* of hidden text as well as the text itself.

4. Liddell and Scott, *A Lexicon, etc.* (Oxford: Clarendon Press, 1944). The word is pronounced "ski-tar-ly," with a short "i," as in "skit."

5. For those unhappy with arguments involving mathematics or probabilities, some analogies may be helpful. Archaeologists often take to the air to spot clues on the ground that may reveal remains of prehistoric enclosures or buildings. "Crop marks" are patches of uneven growth that may indicate soil disturbance in the distant past. Especially noteworthy are circles, ovals, straight lines or rectangles, which are far more likely to have been man-made than chance occurrences. It may be impossible to rule out natural causes, and so the idea of probability comes into play. How likely or unlikely is it that the crop markings point to human activity? So it is with words in an array: how likely or unlikely is it that they were deliberately contrived rather than accidents of chance?

Here is another analogy. Suppose you are visiting the ruins of a grand mansion which has been derelict for a hundred years or more. It is set in a remote part of the country, and is surrounded by overgrown woodland. Exploring the maze of trees and undergrowth you come across three trees in a row, the distance between the first and second being the same as the distance between the second and third. Then you notice a fourth tree in the row, equally spaced with the first three, and then a fifth, also equally spaced. It begins to dawn on you that these trees were carefully planted, equally spaced and in a straight line. How many equally spaced trees in a straight line are needed to show beyond reasonable doubt that they were deliberately planted in this particular manner? I would suggest five, but others may take a different view.

It is considerations such as these which come into play when attempting to assess whether or not the cipher solutions presented here are genuine.

6. Christopher Marlowe, trl., *Lucan's First Booke* (London: Thomas Thorpe, 1600).

7. J. H., trl., *Augustine, or the Citie of God* (London: George Eld, 1610).

8. Io. Healey, trl., *Epictetus, etc.* (London: Thomas Thorpe, 1610).

9. Io. Healey, trl., *Epictetus, etc.* (London: Edward Blount, 1616).

Chapter 20

1. Joel Hurstfield, *The Queen's Wards: Wardship and Marriage under Elizabeth I* (London: 1958), 255.

2. The rumors were spectacularly wrong, as *none* of the four mentioned received a single vote, although one was appointed: Thomas, Fifth Lord Borough (or Burgh) of Gainsborough, Lord Deputy of Ireland. Philip Gawdy had attended a "feast" the day before which was attended by "my Lord Keeper [Sir John Puckering], Lord Buckhurst, Sir John Foscue, and first I should have said my Lord of Canterbury of the Counsayle, my Lord of Rutland, my Lord of Bedford, my Lord Stafford, my Lord Shandowes, my Lord North [and others]." It was evidently from among these highly placed people, one a member of the Queen's Privy Council, that Philip had heard the rumor that Southampton might be nominated; this was no backstairs servants' gossip. Philip Gawdy to his brother Bassingbourne Gawdy, letter, May 1593: British Library, Egerton MS 2804. http://archive.org/stream/reportofroyalcom07grea/reportofroyalcom07grea_djvu.txt.

3. Charlotte Carmichael Stopes, *The Life of Henry, Third Earl of Southampton, Shakespeare's Patron* (Cambridge: Cambridge University Press, 1922), 55.

4. Gilbert Talbot, letter written from the Court to his father, the Earl of Shrewsbury, on 11 May 1573, quoted in Edmund Lodge, *Illustrations of British History etc.*, vol. 2 (London: 1791), 100.

5. The details of the votes cast at chapter meetings from 1553 to 1621 are preserved in the *Liber Caeruleus* (Blue Book), a later copy of the original records. British Library Add. MS 36768 (Phillipps MS 8816). I am indebted to the late Peter R. Moore for bringing it to my attention.

6. G. V. Akrigg, *Shakespeare and the Earl of Southampton* (London: Hamish Hamilton, 1968), 48.

7. *Liber Caeruleus, v. supra.*

8. The story goes that the King immediately wrote to the London authorities to order the release of Southampton, with instructions that he should make all haste to journey north to meet up with him. But when his letter was received in London it turned out that he had not used the correct form of words for his order ("Le Roy le veult," perhaps), so the authorities were unable to carry out his instruction, bureaucracy trumping royalty. When word reached James that his order had not been put into effect he was absolutely furious, and (presumably having been informed of the correct formula) sent word to London a second time that Southampton was to be freed, which was duly carried out on 10 April. (I suspect that this was the date the King's *first* instruction was received, and that Southampton was actually freed some ten days later. It would not have taken him 17 days to meet up with the King [somewhere north of Hinchingbrook] if freed on 10 April, while seven days from [say] 20 April would seem about right for traveling the 70 miles from London to reach Hinchingbrook on 27 April. However, I have been unable to find a source for this story, which I heard broadcast on the BBC in early 2013.) They met up at Huntingdon on 27 April, and Southampton carried the Sword of State before James as he entered Hinchingbrook Priory, the home of Sir Oliver Cromwell (uncle of the Lord Protector). For the facts just mentioned (but not the story), see John Nichols, *The Progresses, Processions and Magnificent Festivities of King James the First* (London: J. B. Nichols, 1828), 52, 98.

9. George Peele, *The Honour of the Garter* (London: 1593). It was dedicated to the Earl of Northumberland, who was elected that year and gave him three pounds for it in June.

10. I can't resist saying that I love this phrase: "*Lords of lively hope,*" applied to the two youngest appointees; such a graceful and musical comment.

11. I have not been able to determine whether this is a quotation from a classical author. The second line was used by John Lyly at the end of his introduction to his play *Midas, King of Phrygia* (London: Thomas Scarlet for I. B., 1591).

12. Roy Strong, *The Cult of Elizabeth* (London: Pimlico, 1977), 68.

13. John Sanford, *Apollinis et Musarum Euktika Ei-*

dullia, in Serenissimæ Reginæ Elizabethae auspicatissimum Oxoniam adventum (Oxford: J. Barnesius, 1592).

14. G. P. V. Akrigg, *Shakespeare and the Earl of Southampton* (London: Hamish Hamilton, 1968), 36.

15. Charlotte Carmichael Stopes, *The Life of Henry, Third Earl of Southampton, Shakespeare's Patron* (Cambridge: Cambridge University Press, 1922), 50.

16. This legal doctrine has occasionally resulted in controversy. The Earl of Banbury was 83 when his wife produced a son, Edward, born in 1627, and 87 when Nicholas was born in 1631. Five weeks after he died in 1632 his widow married Lord Vaux, who was generally assumed to be the children's father. Nevertheless, legally Edward was legitimately the next earl, although when he attempted to enter the House of Lords he was refused admittance. The dispute over the inheritance of the earldom was not finally resolved until 1813, when the then potential heir gave up his claim. http://en.wikipedia.org/wiki/Knollys_%28family%29#Earls_of_Banbury.

17. Alexander Nowell, appendix to *A Catechism* (Cambridge: Cambridge University Press, 1853), 228.

Chapter 21

1. Lawrence Stone, *The Family, Sex and Marriage in England, 1500–1800* (New York: Harper & Row, 1977), 6.

2. Richard Feacham, *The Parish Church of St. Martin, East Horsley, Surrey* (1968).

3. Lawrence Stone, *v. supra*, 100.

4. Historical Manuscripts Commission, *Calendar of Salisbury Papers at Hatfield House*, HMSO, part XVI (1933), 204, 288, 416.

5. Charlotte Carmichael Stopes, *The Life of Henry, Third Earl of Southampton, Shakespeare's Patron* (Cambridge: Cambridge University Press, 1922), 9–13.

6. The vault is said to contain the bodies of the First Earl, Thomas Wriothesley and his wife Jane; the Second Earl, Henry and his wife Mary; the Third Earl, Henry and his wife Elizabeth, his son, James Wriothesley, and the Fourth Earl, Thomas. Anon., *The Parish Church of St. Peter, Titchfield: A Guide to the Church and Village* (1946). To see another under-church vault, go to http://www.okmmetaldetectors.com/metal-detector-finds/hidden-tomb-church-redgrave-uk.php?lang=en.

7. John C. G. Röhl, Martin Warren and David Hunt, *Purple Secret* (London: Bantam, 1998), 186–87, 200–01.

8. It is of interest to note that more portraits of Southampton have survived from early modern times than of any of his contemporaries, with the exception of Queen Elizabeth.

Chapter 22

1. According to John Lingard, *History of England* (London: 1854), the family of Mapother, County Roscommon in Ireland, are reputed to be descended from a daughter of Queen Elizabeth, sent there to be brought up. Whatever the truth of this statement, it serves to illustrate the tenor of mid-nineteenth-century historians' views of the Queen's morals.

2. As mitochondrial DNA is passed unchanged from mother to daughter, Henry Wriothesley's mitochondrial DNA could be compared with the mitochondrial DNA obtained from mother-to-daughter descendants of Anne Boleyn's sister Mary. It was mitochondrial DNA which enabled the remains found under a parking lot in Leicester to be identified as those of Richard III.

Chapter 23

1. Jones Harris had found the name "Dyer" in the second column of actors' names, but had not noticed "Ste(a)nley" in the first column. Sir Edward Dyer has been proposed as an authorship candidate, notably by Alden Brooks, *Will Shakspere and the Dyer's Hand* (New York: Scribner's, 1943). As a word of only four letters, it could easily have occurred by chance.

2. E. K. Chambers, *William Shakespeare*, vol. 2 (Oxford, 1930), 78.

3. *Ibid.*, 73–76.

4. J. Payne Collier, *Memoirs of the Principal Actors* etc. (London: for the Shakespeare Society, 1846), 89.

5. I think it likely that the name was occasionally spelled "Stenley" at the time, as orthography was variable, but no example has so far come to light. The name of Stratford-upon-Avon was spelled "Stretford-upon-Aven" on John Speede's map of Warwickshire, 1630.

6. And all praise to Jones Harris, the *onlie begetter*.

7. William and Elizebeth Friedman, *The Shakespearean Ciphers Examined* (Cambridge: Cambridge University Press, 1957), 100.

8. This consideration still held after James's accession to the throne, since if James and all three of his children died young William would have been the next heir. But by now the low profile afforded by the pen name had probably become ingrained.

Chapter 24

1. Leo Daugherty, *The Assassination of Shakespeare's Patron: Investigating the Death of the Fifth Earl of Derby* (New York: Cambria Press, 2011), *passim*.

2. Leslie Hotson, *I, William Shakespeare* (London: Jonathan Cape, 1937), 154, quoting State Papers 12/249/90. The remark about "kings" shows that William Stanley was regarded as the next heir to Queen Elizabeth by Yorke, and presumably by many others as well.

3. He was later recorded as living in Spain in 1596. Leo Daugherty, *v. supra*, 270–72.

4. Barry Coward, *The Stanleys, Lords Stanley and Earls of Derby, 1385–1672* (Manchester: for the Chetham Society, 1983), 41–55.

5. Alice, Countess of Derby, to Sir Robert Cecil, 9 May [1594], Hatfield Papers. http://www.british-history.ac.uk/catalogue.aspx?gid=144.

6. Harry H. Boyle, "Elizabeth's Entertainment at Elvetham: War Policy in Pageantry," *Studies in Philology*, vol. 68, no. 2 (April 1971), 146–66. It is frequently suggested that this entertainment is referred to in *Midsummer Night's Dream*; for example, see: http://www.thefreelibrary.com/The+Fey+Beauty+of+A+Midsummer+Night%27s+Dream%3A+a+Shakespearean+comedy...-a0125306068.

7. Rather surprisingly, Countess Alice wrote to the Earl of Shrewsbury six weeks later to say that she had

heard of a report of William "matchinge with my Lady Arbella," great-great-granddaughter of Henry VII. As William was the great-great-grandson of Henry VII, the dynastic significance of such a marriage would have been colossal, and whoever originated the report clearly had in mind that William was heir apparent, and that his claim to the throne would be doubly secured by marrying his distant cousin. Countess Alice Derby to Gilbert Talbot, 27 June 1594, Talbot MSS, Shrewsbury Letters; MS 3203, Item 14, Lambeth Palace Library.

8. The Jesuit priest Henry Garnet wrote, "The marriage of the Lady Vere to the new Earl of Derby is deferred, by reason that he standeth in hazard to be unearled again, his brother's wife being with child, until it is seen whether it be a boy or no." Undated letter of 1594. Charlotte Carmichael Stopes, *The Life of Henry, Third Earl of Southampton, Shakespeare's Patron* (Cambridge: Cambridge University Press, 1922), 86. She adds that the child "proved a girl," but in fact there was no child.

9. George Carey to his wife, 22 April 1594, Gloucester Records Office, MF 1161, letter-book 2.

10. "For as well Poets as Poesie are despised, & the name become, of honorable infamous, subiect to scorne and derision, and rather a reproch than a prayse to any that vseth it: for commonly who so is studious in th'Arte or shewes himselfe excellent in it, they call him in disdayne a *phantasticall*: and a light headed or phantasticall man (by conuersion) they call a Poet." George Puttenham, *Arte of English Poesie* (London: 1589), Chapter VIII.

11. The date of the wedding was given by John Stowe as 25 January 1595, and until recently this date was accepted by all historians. It has now been shown by David Wiles that it actually took place on 30 January. If the guests assembled on 25 January, and the play was performed the next day, that would have been four days before the actual wedding ceremony, which would explain the opening lines, spoken by Theseus:

> Now, fair Hyppolyta, our nuptial hour
> Draws on apace; four happy days bring in
> Another moon

On 30 January 1595 there was indeed a new moon. However, Wiles proposes an alternative marriage as explained in note 23 to Chapter 27 below. David Wiles, *Shakespeare's Almanac: "Midsummer Night's Dream": Marriage and the Elizabethan Calendar* (Woodbridge: D. S. Brewer, 1993).

12. "Yow may tell my lady of Darby, she is to blame that she not come to se hir dowghter, which truly is worth the seying." Lord Burghley to Sir Robert Cecil, 8 July 1596, PRO, SP 12/259; fol. 140^{v}. Throughout the early years of the marriage Elizabeth frequently suffered serious ill health.

13. Lady Anne Bacon to the Earl of Essex, 1 December 1596, Lambeth Palace Library, MS 660, fol. 149^{r}. See Paul E. J. Hammer, *The Polarisation of Elizabethan Politics: The Political Career of Robert Devereux, 2nd Earl of Essex, 1585–1597* (Cambridge: Cambridge University Press, 1999), 321, 385.

14. "Yf any on can say that I knowe my wyff to be dishonest of her body or thatt I can justly prove itt by my self or any on else, I challenge him to the combat of lyff. If any one suppose that any speches of myn to have proceded owt of that dowbt, he doth me wronge." Statement by William Stanley, Earl of Derby, 20 August 1597 (or perhaps 1596). Cecil Papers, 14.20, printed in HMCS, 179.140. http://www.proquest.com/products-services/cecil_papers.html.

15. From Lord Cobham (Robert Cecil's father-in-law), the Countess of Warwick and Lady Raleigh. The letters do not appear to have survived. Did Stanley's jealousy and rage later find resolution in *Othello*? Edward Mylar (*recte* ffyton or Fitton, per the late Peter Moore) to Sir Robert Cecil, 9 August 1597, Cecil Papers, MS 54.14.

16. *Ibid.*

17. The Earl and Countess of Derby to Sir Robert Cecil. "We give thanks for your kind remembrance by letters, and have had good occasion to like this country. The discourses of this passing time we leave to the relation of this agent.—Alport our lodge, this 22 of August 1597.—Your loving niece and nephew." 22 August 1597. Cecil Papers, MS 54.77.

18. On 20 September 1597, Thomas Audeley wrote to Edward Smythe in Paris, "My lord of Essex in no great grace, neither with Queen or Commons: with the Queen for that he lay with my Lady of Darbe before he went, as his enemies witness." Cecil Papers, MS 55.45. Essex had set out for his naval expedition to the Azores on 10 July 1597; it was not a success.

19. "I find his lordship most lovingly kind to my very good lady, as not taking any discontentment at anything happened at the departure. But his discontentment grows by reason of her absence, and they do not honourably dispose themselves to live together in like honourable hospitality his lordship's ancestors (the honours of these North parts) have done: which only your Honour may bring to pass." Thomas Ireland to Sir Robert Cecil, 30 July 1598. Cecil Papers, MS 62.100.

20. John Tyndall to Secretary Cecil, 9 May 1599, CSPD 1598–1601, Lincoln's Inn SP 12/270/108; f. 186.

21. James Greenstreet, "A Hitherto Unknown Noble Writer of Elizabethan Comedies," *The Genealogist*, New Series, vol. 7 (1891), 205–08. http://www.rahul.net/raithel/Derby/greenstreet.html.

22. "My Lord Darby hath put up the playes of the children in Pawles to his great paines and charge." Andrew Gurr, *The Shakespearian Playing Companies* (Oxford: Clarendon, 1996). Gurr's source is *Historical Manuscripts Commission, Report on the Manuscripts of Lord de L'Isle and Dudley*, ed. C. L. Kingsford (London: HMSO, 1925–66).

23. Herbert Berry, *The Boar's Head Playhouse* (Folger Books, 1986).

24. Spelling modernized. Cecil Papers, MS 186.24.

25. Perhaps the following report gives an indication of the nature of William's "prodigal courses." According to Mark Eccles, there is a Star Chamber suit showing that the Earl of Derby, "in the intervals of penning comedies, would order his servants to ambush and murder an enemy, promising to save them harmless, or would muster men by the hundreds to defy the law on the Yorkshire moors." Whether these were allegations or actual events is not clear. Mark Eccles, in *Thomas Lodge and other Elizabethans,* ed. C. J. Sisson (Cambridge, Mass.: Harvard University Press, 1933), 208.

26. The votes cast for him at KG Chapter Meetings start one week after he became earl, with 1 out of 11 in April 1594. Thereafter his votes were: in 1595, 5 out of 11; in 1596, 4 out of 12; in 1597, 3 out of 10; in 1598, no vacancies and no voting; in 1599, 4 out of 9; in 1600,

8 out of 13. Clearly he had strong support from his fellow peers, presumably because he was heir-apparent, since he had done nothing exceptional for the good of the country. It has been suggested that the honor indicated that the Queen was prepared to accept him as her successor, as the heir-apparent was traditionally made a KG.

27. Coward, *The Stanleys, Lords Stanley and Earls of Derby*, 41–55.

28. http://www.isle-of-man.com/manxnotebook/people/lords/william6.htm.

29. Madame Guizot de Witt, *The Lady of Latham: Being the Life and Original Letters of Charlotte de la Trémoille, Countess of Derby*, transln. (London: Smith, Elder, 1869), quoted by John Raithel, *The URL of Derby*. http://www.rahul.net/raithel/Derby/.

30. William, Earl of Derby to Sir Robert Cecil, his uncle. "I was wished by my wife to move you for a letter to reprieve a poor young man for whom you have already written once before, at her request. To-morrow the man dies unless he be reprieved: it seems by his petition, his offence was stealing a little silver 'skellett' out of her chamber, which being the first fault, she was loath to have him die, yet nevertheless he was condemned before he could make any mends." January 1598, Cecil Papers, 38.13.

31. Derby wrote to the mayor of Chester on 11 December 1606, asking him to treat Lord Hereford's players well and hoping "that you will pmit [permit] them to use theire quallitie," "quality" being used at the time especially of actors' performing ability. A. W. Titherley, *Shakespeare's Identity: William Stanley 6th Earl of Derby* (Winchester: 1952), 70.

32. William, Earl of Derby, to Robert Cecil, Earl of Salisbury. "I understand by this bearer, Mr. Gamull, Recorder of ye City of Chester, that he intendeth to become an humble petitioner to his Majesty .... And ... as he is one who hath given good testimony of his love towards me, I could do no less than at his request make bold to commend him to your lordship's honorable consideration." 31 October 1607, *Calendar of State Papers Domestic*. Notice the use of the word "love" denoting no more than respect or loyalty. (See the full letter and a transcript in Chapter 29.)

33. A. W. Titherley, *v. supra,* 95.

Chapter 25

1. Robert Parsons was a Jesuit priest who is believed to have written *A Conference about the next Succession to the Crown of Ingland*, published in 1594 under the pen name R. Doleman (Parsons's authorship of the work has been questioned). In it he finally settled for the children of Margaret, Countess of Derby, and preferred William over his elder brother on the grounds that as he was unmarried, he might make a match with some continental princess for good political reasons.

> Lastly I do name, the children of this countesse [the Countess of Derby] in general, and not the earle of Darby [Ferdinando] particulerly aboue the other, though he be the eldest, for two respects, first, for that his yonger brother is vnmarried, ... & secondly for that diuers men remaine not so fully satisfied & contented with the course of that Lord [Ferdinando] hitherto, and do thinke that they should do better with his brother [p. 267]

Suspicions attached to Ferdinando as he was thought to have communicated with Catholics on the Continent in 1591. http://books.google.ca/books?id=kOQbU56suzcC&q=267#v=onepage&q=267&f=true.

2. The throne of England at this time was elective; it did not become strictly hereditary until the reign of George I. When a monarch died, the noblemen and leading government and parliamentary officials met as the "Great Council," which was formed to choose the next monarch. Normally heredity would be a major consideration, but other factors were taken into account, for example Roman Catholics were barred. Even today, Parliament has the final say over who should inherit.

3. *Henry IV, Part 2*, Act 3, scene 1, line 31.

4. In the event, as the reader will know, James VI of Scotland was chosen, and the reasons for rejecting him ignored. After all, he was already a successful king, familiar with the duties of a king, and *father of two sons*. The uniting of the two kingdoms was a valuable and long-desired bonus.

Incidentally, in the secret correspondence between Sir Robert Cecil and James there is occasional mention of a mysterious "40," who occupies some unrecorded recent "office." Names of people in the correspondence were replaced by numbers, and the higher the number, the higher the status of the individual. It so happens that number "40" was the highest number employed (King James was "30," the next highest number, and Queen Elizabeth was "24"); he has not been identified. I think it likely that "40" represented Derby, and that his unspecified office was that of heir-apparent. James calls "40" cousin (they were third cousins), and takes pains to ensure that no one else approaches "40" except through Cecil, and of course Cecil was both Derby's uncle and also clearly fond of him, and would have known what his feelings were about inheriting the throne. The identity of "40" is something that merits further research.

5. These remarks and those quoted from sonnet 81 make little sense if the author's *real* name is on the front of the book and at the top of every other page.

6. Anon. [Richard Barnfield], *The Affectionate Shepheard Concerning the Complaint of Ganymede* (London: November 1594). The collection was dedicated "with familiar devotion" to Lady Penelope Rich, sometimes thought to be the "Dark Lady" of the sonnets. http://www.shakespearesdarklady.com/.

7. Richard Barnfield, *Cynthia, with Certain Sonnets* (London: Humfrey Lownes, 1595).

8. C. S. Lewis, *English Literature in the Sixteenth Century, Excluding Drama* (London: Oxford University Press, 1973), 503–05.

Chapter 26

1. Leo Daugherty, *William Shakespeare, Richard Barnfield, and the Sixth Earl of Derby* (Amherst, NY: Cambria Press), 43. Other commentators agree with this finding, including Paul Hammond, *Figuring Sex between Men from Shakespeare to Rochester* (Oxford: Oxford University Press, 2002), and Stanley Wells and Paul Edmondson, *Shakespeare's Sonnets* (Oxford: Oxford University Press, 2004). Daugherty's priority of discovery derives from a presentation of his at the "Lancastrian Shakespeare" Conference, July 1999.

2. Explicit to and fro influences have been found by Paul Hammond in sonnets 1, 15, 20, 27, 33, 35, 46, 87, 94, 97, and 126. Paul Hammond, *passim*, *v. supra*, and Leo Daugherty, *v. supra*, 75–84. There is also a raft of less clear echoes, *ibid.*, 85–91.

3. *Early English Books Online*, http://eebo.chadwyck.com/home.

4. Leo Daugherty, *v. supra*, 43, 60, 88, 95, 106.

5. R. B., Gent. [Richard Barnfield], *Greene's Funeralls* (London: John Danter, November 1594).

6. The meaning of "hobby horse" is puzzling. It may be a jibe at Shakespeare for writing so many sonnets addressing Henry Wriothesley. It can also refer to a loose woman (*OED*). If we now reflect that Barnfield's *The Affectionate Shepheard* (1594) was about a lady of dubious morals and dedicated to Lady Penelope Rich, who has been suggested as the Dark Lady and also as "Avisa" of *Willobie his Avisa* (also 1594), we may wonder—speculating wildly—whether Barnfield is hinting at Stanley's involvement with a "woman colored ill." If so, he must have known Stanley rather better than at first might appear. Lady Penelope Rich and her lover Charles Blount accused Barnfield of using them as models for Queen Guendolena and Ganymede, two characters in the first part of the poem. http://www.folger.edu/html/folger_institute/mm/EssayMR.html.

7. These include Henry Chettle, *Kind-Heart's Dream* (1592), Barnaby Rich, *Greene's Newes both from Heaven and Hell* (1593), R. B. [Richard Barnfield], *Greene's Funeralls* (1594) and John Dickenson, *Greene in Conceipt* (1598), all of which summon up Greene's ghost. Leo Daugherty, *v. supra*, 62.

8. George Klawitter, Barnfield's champion and editor of several books of his poetry, regards it as very likely that Barnfield's Ganymede was Southampton. Michael Mooten, http://willobiehisavisadecoded.webs.com/faq.htm.

9. Richard Barnfield, *Cynthia, with Certain Sonnets* (London: Humfrey Lownes, January 1595).

10. T. T.'s poem, lines 7–9, contains an interesting phrase, "double grace" (*ibid.*, 88):

> Fair CYNTHIA lov'd, fear'd, of Gods and men,
> Downe sliding from that cloudes ore-peering mountain:
> Decking with **double grace** the neighbour plains

This echoes, or is echoed, in Shakespeare's sonnet 78, line 8:

> And given **grace** a **double** majesty.

It therefore seems either that T. T. also saw Shakespeare's sonnets in manuscript as well as Barnfield, or that Shakespeare saw T. T.'s commendatory poem whether in manuscript or after the publication of *Cynthia*. It is tempting (but probably pointless) to speculate that T. T. is Thomas Thorpe, who later printed the sonnets (1609).

11. Francis Meres, *Palladis Tamis, Wit's Treasury* (London: Cuthbert Burbie, 1598), 284v.

12. Joseph Sobran in *Alias Shakespeare* (1997) draws attention to "the wealth of legal terminology used in the sonnets," although on the face of it such specialized language might not seem particularly appropriate for a series of poems about love and devotion. But if, as we believe, the poet was studying law at Lincoln's Inn at the time (Southampton was also studying law, at Gray's Inn) the explanation becomes immediately apparent. Joseph Sobran, *Alias Shakespeare: Solving the Greatest Literary Mystery of All Time* (New York: Free Press, 1997), p. 201. Most of the sonnets from 1 to about 105 (and from 127 to 152) seem to have been written between 1591 and 1595. R. J. C. Wait, *The Background to Shakespeare's Sonnets* (London: Chatto & Windus, 1972).

13. W. Shakespeare, *The Passionate Pilgrim* (London: I. Jaggard, 1599).

Chapter 27

1. William Shakespere, *A Pleasant Conceited Comedy called Loves Labors Lost* (London: Cutbert Burby, 1598).

2. R. W. David, ed., *Love's Labour's Lost* (London: Arden 2, 1951).

3. H. R. Woudhuysen, "Love's Labour's Lost" in Richard Proudfoot *et al., The Arden Shakespeare Complete Works*, rev. ed. (London: Thomson, 2011), 743.

4. Abel Lefranc, "Les Éléments français de 'Peines d'amour perdues' de Shakespeare," *Revue Historique* 178 (1936), 411–12, 414–15. Lefranc's views about the French atmosphere of the play had been anticipated some 70 years earlier by Émile Montégut, who wrote:

> It is extraordinary to observe Shakespeare's fidelity to the most minute details of historic truth and local color.... The conversations of his Lords and Ladies are thoroughly French: vivacious, alert, witty, an unbroken game of shuttlecock, a skirmish of *bons mots*, a miniature war of repartee. Even their bad taste is French, and their language honed and refined to excess...

It would seem likely that its author had spent at the least a few months moving in high French society. Émile Montégut, *Oeuvres de Wm. Shakespeare* (Hachette, 1867), vol. 2, p. 340, quoted in *Sous le masque de William Shakespeare, VIe Comte de Derby* (Paris, Payot et cie., 1918), vol. 2, 5. Trl. Cecil Cragg (Braunton, Devon, 1988), 226.

5. Francois Rabelais, *Gargantua and Pantagruel*, Book 1 (1653). http://www.gutenberg.org/files/8166/8166.txt.

6. James Greenstreet, "A Hitherto Unknown Noble Writer of Elizabethan Comedies," *The Genealogist*, New Series, vol. 7 (London: 1891), 205–08. http://www.rahul.net/raithel/Derby/greenstreet.html.

7. Richard Lloyd, *A brief discourse of the most renowned actes and right valiant conquests of these puisant Princes, called the Nine Worthies* (London: R. Warde, 1584).

8. Note the midline rhymes: conquer<u>or</u> / Lyon <u>or</u>; h<u>ent</u> / arg<u>ent</u>.

9. John Raithel, *The URL of Derby*. http://www.rahul.net/raithel/Derby/plays.html#LLL referring to Abel Lefranc, *v. supra*, trl., 236.

10. Robert Gittings, *Shakespeare's Rival* (London: Heineman, 1960), 53–61.

11. Frances Yates, *A Study of Love's Labour's Lost* (Cambridge: Cambridge University Press, 1936).

12. You won't find this actorly business in any modern production of the play, as modern producers are not disposed to read widely about the plays they put on.

13. "...gallant young Iuvenall," Francis Meres, *Palladis Tamia. Wit's Treasury* (London: P. Short for Cuthbert Burbie, 1598), 286r.

14. Robert Gittings, *v. supra*, 82–83. Gittings also points out that Shakespeare was writing *Henry IV, Part*

1, at this time, and that there are "a number of exact images from Nashe's prose works that pervade it." These are two of many examples which show that Shakespeare was heavily indebted to Nashe and must have made a habit of reading everything he wrote (see Chapter 7).

15. *Mémoires de Marguerite de Valois* (Elzevir edition, 108–113), trans. Richard Macdonald Lucas, *Shakespeare's Vital Secret* (Keighly: Wadsworth, 1937), 173–176, following Lefranc, *ibid.*, vol. 2, p. 79ff..

16. *Ibid.*

17. *Ibid.* See also http://www.siefar.org/dictionnaire/fr/Claude_de_La_Tour_d%27Auvergne/Hilarion_de_Coste.

18. The first mention of a Hamlet play occurs in Nashe's Epistle prefaced to Robert Greene's *Menaphon*, printed in 1589. Nashe refers to "whole Hamlets, I should say handfuls of Tragical speeches." This is usually supposed to refer to a precursor of Shakespeare's play, called *Ur-Hamlet*, but Carl Nordling makes a strong case for his theory that a play written in German, but apparently by an Englishman, *Der bestrafte Brudermord oder: Prinz Hamlet aus Dännemark,* might well have been written by William Stanley while on his continental travels with his tutor. http://carlonordling.se/shakespeare/4.html.

19. Beryl Hughes, *Shakespeare's Friend of the Sonnets: A Mystery Solved* (London: Minerva Press, 2000), 28–36. *Antonio's Revenge*, written by Marston (1602), has a plot modeled very closely on that of *Hamlet.* Antonio has lost his father, and is repeatedly spurred on to vengeance by his father's ghost. The fact that the chastity of his intended bride, Mellida, is in question is one of the factors which drives him, like Hamlet, to feign madness. So it would seem that Hamlet's having doubts about Ophelia's chastity was evident in the original production of the play. http://archive.org/stream/jstor-456606/456606_djvu.txt

20. The origin of the name Ophelia is obscure. It may be derived from the Greek *'Οφειλη*, "a debt, that which is owed, a forfeit, a sacrifice." Her honor, and later her life, are sacrificed to Claudius's greed.

21. There was a nineteenth-century tradition in British dramatic circles that Ophelia was pregnant in the mad scene. The line "O, how the wheel becomes it!" (IV.v.173) was taken to be a reference to a wheel farthingale, a style of dress which would conceal a pregnancy. Suicide has often been committed by young girls who find themselves pregnant.

Ophelia's position at the Danish Court is not dissimilar to that of a Maid of Honor at Elizabeth's Court, where despite the Queen's best efforts irregularities occurred, to such an extent that their reputation was often called in question, as in the following verse.

Here lyeth interred under this Mound [? Mould
A Female of Sixteen yeares old.
More Men than yeares have been upon her
And yet she died a Maid of Honor.

Lambeth Palace Library, MS 2086, 67, quoted in Charlotte Isabelle Merton, *The Women Who Served Queen Mary and Queen Elizabeth etc.,* PhD. Thesis 17227, Trinity College Cambridge, 1991, 128 (CUL).

22. There are many other hints as to the true situation, for example Hamlet's teasing Ophelia during the play-within-the-play scene. He is not tormenting her for fun; he is really upset at the thought that she may have lost her innocence.

23. In May 1601 Robert Cecil started a secret correspondence with King James of Scotland, who by this time had effectively become Elizabeth's successor. William is very likely to have known about this, especially if (as I have suggested) he was the person referred to as "40" in that correspondence, someone of high status whom the King called his "cousin" (they were third cousins). So, also like Hamlet, William has been deprived of a crown that he might have expected to inherit. But loss of the crown seems to have been the least of Hamlet's concerns (he refers to it only once), and similarly William seems to have had little appetite for succeeding Queen Elizabeth, as his self-abasement in several of the sonnets might indicate.

24. Leo Daugherty, *The Assassination of Shakespeare's Patron: Investigating the Death of the Fifth Earl of Derby* (New York: Cambria Press, 2011), 181–82.

25. Ian Wilson, an orthodox Stratfordian, speculates that Ferdinando's death by poison may have been in William Shakespeare's mind (that is, William Shakspere's mind) when he came to write *Hamlet.* He suggests that William Stanley, who was associated with John Marston in the revival of the Paul's Boys acting troupe in 1599, might have mentioned this to Marston, who might then have mentioned it to Shakespeare (that is, Shakspere). The official verdict was witchcraft, so only an insider such as Stanley would attribute the death to poison. Ian Wilson, *Shakespeare: The Evidence* (New York: St. Martin's Press, 1993), 269.

26. As mentioned above, note 11 to Chapter 24, John Stowe gave the date of the marriage as 25 January. If that was the date when everyone arrived at Greenwich, and the play was performed the next day, this would be precisely four days before the actual date of the wedding on 30 January, thereby explaining Theseus's and Hippolyta's emphasizing "four days" in the opening lines of the play. However, David Wiles (who determined the true date of the Stanley-Vere wedding) argues that the play was almost certainly designed to be performed at the wedding of Thomas Berkeley and Elizabeth Carey on 19 February 1596; Elizabeth was the daughter of Sir George Carey, whose wife was a sister of Derby's elder brother's wife. The two marriages in question are therefore either Derby's own, or that of his niece by marriage. David Wiles, *Shakespeare's Almanac: "Midsummer Night's Dream," Marriage and the Elizabethan Calendar* (Woodbridge: D.S. Brewer, 1993).

27. E. K. Chambers, *Shakespearean Gleanings* (Oxford: Oxford University Press, 1944).

28. E. A. J. Honigmann, *Shakespeare, the "Lost Years"* (Manchester: Manchester University Press, 1985), 150–54.

29. A. W. Titherley, *Shakespeare's Identity: William Stanley 6th Earl of Derby* (Winchester, 1952), 72.

30. Georges Lambin, *Voyages de Shakespeare en France et en Italie* (Geneva: Droz, 1962), trans. Tal G. Wilson *et al.* in W. Ron Hess, *The Dark Side of Shakespeare*, vol. 1 (New York: Writers Club Press, 2002), 483–520.

31. *Ibid.*, 487–88.

32. John Raithel, *The URL of Derby.* http://www.rahul.net/raithel/Derby/plays.html#wives.

33. *Ibid.*, referencing A. W. Titherley, *Shakespeare's Identity: William Stanley 6th Earl of Derby* (Winchester: 1952), 78.

34. Roger Prior, "The Date of *Edward III*," *Notes & Queries*, ccxxxv (1990), 178–80, and "Was *The Raigne of King Edward III* a Compliment to Lord Hunsdon?" *Connotations*, vol. 3, no. 3 (1993–94), 243–64.

35. Brian Vickers, *Shakespeare, Co-Author* (Oxford: Oxford University Press, 2002).

36. Brian Vickers, "Incomplete Shakespeare: Denying Co-Authorship in 1 Henry VI," *Shakespeare Quarterly*, vol. 58 (2007), 311–52. Later Vickers proposed that Kyd wrote most of *1 Henry VI*; *Times Literary Supplement*, 18 April 2009.

37. Hugh Craig and Arthur F. Kinney, *Shakespeare, Computers, and the Mystery of Authorship* (Cambridge: Cambridge University Press, 2009).

38. Brian Vickers was reported by *Time* magazine in October 2009 to have concluded that Shakespeare wrote the first three acts, and most of the rest was written by Kyd, some time around 1590. I do not know whether Vickers has since published a paper on this finding. http://www.time.com/time/arts/article/0,8599,1930971,00.html.

39. MacDonald Jackson, "Shakespeare and the Quarrel Scene in Arden of Faversham," *Shakespeare Quarterly*, vol. 57, no. 3 (Fall 2006), 249–93.

40. Thomas Merriam, *Marlowe in Henry V: A Crisis of Shakespearian Identity?* (Oxford: Oxquarry Books, 2002).

41. Laurie Maguire, http://www.cems-oxford.org/sites/default/files/MaguireSmithSh Collaboration.pdf.

42. Gary Taylor, *Thomas Middleton: The Collected Works* (Oxford: Oxford University Press, 2007).

43. "My Lord Darby hath put up the playes of the children in Pawles to his great paines and charge." Andrew Gurr, *The Shakespearian Playing Companies* (Oxford: Clarendon, 1996). Gurr's source is *Historical Manuscripts Commission, Report on the Manuscripts of Lord de L'Isle and Dudley*, ed. C. L. Kingsford (London: HMSO, 1925–66). Herbert Berry, *The Boar's Head Playhouse* (Folger Books, 1986). According to Leo Daugherty, both John Marston and Thomas Middleton wrote for Paul's Boys at this time, and "Derby would necessarily have worked in association with them." *ODNB*.

44. Gary Taylor and John Jowett, *Shakespeare Reshaped, 1606–1623* (Oxford: Oxford University Press, 1993).

45. Frances Yates, *Shakespeare's Last Plays: A New Approach* (London: Routledge and Kegan Paul, 1975), and *The Occult Philosophy in the Elizabethan Age* (London and New York: Routledge, 1979, reprinted 2001). Dee's benevolent angel was called Uriel, who became Ariel in *The Tempest*. While magic was generally malevolent in Elizabethan and Jacobean times, Dee's magic was invariably benign, as are the magical elements in *Midsummer Night's Dream* and *The Tempest*.

46. Dee's diary records him dining with Derby on 13 and 22 September 1595, and a visit by Derby on 26 June 1596 to him in Manchester, where he had been appointed warden of Christ's College apparently with Derby's support. On 19 August 1597 Derby and his wife visited Dee in Manchester, and two days later had a "banket" (banquet) with him at his lodging. J. O. Halliwell, ed., *The Private Diary of Dr. John Dee* (London: J. B. Nichols and Son, 1842), http://www.gutenberg.org/ebooks/19553.

Chapter 28

1. *Taming of the Shrew*, Induction 2.20: "Marion Hackett, fat ale-wife of Wincot" (There are still Hacketts living in modern Wilnecote; see reference 2 below). *TS* Induction 2.17: "Sly, old Sly's son of Burton-heath." *Merry Wives*, I.i.84: "He was outrun on Cotsall."

2. A.J. Pointon, *The Man Who Was Never Shakespeare: The Theft of William Shakspere's Identity* (Tunbridge Wells, U.K.: Parapress, 2011), 146–49.

3. Thomas Edwards, *Cephalus and Procris. Narcissus* (entered Stationers' Register October 1593, published 1595), ed. W. E. Buckley (London: Nichols and Sons, for the Roxburghe Club, 1878, 1882).

4. Charlotte Carmichael Stopes, "Thomas Edwards, Author of 'Cephalus and Procris. Narcissus,'" *Modern Language Review*, vol. 16, no. 3–4 (July–October 1921), 209–23.

5. A. W. Titherley, *Shakespeare's Identity: William Stanley 6th Earl of Derby* (Winchester: 1952), 93.

6. http://en.wikipedia.org/wiki/Meriden,_West_Midlands.

7. Andrew Gurr, "A Jibe at Shakespeare in 1606," *Notes & Queries*, vol. 49, no. 2 (June 2002), 245–47. Gurr omits the final words: "It ([Shakspere's] mouth) will swear but it will lye, hear it not," which he may have found an unpalatable slur on the man from Stratford-upon-Avon.

8. Julia Cleave, private communication.

9. John Marston, *The Works of John Marston*, ed. A. H. Bullen, 3 vols. (London: John C. Nimmo, 1887). *Histriomastix* was first performed at Christmas 1598/9, and if these lines occurred in the play at that date they cannot refer to Derby. But as it was not printed until 1610 the lines may have been added any time after 1601, when Derby was appointed KG.

10. John Davies, *The Scourge of Folly*, to be found in *The Complete Works of John Davies of Hereford*, ed. Alexander B. Grosart, 2 vols. (London: 1878).

11. Diana Price, *Shakespeare's Unorthodox Biography* (Westport, Conn.: Greenwood Press, 2002), 63.

12. This view was held by A. W. Titherley, *v. supra* 45–46. I am unable to attach much credence to it, nor do I know of anything that might corroborate it. Alternatively, "companion" may simply suggest a close friendship, such as might be appropriate between a monarch and the next heir. Elizabeth was of course famous for refusing to name an heir, since that would undermine her own authority. Once again, the interpretation of writings of this period presents problems which greater clarity and openness at the time would have obviated.

13. Brian Vickers, *Shakespeare, A Lover's Complaint, and John Davies of Hereford* (Cambridge: Cambridge University Press, 2007).

14. John Davies [of Hereford], *Microcosmos: The Discovery of the Little World, with the Government Thereof* (Oxford: Joseph Barnes, 1603).

15. John Raithel, *The URL of Derby*. http://www.rahul.net/raithel/Derby/plays.html#wives.

16. Robert Chester, *Love's Martyr, or, Rosalyn's Complaint (1601)*, ed. Alexander B. Grosart (London: Trübner, 1878).

17. Dennis Flynn, "'Awry and Squint': The Dating of Donne's Holy Sonnets," *John Donne Journal*, vol. 7, no. 1 (1988), 35–46.

18. In *Antony and Cleopatra*, Act II, scene vii, lines 26 and 27, Lepidus says:

Your serpent of Egypt is bred now of your mud
by the operation of your sun[.]

19. Shakespeare Birthplace Trust. http://www.shakespeare.org.uk/explore-shakespeare/collections/treasures/plutarch-039-s-lives-of-the-noble-grecians-and-romans.html.

20. Henry Peacham, *The Compleat Gentleman etc.* (London: Francis Constable, 1622).

21. These words come from Ben Jonson's poem in the early pages of the First Folio. The poem is dedicated "To the memory of my beloved, the Author, Mr. William Shakespeare, and what he hath left us." Authorship doubters interpret this in the following way: "To the memory of my beloved, the Author, [who wrote under the pen name] Mr. William Shakespeare, and what he hath left us."

22. Matthew W. Black and Matthias A. Shaaber, *Shakespeare's Seventeenth Century Editors* (New York and London: Oxford University Press, 1937).

23. There was a convention, not always adhered to, that the initial "u" or "v" in a word was printed as "v," and all subsequent "u's" and "v's" were printed "u."

24. First pointed out by James Greenstreet (by now "the late"), "Testimonies against the accepted authorship of Shakespear's Plays," *The Genealogist*, New Series, vol. 8 (London: 1892), 137–146.

25. Paul Werstine, "William Shakespeare," in David C. Greetham (ed.), *Scholarly Editing: A Guide to Research* (New York: 1995), 253–82.

26. René Weis, *Shakespeare Revealed: A Biography* (London: John Murray, 2007), 418.

27. E. K. Chambers, *William Shakespeare*, vol. 1 (Oxford: 1930), 551–54.

28. Helen Moorwood, *Shakespeare's Stanley Epitaphs in Tong, Shropshire* (Much Wenlock, 2013), 14.

29. E. A. J. Honigmann, *Shakespeare, the "Lost Years"* (Manchester: Manchester University Press, 1985), 78–81.

30. Carl O. Nordling, http://carlonordling.se/shakespeare/3.html.

Chapter 29

1. E. A. J. Honigmann, *The Texts of Othello and Shakespearian Revision* (London: Routledge, 1996), 82–91.

2. J. Dover Wilson, *The Manuscript of Shakespeare's "Hamlet" etc.*, vol. 1 (Cambridge: 1934), 106 ff.

3. E. A. J Honigmann, *v. supra*, 86.

4. Sidney Lee, *Shakespeare's Sonnets* (Oxford: Clarendon Press, 1905), 44–46.

5. Anonymous review of Gerald H. Rendall, *Shake-speare: Handwriting and Spelling* (London: Cecil Palmer, 1931). Undated newspaper cutting in G. H. Rendall's *nachlass* deposited in Liverpool University Library, perhaps from the *Times Literary Supplement.*

6. What seems to have happened is that the players would have arranged for Shakespeare's manuscript, frequently difficult to read, to be copied legibly. This text would have been used for producing the actors' slips (abbreviated parts, containing just cues and speeches) and also as prompt copy. After several performances, perhaps spread over two or more years, Shakespeare's original manuscript would be offered to a publisher for a few shillings, as the players had no further use for it. The compositor would then produce his own version of the manuscript, which was still just as difficult to read as before; his readings of obscure words might occasionally differ from those in the players' copy.

7. Eric Sams has considerably extended Honigmann's analysis of Shakespeare's spelling habits. "Shakespeare's Hand in the Copy for the 1603 First Quarto of *Hamlet*," *Hamlet Studies*, vol. 20 (1998), 80–88.

8. E. A. J. Honigmann, *v. supra*, 158–161.

9. A photograph of this letter appears in Professor Abel Lefranc, *Sous le masque de William Shakespeare, VIe comte de Derby*, vol. 2 (Paris: Payot et cie., 1918) and also in A. W. Titherley, *Shakespeare's Identity: William Stanley 6th Earl of Derby* (Winchester: 1952), Plate VIII, from which this reproduction is taken by courtesy of the publisher. William, Earl of Derby to Salisbury, CSPDom, 31 October 1607, 80.

10. Note the use of the word "love" to mean no more than dutiful loyalty, which may help towards an understanding of the way the word is used in the sonnets.

11. The reproduction comes from A. W. Titherley, *v. supra*, Plate VII, by courtesy of the publisher. William, Earl of Derby to Salisbury, 16 December 1605. BL Add. MS 12506, f. 207.

12. E. A. J. Honigmann, *v. supra*, 161.

Conclusion

1. Further thoughts on Southampton's perceived status are discussed in Appendix E.

2. It is sometimes asked why Shakespeare wrote plays about Henry VI and Henry VIII but never wrote a play about Henry VII. This question finds a simple answer if Shakespeare was descended from him.

3. I think it worth repeating here that plays were mostly written in collaboration by two or more writers. Those who knew that Stanley had written plays in the late 1580s or the 1590s would also know that some of the early plays had been co-written with others. They would not know how many of the later plays had been co-written or whether Stanley was the sole author of most of them. They would know that the name "William Shakespeare" was a pen name, but would not be so aware (as we are today) that the main writer and by far the most gifted was Stanley himself (supposedly). In other words, the secret was that Stanley had *played some part* in the writing of the plays issued under the pen name rather than that they were nearly all written wholly by him. That he associated with poets, playwrights and players would of course have been regarded as very much below his dignity as an earl.

4. King James's elder son, Prince Henry Frederick, died in 1612 aged 18, apparently of typhoid. His younger son Charles inherited the throne in 1625 on the death of his father. If Charles had died before James, his sister Elizabeth of Bohemia might well have inherited; she was very popular in the country and a woman of character. She married in 1613 Frederick, Count Palatine of the Rhine, elector of the Holy Roman Empire and later King of Bohemia.

5. Undoubtedly there will arise the temptation to relate what is known of Derby's life to lines or episodes

in the plays. I cannot resist giving an example of my own. At the end of *Hamlet* Fortinbras says of the dead Hamlet:

For he was likely, had he been put on,
To have proved most royal.

One might wonder if anyone else was in the back of Stanley's mind when he wrote these words. Was he thinking of Ferdinando, his elder brother, tragically denied the possibility of inheriting the throne? Or of Henry Wriothesley, supposedly the son of the Queen, whom he had urged to father a son (in my view) in order to increase his chances (such as they were) of being chosen to succeed Elizabeth? Or was he thinking of himself, not keen to become King, but confident that he could pull it off if called upon? This is merely idle speculation, of course, and I apologize for indulging in it.

Appendix A

1. Nina Green, http://oxford-shakespeare.com.
2. Alan Nelson, http://socrates.berkeley.edu/~ahnelson/authorsh.html.
3. Jonathan Hope, *The Authorship of Shakespeare's Plays* (Cambridge: Cambridge University Press, 1994), 11–26.
4. Terry Ross, *Shakespeare Fellowship Discussion Group*, 12 June 2003.
5. T. C. Banks, *An Historical and Critical Enquiry into the Nature of the Kingly Office, etc.* (London: Sherwood, Neely and Jones, 1814), 60–61.
6. R. J. C. Wait, *The Background to Shakespeare's Sonnets* (London: Chatto and Windus, 1972), 14–16, 123, 189–92, 199.
7. A similar thought occurs in: "But spurn'd in vain, Youth waineth by increasing," line 4 from "A Sonnet" printed in *Polyhymnia* by George Peele (London: 1590). The thought also occurs (we are told) in classical authors, e.g., Ovid.
8. Gerard Ledger, http://www.shakespeares-sonnets.com/sonnet/126.
9. Nina Green, private communication.

Appendix B

The numerous obscurities of Nashe's text are discussed by the editors of his works, Ronald McKerrow (London: A. H. Bullen etc., 1904) and F. P. Wilson (Oxford: B. Blackwell, 1958). Passages referred to in Chapter 7 are underlined.

1. Nina Green, quoted with grateful acknowledgments. http://www.oxford-shakespeare.com/nashe.html.
2. Gabriel Harvey's father, a rope-maker, who had three sons.
3. The offensive text between # and ## was replaced in later editions.
4. Gabriel Harvey, whom Nashe is angry with because of his gloating over the fact of and the manner of Greene's death. Both Nashe and Stanley were admirers of Greene and held him in high esteem: "*Gabriell Harvey* hath shewed the same inhumanitie to *Greene* that lies full low in his grave." Francis Meres, *Palladis Tamia. Wit's Treasury* (London: P. Short for Cuthbert Burbie, 1598), 286[r].
5. These are all terms (obscure to us) used by Robert Greene in his popular pamphlets about London lowlife.
6. Harvey felt mortally insulted when Greene twitted him for having a father who was a rope-maker (a kind of snub that his origins were working-class).

Appendix C

1. Conversely, if the name of someone hitherto unknown had been found, the cipher would be less likely to be judged authentic, a somewhat paradoxical situation.

Appendix D

1. William, Earl of Derby, to Sir Julius Cæsar, with a deputation, 25 March 1606. BL Lansdowne 167, ff. 153, 155.
2. William, Earl of Derby, to Sir John Salusburie, 27 November 1598. National Library of Wales, MS 1603D, fol. 206 (a handwritten copy of the original).
3. William, Earl of Derby, to his uncle Sir Robert Cecil, 4 January 1596. Cecil Papers 29. 96.
4. William, Earl of Derby, to Sir Robert Cecil, 30 November 1599. Cecil Papers 74.107.
5. William, Earl of Derby, to Sir William More (dictated), 6 January 1598. Surrey History Centre, 6729/6/50.
6. William, Earl of Derby, to "Sir G. M.," Sir George More (dictated), 6 May 1619. Surrey History Centre, 6729/6/51.
7. These letters are found in the Cecil Papers located at Hatfield House. http://www.proquest.com/products-services/cecil_papers.html.

Appendix E

1. Normally a cryptographer would attach little importance to a four-letter word found in a transposition cipher, as explained in Chapter 19; the odds of EIR appearing adjacent to the H of "Mr. W. H." are about 1 in 900. But the resonance of this word with the material discussed in Chapters 14–17 and 20–21 is so remarkable that it is almost impossible to believe that this is chance at work. The Dedication does indeed appear to be a masterpiece of cryptography, preserving both the name Henry Wriothesley and his status as perceived by the cryptographer's patron (who may himself have been the cryptographer).

Bibliography

Abbreviations

BL	British Library
CSPDom	Calendar of State Papers Domestic
FF	First Folio
HMCS	Historical Manuscripts Commission Salisbury. Cecil Papers
HMSO	Her Majesty's Stationery Office
KG	Knight of the Garter
ODNB	*Oxford Dictionary of National Biography*
OED	*Oxford English Dictionary*
PRO	Public Record Office, now the National Archives
PRO, SP	Public Record Office, State Papers
TNA	The National Archives
UP	University Press

Manuscripts

Cecil Papers at Hatfield House, HMCS. http://www.proquest.com/products-services/cecil_papers.html.

College of Arms. MS R.20 Funeral Ceremony. Anstis.

Historical Manuscripts Commission. *Calendar of State Papers, Spain. Simancas*. London: 1896. http://www.british-history.ac.uk/catalogue.aspx?gid=138.

Historical Manuscripts Commission. *Calendar of State Papers, Venetian*. London: 1900. http://www.british-history.ac.uk/report.aspx?compid=95611.

Historical Manuscripts Commission. *Calendar of the Cecil Papers in Hatfield House* London: many volumes, 1883–1976. http://www.british-history.ac.uk/catalogue.aspx?gid=144.

Historical Manuscripts Commission. MSS Rye and Herefordshire Corporations. London: 1892. http://www.british-history.ac.uk/report.aspx?compid=67148.

Historical Manuscripts Commission. *Report on the Manuscripts of Lord de L'Isle and Dudley*, ed. C. L. Kingsford. London: HMSO, 1925–66.

Historical Manuscripts Commission. Seventh Report. London: 1879. http://archive.org/stream/reportofroyalcom07grea/reportofroyalcom07grea_djvu.txt.

Liber Caeruleus, a later copy of the original records of the voting at KG Chapter Meetings. British Library Add. MS 36,768. Phillipps MS 8816.

Reference Resources

Harvard Concordance to Shakespeare, Martin Spevack. Cambridge, Mass.: Belknap, 1974.

Oxford Dictionary of National Biography. New York: Oxford University Press, 2004–2013.

Oxford English Dictionary. New York: Oxford University Press, 2013.

Works Cited

Akrigg, G. P. V. *Shakespeare and the Earl of Southampton*. London: Hamish Hamilton, 1968.

Alden, Raymond Macdonald. *The Sonnets of Shakespeare*. Boston & New York: Houghton Mifflin, 1916.

Anon. "A Problem for the Trade," *The Gentleman's Tailor*, vol. 46, 1911.

Anon. [Richard Barnfield]. *The Affectionate Shepherd Concerning the Complaint of Ganymede*. London: 1594.

Anon. Review of Gerald H. Rendall, *Shake-speare: Handwriting and Spelling*. London: Cecil Palmer, 1931. Undated newspaper cutting in G. H. Rendall's *nachlass* deposited in Liverpool University Library, perhaps from the Times Literary Supplement.

Anon. *The Ceremonies, Form of Prayer, and Services Used in Westminster-Abby at the Coronation of King James the First and Queen Ann His Consort*. London: Randal Taylor, 1685.

Anon. *The Parish Church of St. Peter, Titchfield: A Guide to the Church and Village*, 1946.

Audeley, Thomas. Letter to Edward Smythe, 20 September 1597, perhaps 20 December 1597. Cecil Papers, MS 55.45, printed in HMCS, 7:391.

B. R., Gent. [Richard Barnfield] *Greene's Funeralls*. London: John Danter, 1594.

Bacon, Lady Anne. Letter to the Earl of Essex, 1 De-

cember 1596. Lambeth Palace Library, MS 660, fol. 149r.
Bagley, J. J. *The Earls of Derby, 1485–1985*. London: Sidgwick & Jackson, 1985.
Banks, T. C. *An Historical and Critical Enquiry into the Nature of the Kingly Office, Etc.* London: Sherwood, Neely and Jones, 1814.
Barnfield, Richard. *Cynthia, with Certain Sonnets*. London: 1595.
_____. *Poems in Divers Humors*. London: 1598.
Bedingfield, Thomas. *Cardanus Comforte Translated into Englishe and Published by Commandment of the Righte Honourable the Earle of Oxenforde*. London: Thomas Marsh, 1576.
Begent, Peter J., and Hubert Chesshyre. *The Most Noble Order of the Garter 650 Years*. London: Spink, 1999.
Bernard, E. A. B. *Evesham and a Reputed Son of Queen Elizabeth*. Old Evesham Pamphlets, 1926.
Berry, Herbert. *The Boar's Head Playhouse*. Folger Books, 1986.
Black, Matthew W., and Matthias A. Shaaber, *Shakespeare's Seventeenth Century Editors*. New York and London: Oxford University Press, 1937.
Blayney, Peter M. *The First Folio of Shakespeare*. Folger Library Publications, 1991.
Booth, Stephen, ed. *Shakespeare's Sonnets*. New Haven: Yale University Press, 1977.
Boyle, Harry H. "Elizabeth's Entertainment at Elvetham: War Policy in Pageantry," *Studies in Philology*, vol. 68, no. 2. April 1971, 146–166.
Bradley, A. C. *Oxford Lectures on Poetry*. Bloomington: Indiana University Press, 1961.
Brooks, Alden. *Will Shakspere and the Dyer's Hand*. New York: Scribner's, 1943.
Burghley, Lord. Letter to Sir Robert Cecil, 8 July 1596, PRO, SP 12/259; fol. 140v.
Burrow, Colin, ed. *The Complete Sonnets and Poems, by William Shakespeare*. Oxford University Press, 2002.
Camden, William. *The History of the Most Renowned and Victorious Princess Elizabeth, Late Queen of England*, a translation of *Annales etc.*, 1615. London: 1675.
Campbell, S. C. *Shake-speare's Sonnets: The Alternative Text*. Cambridge: Cassandra Press, 2009.
Carey, George. Letter to his wife, 22 April 1594. Gloucester Records Office, MF 1161, letter-book 2.
Chamberlin, Frederick. *The Private Character of Queen Elizabeth*. London: John Lane, 1921.
Chambers, E. K. *Shakespearean Gleanings*. Oxford University Press, 1944.
_____. *William Shakespeare: A Study of Facts and Problems*, 2 vols. Oxford: Clarendon Press, 1930.
Chester, Robert. *Love's Martyr, or, Rosalyn's Complaint* (1601), ed. Alexander B. Grosart. London: Trübner, 1878.
Chettle, Henry. *England's Mourning Garment*. London: Thomas Millington, 1603, repr. Amsterdam: Da Capo Press, 1973.
Cinthio, Giovanni Battista Giraldi. *Hecatommithi*. Mondovi, 1565.
Cleave, Julia. "More a Player Than a Playwright?" *De Vere Society Newsletter*. March 2008, 17–19.
Collier, J. Payne. *Memoirs of the Principal Actors*. London: Shakespeare Society, 1846.
Collier, John Payne. *The Works of Edmund Spenser*. London: Bell and Daldy, 1862.
Colonna, Francesco. *Hypnerotomachia: The Strife of Love in a Dreame*, translation by R. D., London: 1592. Facsimile edn., introduced by Lucy Gent. Scholars' Facsimiles & Reprints, 1973.
Cooper, Tarnya. *Searching for Shakespeare*. London: National Portrait Gallery, 2006.
Cooper, Thomas. *Thesaurus Linguæ Romanæ & Britannicæ*. London, 1565.
Covell, William. *Polimanteia, etc.* London: R. Bankworth, 1595.
Coward, Barry. *The Stanleys, Lords Stanley and Earls of Derby, 1385–1672*. Manchester: for the Chetham Society, 1983.
Craig, Hugh, and Arthur F. Kinney, *Shakespeare, Computers, and the Mystery of Authorship*. Cambridge University Press, 2009.
Daniel, Samuel. *The Civil Wars Between the Houses of Lancaster and York*. London: Simon Waterson, 1609.
Daugherty, Leo. *The Assassination of Shakespeare's Patron: Investigating the Death of the Fifth Earl of Derby*. New York: Cambria Press, 2011.
_____. *William Shakespeare, Richard Barnfield, and the Sixth Earl of Derby*. Amherst, New York: Cambria Press, 2010.
David, R. W., ed. *Love's Labour's Lost*. London: Arden 2, 1951.
Davies, John, of Hereford. *Microcosmos: The Discovery of the Little World, with the Government Thereof.* Oxford, Joseph Barnes, 1603.
_____. *The Scourge of Folly*, to be found in *The Complete Works of John Davies of Hereford*, ed. Alexander B. Grosart, 2 vols. London: 1878.
Davies, Sir John. *Hymnes of Astraea, in acrosticke verse*. London: I. S., 1599.
Davison, Francis. *Anagrammata in Nomina Illustrissimorum Heroum*. London: Simon Stafford, 1603. http://www.philological.bham.ac.uk/anagrams/
Deacon, Richard (real name Donald McCormick). *John Dee*. London: Frederick Muller, 1969.
Derby, Alice, Countess of. Letter to Sir Robert Cecil, 9 May [1594], Hatfield Papers. http://www.british-history.ac.uk/catalogue.aspx?gid=144
_____. Letter to the Earl of Shrewsbury, 27 June 1594, Talbot MSS, Shrewsbury Letters; Lambeth Palace Library, MS 3203 Item 14.
Derby, the Earl and Countess of. Letter to Sir Robert Cecil, 22 August 1597. Cecil Papers, MS 54.77.
Derby, Will. Letter (dictated) to Sir G. M., 6 May 1619. Surrey History Centre, 6729/6/51.
_____. Letter (dictated) to Sir William More, 6 January 1598. Surrey History Centre, 6729/6/50.
_____. Letter to Robert Cecil, Lord Salisbury, 16 December 1605. BL Add. MM 12,506/7, vol. i, f. 207.
_____. Letter to Robert Cecil, Lord Salisbury, 31 October 1607. Calendar of State Papers Domestic.
_____. Letter to Sir John Salusbury, 27 November 1598. National Library of Wales MS 1576B, 18–19.
_____. Letter to Sir Julius Caesar, 25 March 1606. BL Lansdowne 167, ff.153, 155.
_____. Letter to Sir Robert Cecil, 30 November 1599. Cecil Papers, MS 74.107.
_____. Letter to Sir Robert Cecil, 4 January 1596. Cecil Papers, MS 29.96.
D'Ewes, Simonds. *The Journals of All the Parliaments During the Reign of Queen Elizabeth*. London: 1682.
Dickenson, John. *Greene in Conceipt*. London, 1598.

Dickinson, Warren D. *The Wonderful Shakespeare Mystery*. Nashville, TN: OMNI PublishXpress, 2001)

Doleman R. (Robert Parsons?). *A Conference About the Next Succession to the Crown of Ingland*. Amsterdam, 1593). http://books.google.ca/books?id=kOQbU56suzcC&q=267#v=onepage&q=267&f=true

Dowden, Edward, ed. *The Sonnets of William Shakespeare*. London: Kegan Paul, Trench, 1881.

Duffield, Captain. Letter of 9 November 1593. *Cecil Papers at Hatfield House*. http://www. britishhistory.ac.uk/report.aspx?compid =112054

Dugdale, William. *The Antiquities of Warwickshire*. London: Thomas Warren, 1656.

Duncan Jones, Katherine. *Shakespeare's Sonnets*. London: Arden, 1997.

Dutton, Richard. *William Shakespeare: A Literary Life*. London: Macmillan, 1989.

Eccles, Mark. Article in *Thomas Lodge and Other Elizabethans* ed. C. J. Sisson *et al.* Cambridge, MA: Harvard University Press, 1933.

Edwards, Philip. *Shakespeare: A Writer's* Progress. New York: Oxford University Press, 1986.

Edwards, Thomas. *Cephalus and Procris. Narcissus* (entered Stationers' Register October 1593, published 1595), ed. W. E. Buckley. London: Nichols and Sons, for the Roxburghe Club, 1878, 1882.

Elizabeth I, *Collected Works*, eds. Leah S. Marcus, Janel Mueller, and Mary Beth Rose. University of Chicago Press, 2000.

Erne, Lukas. *Shakespeare as Literary Dramatist*. Cambridge: Cambridge University Press, 2003, revised ed. 2013.

Farey, Peter. "Sonnet 125," *The Shakespeare Conference,* 17 Oct. 2006. http://shaksper.net/archive/2006/242-october/25009-sonnet-125.

Feacham, Richard. *The Parish Church of St. Martin, East Horsley, Surrey*, 1968.

Finnis, John, and Patrick H. Martin. "An Oxford Play Festival in February 1582," *Notes and Queries*, vol. 248, no. 4. December 2003, 391–94.

Flynn, Dennis. "'Awry and Squint': The Dating of Donne's Holy Sonnets," *John Donne Journal,* vol. 7, no. 1. 1988, 35–46.

Foakes, R. A., ed. *Henslowe's Diary*, 2nd ed. Cambridge University Press, 2002.

Frazer, Robert. *The Silent Shakespeare*. Philadelphia: William J. Campbell, 1915.

Friedman, William F., and Elizebeth S Friedman. *The Shakespearean Ciphers Examined*. Cambridge: Cambridge University Press, 1957.

Frye, Northrop. "How True a Twain" in Edward Hubler, ed. *The Riddle of Shakespeare's Sonnets*. New York: Basic Books, 1962.

Gaines, Helen Fouché. *Elementary Cryptanalysis*. London: Chapman and Hall, 1940.

Gawdy, Philip. Letter to his brother Bassingbourne Gawdy, May 1593. BL Egerton MS 2804.

Gebert, Clara, ed. *An Anthology of Elizabethan Dedications & Prefaces*. Philadelphia: University of Philadelphia Press, 1933.

Gibson, H. N. *The Shakespeare Claimants*. London: Methuen, 1962.

Giroux, Robert. *The Book Known as Q: A Consideration of Shakespeare's Sonnets*. London: Weidenfeld and Nicolson, 1982.

Gittings, Robert. *Shakespeare's Rival*. London: Heinemann, 1960.

Goldstone, Jack A. "The Latin Inscription on the Stratford Monument Unraveled, and Its Bearing on the Authorship Controversy." *De Vere Society Newsletter*, vol. 19, no. 2. July 2012, 11–14.

Green, Nina. http://oxford-shakespeare.com.

Greene, Robert. *Greene's Groatsworth of Wit Bought with a Million of Repentance*. London: William Wright, 1592.

_____. *Menaphon, Camila's Alarm to Slumbering Euphues in His Melancholy Cell at Silexedra, &c*. London: 1589.

Greenstreet, James (the late). "Testimonies Against the Accepted Authorship of Shakespeare's Plays," *The Genealogist*, New Series, vol. 8. London, 1892, 137–146.

Greenstreet, James. "A Hitherto Unknown Noble Writer of Elizabethan Comedies," *The Genealogist*, New Series, vol. 7. London, 1891, 205–08.

_____. "Further Notices of William Stanley, 6th Earl of Derby, K. G., as Poet and Dramatist." *The Genealogist*, New Series, vol. 8. London, 1892, 8–15.

Greg, W. W. *The Shakespeare First Folio, Its Bibliographical and Textual History*. Oxford: Clarendon Press, 1955.

Gunstone, John. Letter, 25 July 1587, *Calendar of State Papers Domestic*, 1598–1601, 373. PRO SP 12/273/103, f. 185v.

Gurr, Andrew. "A Jibe at Shakespeare in 1606." *Notes & Queries*, vol. 49, no. 2. June 2002, 245–47.

_____. *The Shakespearian Playing Companies*. Oxford: Clarendon, 1996.

H., J. Trl. *Augustine, or the Citie of God*. London: George Eld, 1610.

H., T. [Thomas Heywood] *Oenone and Paris*. London: Richard Jones, 1594.

Hall, Joseph. *Virgidemiarum: Sixe Bookes. First Three Bookes, of Tooth-lesse Satyrs*. London: Robert Dexter, 1602.

Halle, Edward. *The Union of the Two Noble and Illustrate Families of Lancastre and Yorke*. London: 1542; later editions 1548 and 1550, commonly called *Halle's Chronicle*.

Halliwell, J. O., ed. *The Private Diary of Dr. John Dee*. London: J. B. Nichols and Son, 1842. http://www.gutenberg.org/ebooks/19553.

Hammer, Paul E. J. *The Polarisation of Elizabethan Politics: The Political Career of Robert Devereux, 2nd Earl of Essex, 1585–1597*. Cambridge University Press, 1999.

Hammond, Paul. *Figuring Sex Between Men from Shakespeare to Rochester*. Oxford University Press, 2002.

Harris, John. http://www.forumgarden.com/forums/members/spot.html.

Harris, Robert. *The Ghost*. London: Arrow Books, 2008.

Harvey, Gabriel. *Four Letters and Certain Sonnets*. London: John Wolfe, 1592.

_____. *Pierce's Supererogation, or a New Praise of the Old Ass*. London: John Wolfe, 1593.

Healey, Io., trl. *Epictetus, etc*. London: Thomas Thorpe, 1610.

_____, trl. *Epictetus, etc*. London: Edward Blount, 1616.

Heywood, Thomas. *Oenone and Paris*. London: Richard Jones, 1594.

_____. *The Hierarchie of the Blessed Angels*. London: A. Islip, 1635. Lib. 4.

Holmes, Edward. *Discovering Shakespeare: A Handbook for Heretics*. Chester-le-Street: Mycroft Books, 2001.

Holmes, Nathaniel. *The Authorship of Shakespeare*. New York: Hurd and Houghton, 1875.

Honigmann, E. A. J. *John Weever: A Biography of a Literary Associate of Shakespeare and Jonson*. Manchester: Manchester University Press, 1987.

_____. *Shakespeare: The "Lost Years."* Manchester: Manchester University Press, 1985.

_____. *The Texts of Othello and Shakespearian Revision*. London: Routledge, 1996.

Hope, Jonathan. *The Authorship of Shakespeare's Plays*. Cambridge University Press, 1994.

Hotson, Leslie. *I, William Shakespeare*. London: Jonathan Cape, 1937.

_____. *Mr. W. H.* London: Rupert Hart-Davis, 1964.

_____. *Shakespeare by Hilliard*. London: Chatto & Windus, 1977.

_____. *Shakespeare's Motley*. London: Hart-Davis, 1952.

Hughes, Beryl. *Shakespeare's Friend of the Sonnets: A Mystery Solved*. London: Minerva Press, 2000.

Hume, Martin, ed. *Calendar of State Papers, Spain (Simancas)*, vol. 4. London, 1899.

Hurstfield, Joel. *The Queen's Wards: Wardship and Marriage Under Elizabeth I*. London: Longmans Green, 1958.

Ireland, Thomas. Letter to Sir Robert Cecil, 30 July 1598. Cecil Papers, MS 62.100.

Jackson, MacDonald P. "Shakespeare and the Quarrel Scene in Arden of Faversham." *Shakespeare Quarterly*, vol. 57, no. 3. Fall 2006, 249–293.

Jenkins, Elizabeth. *Elizabeth and Leicester*. London: V. Gollancz, 1961.

Jones, Philippa. *Elizabeth: Virgin Queen?*, New Holland, 2010.

Jonson, Benjamin. *Workes of Beniamin Ionson*, vol. 1. London: 1616, repr. 1640.

Kerrigan, John, ed. *The Sonnets; and, a Lover's Complaint, by William Shakespeare*. Harmondsworth, UK: Viking, 1986.

Kingsford, C. L., ed. *Historical Manuscripts Commission, Report on the Manuscripts of Lord de L'Isle and Dudley*. London: HMSO, 1925–66.

Klawitter, George, ed. *Richard Barnfield: The Complete Poems*. Selinsgrove, Pa.: Susquehanna University Press, 1990.

Knight, G. Wilson. *The Mutual Flame: On Shakespeare's Sonnets & the Phoenix & the Turtle*. London: Methuen, 1955.

Lambin, Georges. *Voyages de Shakespeare en France et en Italie*. Geneva, Droz, 1962, trans. Tal G. Wilson *et al.* in W. Ron Hess, *The Dark Side of Shakespeare*, vol. 1. New York: Writers Club Press, 2002, 483–520.

Ledger, Gerard. *Shakespeare's Sonnets*. http://www.shakespeares-sonnets.com/; http://www.shakespeares-sonnets.com/Archive/ded2comm.htm.

Lee, Sidney. *A Life of William Shakespeare*, third edition of revised version. London: John Murray, 1922.

_____. *Shakespeare's Sonnets*. Oxford: Clarendon Press, 1905.

Lefranc, Abel. "Les Éléments français de 'Peines d'amour perdues' de Shakespeare," *Revue Historique* 178 (1936), pp. 411–12, 414–15.

_____. *Sous le masque de William Shakespeare, VIe comte de Derby*. Paris: Payot et cie., 1918, 2 vols., translated by Cecil Cragg. Braunton, Devon, 1988.

Leti, Gregorio. *La Vie d'Elizabeth, reine d'Angleterre*, vol. 1. Amsterdam, 1704, trans. of suppressed Italian original, pub. 1682.

Lewis, C. S. *English Literature in the Sixteenth Century, Excluding Drama*. London: Oxford University Press, 1973.

Lingard, John. *History of England*. London: 1854.

Lloyd, Richard. *A Brief Discourse of the Most Renowned Actes and Right Valiant Conquests of These Puisant Princes, Called the Nine Worthies*. London: R. Warde, 1584.

Lodge, Edmund. *Illustrations of British History etc.* London, 1791.

Looney, J. Thomas. *"Shakespeare" Identified in Edward de Vere, the Seventeenth Earl of Oxford*. London: C. Palmer, 1920.

Lucas, Richard Macdonald. *Shakespeare's Vital Secret*. Keighley: Wadsworth, 1937.

Maguire, Laurie. A New Shakespeare Collaboration? http://www.cems-oxford.org/sites/default/files/MaguireSmithSh Collaboration.pdf.

Malone, Edmond. "Life of Shakespeare," in *The Plays and Poems of William Shakespeare etc.*, vol. 2. London: 1821.

Manley, Lawrence. "From Strange's Men to Pembroke's Men: 2 'Henry VI' and 'The First Part of the Contention.'" *Shakespeare Quarterly*, vol. 54, no. 3 (Autumn 2003), 253–287.

Marcus, Leah S. *Puzzling Shakespeare: Local Reading and Its Discontents*. Berkeley: University of California Press, 1988.

Marlowe, Christopher, trl. *Lucan's First Booke*. London: Thomas Thorpe, 1600.

Marston, John. *The Works of John Marston*, ed. A. H. Bullen, 3 vols. London: John C. Nimmo, 1887.

Meres, Francis. *Palladis Tamia. Wit's Treasury*. London: P. Short for Cuthbert Burbie, 1598.

Merriam, Thomas. *Marlowe in Henry V: A Crisis of Shakespearian Identity?* Oxford: Oxquarry Books, 2002.

Merton, Charlotte Isabelle. *The Women Who Served Queen Mary and Queen Elizabeth: Ladies, Gentlemen and Maids of the Privy Chamber, 1553–1603*. Ph.D. Thesis, 17227. Trinity College, Cambridge, 1991, CUL.

Michell, John. *Who Wrote Shakespeare?* London: Thames and Hudson, 1996.

Montégut, Emile. *Oeuvres de Wm. Shakespeare*. Paris: Hachette, 1876.

Moore, Peter R. *The Lame Storyteller, Poor and Despised*. Verlag Uwe Laugwitz, 2009.

Moorwood, Helen. *Shakespeare's Stanley Epitaphs in Tong, Shropshire*. Much Wenlock, 2013.

Mooten, Michael. http://willobiehisavisadecoded.webs.com/faq.htm.

Muir, Kenneth. *Shakespeare's Sonnets*. London: George Allen and Unwin, 1982.

_____. *Shakespeare's Sonnets*. London: Routledge, 2005.

_____. *Shakespeare's Sources*. London: Methuen, 1957.

Mylar (*recte* ffyton or Fitton), Edward. Letter to Sir Robert Cecil, 9 August 1597, Cecil Papers, MS 54.14.

Nashe, Thomas. *The Apologie of Pierce Pennilesse, or Strange Newes of the Intercepting Certain Letters and a Convoy of Verses as They Were Going Privily to Victual the Low Countries*. London: John Danter, 1592.

Nina Green, version in modernized English. http://www.oxford-shakespeare.com/Nashe/Strange_News.pdf.
_____. *Pierce Pennilesse His Supplication to the Devil.* London: Richard Ihones, 1592; repr. by J. Payne Collier, London: 1842. http://books.google.co.uk/books?id= KY9VdGNg4QcC&printsec =titlepage &as_brr=1&redir_esc=y#v=onepage&q&f=true.
Nashe, Thomas. F. P. Wilson, ed.: *Works Edited from the Original Texts by Ronald B. McKerrow; Reprinted from the Original Ed. with Corrections and Supplementary Notes.* Oxford: B. Blackwell, 1958.
Nashe, Thomas, Ronald B. McKerrow, ed., *The Works of Thomas Nashe ed. from the Original Texts.* London: A. H. Bullen etc., 1904.
Nelson, A. H. http://socrates.berkeley.edu/~ahnelson-/authorsh.html.
Nicholas, Harris. *Memoirs of the Life and Times of Sir Christopher Hatton KG.* London: 1847.
Nicholl, Charles. *The Lodger: Shakespeare on Silver Street.* London: Alan Lane, 2007.
Nichols, John. *The Progresses and Public Processions of Queen Elizabeth,* 2 vols. London: John Nichols, 1788.
_____. *The Progresses and Public Processions of Queen Elizabeth,* 3 vols. London: John Nichols and son, 1823.
_____. *The Progresses, Processions and Magnificent Festivities of King James the First.* London: J. B. Nichols, 1828.
Nordling, Carl O. http://carlonordling.se/shakespeare/.
Nowell, Alexander. *A Catechism.* Cambridge University Press, 1853, Appendix.
Ogburn, Charlton. *The Mysterious William Shakespeare.* McLean, Va.: EPM Publications, 1984.
Osborne, Francis. *Historical Memoires of the Reigns of Queen Elizabeth and King James.* London: J. Grismond, 1658.
Padel, John. *New Poems by Shakespeare: Order and Meaning Restored to the Sonnets.* London: Herbert Press, 1981.
Peacham, Henry. *The Compleat Gentleman etc.* London: Francis Constable, 1622.
Peele, George. *The Honour of the Garter.* London, 1593.
_____. *Polyhymnia.* London, 1590.
Petowe, Henry. *Continuation to Hero and Leander.* London: Andrew Harris, 1598.
Pointon, A. J. *The Man Who Was Never Shakespeare: The Theft of William Shakspere's Identity.* Tunbridge Wells, U.K.: Parapress, 2011.
_____. "The Rest Is Silence: The Absence of Tributes to the Author Shakespeare at the Time of Shakspere's Death," in *Shakespeare Beyond Doubt?* Tamarac, Fla.: Llumina, 2013, pp. 69–70.
Price, Diana. *Shakespeare's Unorthodox Biography: New Evidence of an Authorship Problem.* Westport, CN: Greenwood Press, 2001.
Prior, Roger. "The Date of *Edward III*," *Notes & Queries*, ccxxxv, 1990.
_____. "Was *The Raigne of King Edward III* a Compliment to Lord Hunsdon?" *Connotations*, vol. 3, no. 3. (1993–94), 243–64.
Prothero, G. W., ed. *Select Statutes and Other Constitutional Documents, 4th ed.* Oxford: Clarendon Press, 1913.
Puttenham, George. *Arte of English Poesie.* London: 1589, chapter 8.
Rabelais, François. *Gargantua and Pantagruel*, Book 1. 1653. http://www.gutenberg.org/files/8166/8166.txt.
Raithel, John. *The URL of Derby.* http://www.rahul.net/raithel/Derby/.
Ramsey, Paul. *The Fickle Glass.* New York: AMS Press, 1979.
Reed, Edwin. *Francis Bacon Our Shakespeare.* London: Gay and Bird, 1902.
Rich, Barnaby. *Greene's Newes Both from Heaven and Hell.* London: 1593.
Roe, Richard Paul. *The Shakespeare Guide to Italy: Retracing the Bard's Unknown Travels.* New York: HarperCollins, 2011.
Röhl, John C. G., Martin Warren, and David Hunt. *Purple Secret.* London: Bantam, 1998.
Rollett, John M. "Shakespeare's Impossible Doublet: Droeshout's Engraving Anatomized." *Brief Chronicles*, vol. 2, 2010, 9–24. http://www.briefchronicles.com/.
_____. "Shakespeare's Sonnet 125: Who Bore the Canopy?" *Notes and Queries*, vol. 258, no. 3 (September 2013), 438–441.
Rollins, Hyder Edward, ed. *A New Variorum Edition of Shakespeare: The Sonnets*, vol. 2. Philadelphia & London: J. B. Lippincott, 1944.
Ross, Terry. *Shakespeare Fellowship Discussion Group*, 12/06/2003.
Rowe, Nicholas. *The Works of Mr. William Shakespear.* London: Jacob Tonson, 1709.
Rowse, A. L. *Shakespeare's Sonnets.* London: Macmillan, 1964.
Sams, Eric. "Shakespeare's Hand in the Copy for the 1603 First Quarto of Hamlet," *Hamlet Studies*, vol. 20 (1998), 80–88.
Sandford, Francis. *The History of the Coronation of James II.* London: 1687.
Sanford, John. *Apollinis et Musarum Euktika Eidullia, in Serenissimæ Reginæ Elizabethae auspicatissimum Oxoniam adventum.* Oxford: J. Barnesius, 1592.
Sargent, Ralph M. *The Life and Lyrics of Sir Edward Dyer.* Oxford: Clarendon Press, 1968.
Schlueter, June. "Martin Droeshout *Redivivus*: Reassessing the Folio Engraving of Shakespeare," *Shakespeare Survey*, vol. 60 (2007), 237–251.
Schoenbaum, S. *William Shakespeare: A Documentary Life.* Oxford: Clarendon Press, 1975.
Schoenbaum, Samuel. *Shakespeare's Lives.* Oxford: Clarendon Press, 1970.
Shahan, John, and Alexander Waugh, eds., *Shakespeare Beyond Doubt?.* Tamarac, FL: Llumina, 2013, pp. 114–125.
Shake-speare [William]. *Shake-speares Sonnets: Neuer Before Imprinted.* London: by G. Eld for T. T., 1609.
Shake-speare, Wil. *Poems: Written by Wil. Shake-speare, Gent.* London: John Benson, 1640.
Shakespeare, W. *The Passionate Pilgrim.* London: I. Jaggard, 1599.
Shakespeare, William. *Comedies, Histories, & Tragedies.* London: Isaac Jaggard and Ed. Blount, 1623.
_____. *Lucrece.* London: Richard Field, 1594.
_____. *Venus and Adonis.* London: Richard Field, 1593.
Shakespere, William. *A Pleasant Conceited Comedie Called Loves Labors Lost.* London: Cutbert Burby, 1598.
Sidney, Robert. Letter to Lord Burghley, 26 January 1591. PRO SP 84/44/60.

Sobran, Joseph. *Alias Shakespeare: Solving the Greatest Literary Mystery of All Time*. New York: Free Press, 1997.

Spenser, Edmund. *Colin Clouts Come Home Againe*. London: William Ponsonby, 1595.

_____. *Teares of the Muses. Thalia*. London: William Ponsonbie, 1591.

Stanley, William, Earl of Derby. Statement, 20 August 1597 (or perhaps 1596). Cecil Papers, 14.20, printed in HMCS, 179.140

Stone, Lawrence. *The Family, Sex and Marriage in England, 1500–1800*. London: Weidenfeld and Nicolson, 1977.

Stopes, Charlotte Carmichael. *The Life of Henry, Third Earl of Southampton, Shakespeare's Patron*. Cambridge: Cambridge University Press, 1922.

_____. "Thomas Edwards, Author of 'Cephalus and Procris. Narcissus,'" *Modern Language Review*, vol. 16, no. 3–4. Jul.–Oct. 1921.

Strong, Roy. *The Cult of Elizabeth*. London: Pimlico, 1977; 2nd ed., 1999.

Taylor, Gary. *Thomas Middleton: The Collected Works*. Oxford, 2007.

Taylor, Gary, and John Jowett, *Shakespeare Reshaped, 1606–1623*. Oxford: Oxford University Press, 1993.

Thompson, Edward Maunde. "Handwriting," in *Shakespeare's England: An Account of the Life and Manners of His Age*, vol. 1. Oxford: Clarendon Press, 1916.

Titherley, A. W. *Shakespeare's Identity: William Stanley 6th Earl of Derby*. Winchester, 1952.

Tobin, J. M. "A Touch of Greene, Much Nashe, and All Shakespeare." ed. T. A. Pendleton, *"Henry VI": Critical Essays*. New York: Routledge, 2001.

Tyndall, John. Letter to Secretary Cecil, 9 May 1599, CSPD 1598–1601; Lincoln's Inn SP 12/270/108; f. 186.

Urkowitz, Stephen. "Good News about 'Bad' Quartos," in Maurice Charney, ed., *"Bad" Shakespeare: Revaluations of the Shakespeare Canon*. London and Toronto: Associated University Presses, 1988, 189–206.

Valois, Marguerite de. *Mémoires de Marguerite de Valois*. Leiden: Elzevir, 1624.

Vickers, Brian. "The Face of the Bard?" *Times Literary Supplement*. London: 18 and 26 August 2006, 15–16.

_____. "Incomplete Shakespeare: Denying Co-authorship in 1 Henry VI," *Shakespeare Quarterly*, vol. 58 (2007), 311-352.

_____. *Shakespeare, A Lover's Complaint, and John Davies of Hereford*. Cambridge: Cambridge University Press, 2007.

_____. *Shakespeare, Co-Author*. Oxford: Oxford University Press, 2002.

Wait, R. J. C. *The Background to Shakespeare's Sonnets*. London: Chatto & Windus, 1972.

Walker, Alice. "The 1622 Quarto and the First Folio Texts of *Othello*," *Shakespeare Survey*, vol. 5 (1952), 16–24.

Weever, John. *Epigrammes in the Oldest Cut, and Newest Fashion*. London: Thomas Bushell, 1599.

Weis, René. *Shakespeare Revealed: A Biography*. London: John Murray, 2007.

Wells, Stanley. *Shakespeare's Sonnets*. Oxford: Oxford University Press, 1987.

Wells, Stanley, and Paul Edmondson. *Shakespeare's Sonnets*. Oxford: Oxford University Press, 2004.

Werstine, Paul. "William Shakespeare." ed. David C. Greetham, *Scholarly Editing: A Guide to Research*. New York: Modern Language Association, 1995.

Whetstone, George. *The Right Excellent and Famous Historye of Promos and Cassandra*. London: 1578; prose version 1582.

White, Richard Grant. *Memoirs of the Life of William Shakespeare*. New York: Little, Brown, 1866.

Wiles, David. *Shakespeare's Almanac: "Midsummer Night's Dream," Marriage and the Elizabethan Calendar*. Woodbridge: D.S. Brewer, 1993.

Wilkins, John. *Mercury, or the Secret and Swift Messenger*. 1641; repr. London: Frank Cass, 1970.

William, Earl of Derby. Letter to Robert Cecil, Earl of Salisbury, 31 October 1607, *Calendar of State Papers Domestic*.

_____. Letter to Sir Robert Cecil, n.d., January 1598, Cecil Papers, MS 38.13.

Williams, F. B. "An Initiation in Initials," *Studies in Bibliography*, vol. ix, 1957.

Willoughby, Henry. *Willobie His Avisa*. London: John Windet, 1594.

Wilson, Ian. http://www.shakespearesdarklady.com/.

_____. *Shakespeare: The Evidence*. New York: St. Martin's Press, 1993.

Wilson, J. Dover. *The Manuscript of Shakespeare's "Hamlet," etc*. Cambridge University Press, 1934. 2 vols.

Wilson, John Dover. *The Essential Shakespeare: A Biographical Adventure*. Cambridge University Press, 1932.

Wilson, John Dover, ed. *William Shakespeare: The Sonnets*. Cambridge: Cambridge University Press, 1976.

Witt, Madame Guizot de. *The Lady of Latham: Being the Life and Original Letters of Charlotte de la Trémoille, Countess of Derby*, trln. London: Smith, Elder, 1869.

Woudhuysen, H. R. "Love's Labour's Lost" in Richard Proudfoot, *et al. The Arden Shakespeare Complete Works*, 2nd ed. London: Thomson, 2001.

Yates, Frances. *The Occult Philosophy in the Elizabethan Age*. London and New York: Routledge, c. 1979; repr. 2001.

_____. *Shakespeare's Last Plays: A New Approach*. London: Routledge and Kegan Paul, 1975.

_____. *A Study of Love's Labour's Lost*. Cambridge: Cambridge University Press, 1936.

Yates, Frances M. *Lull and Bruno: Collected Essays*, vol. 1. London and Boston: Routledge and Kegan Paul, 1982.

Index

Page numbers in ***bold italics*** indicate pages with illustrations.